Dedication

This book is for you, dear colorist.

May your time spent coloring these pages
bring you joy, plus lots of fun
mixed in with plenty of relaxation..

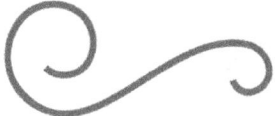

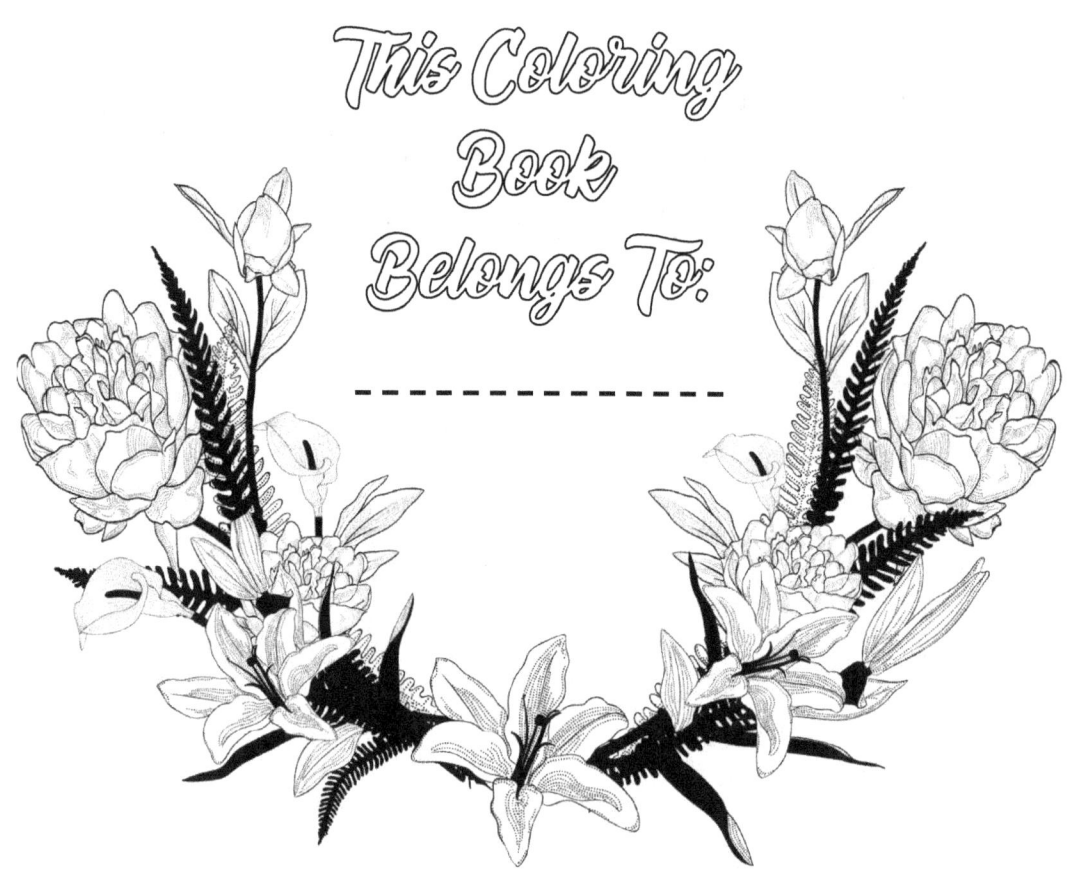

This Coloring
Book
Belongs To:

_ _ _ _ _ _ _ _ _ _ _ _ _

Sample Colors

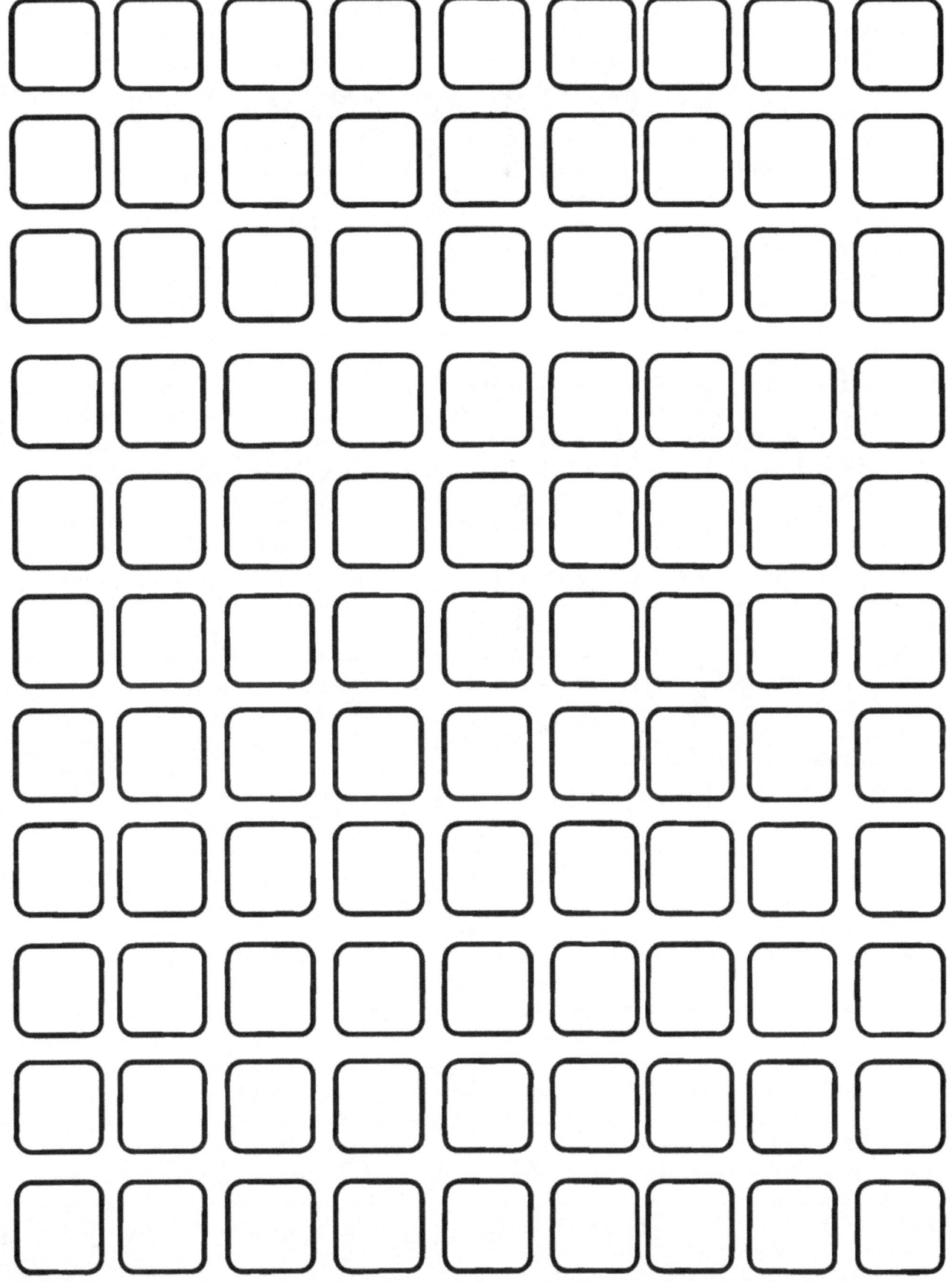

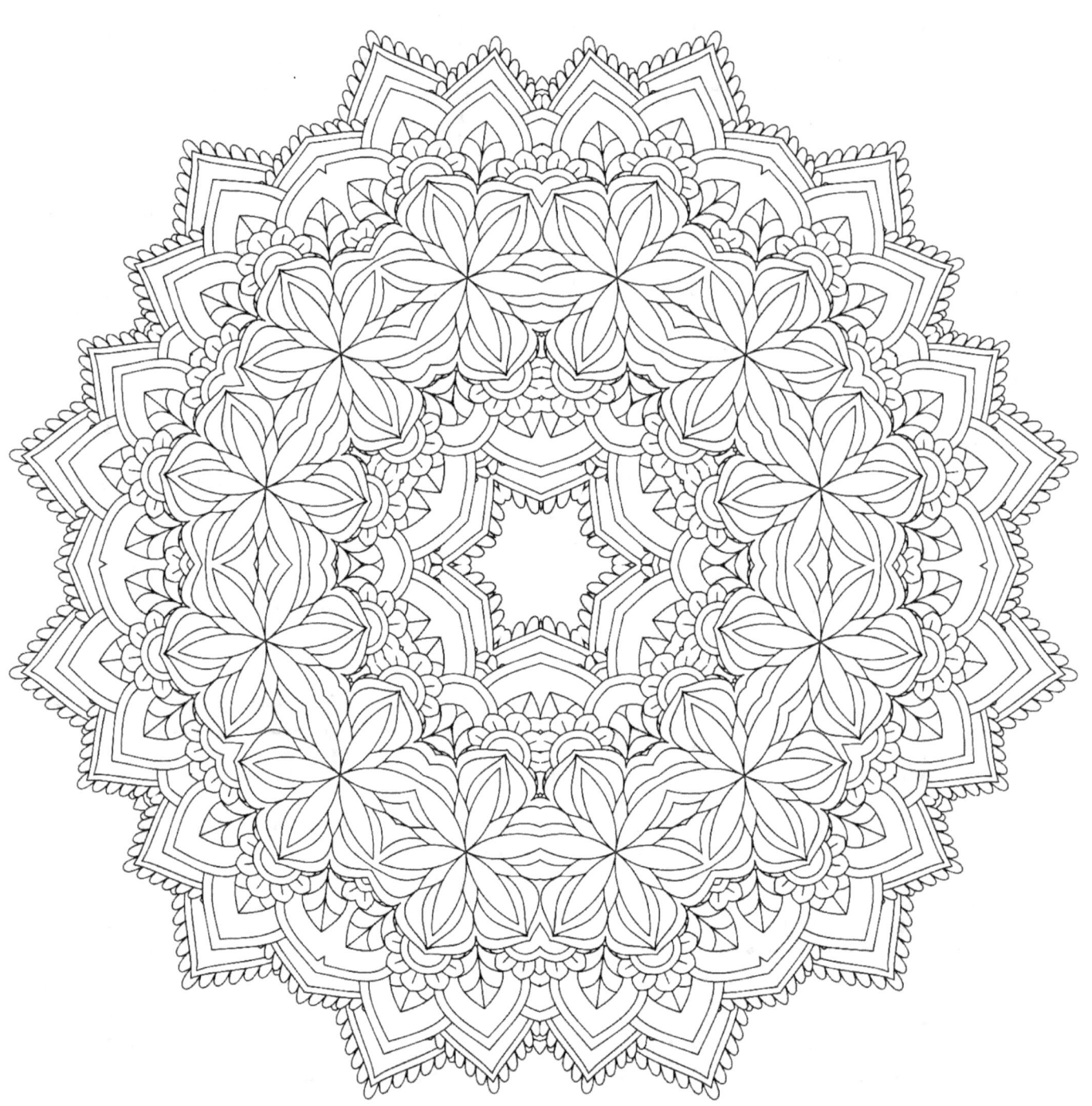

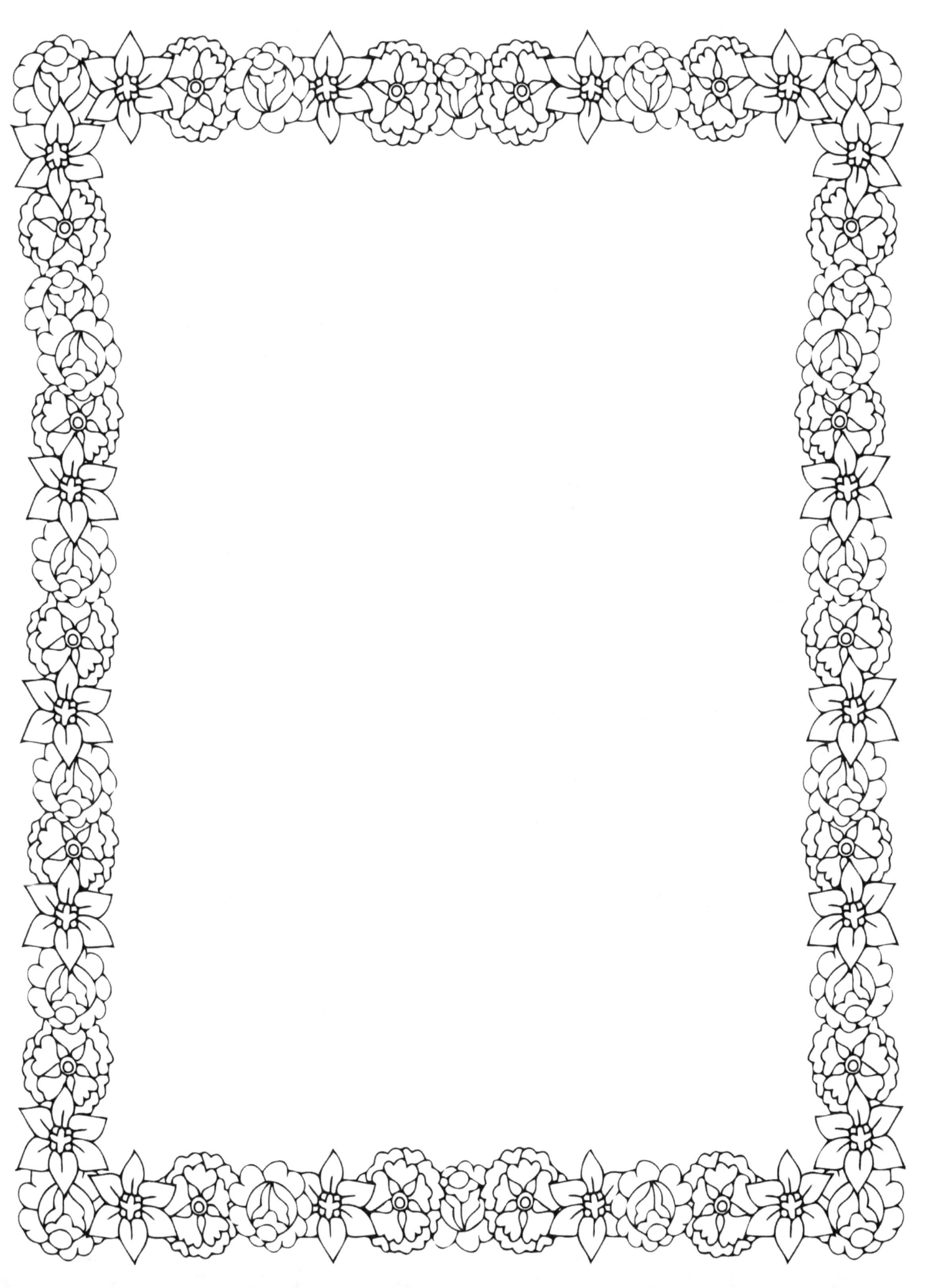

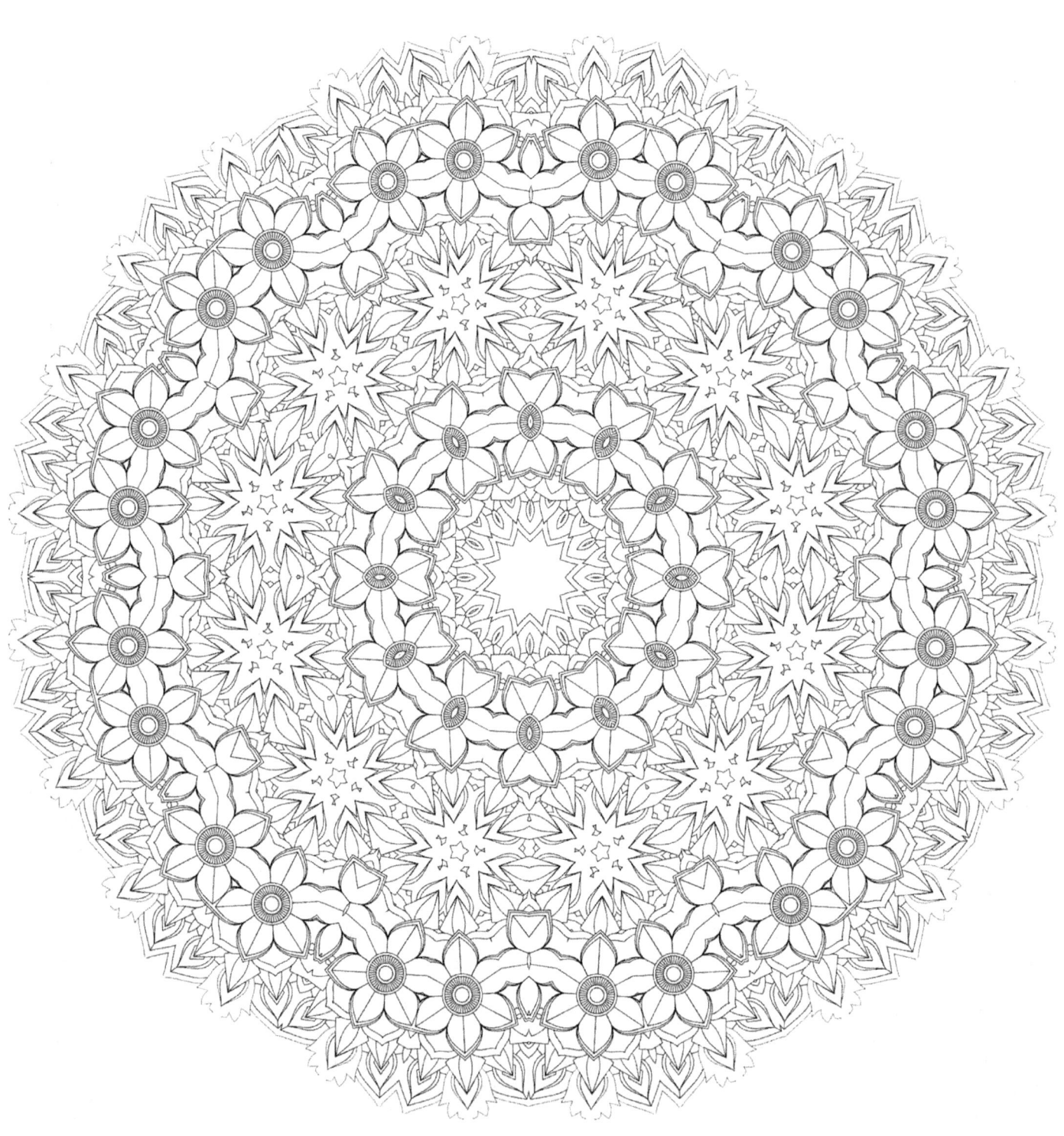

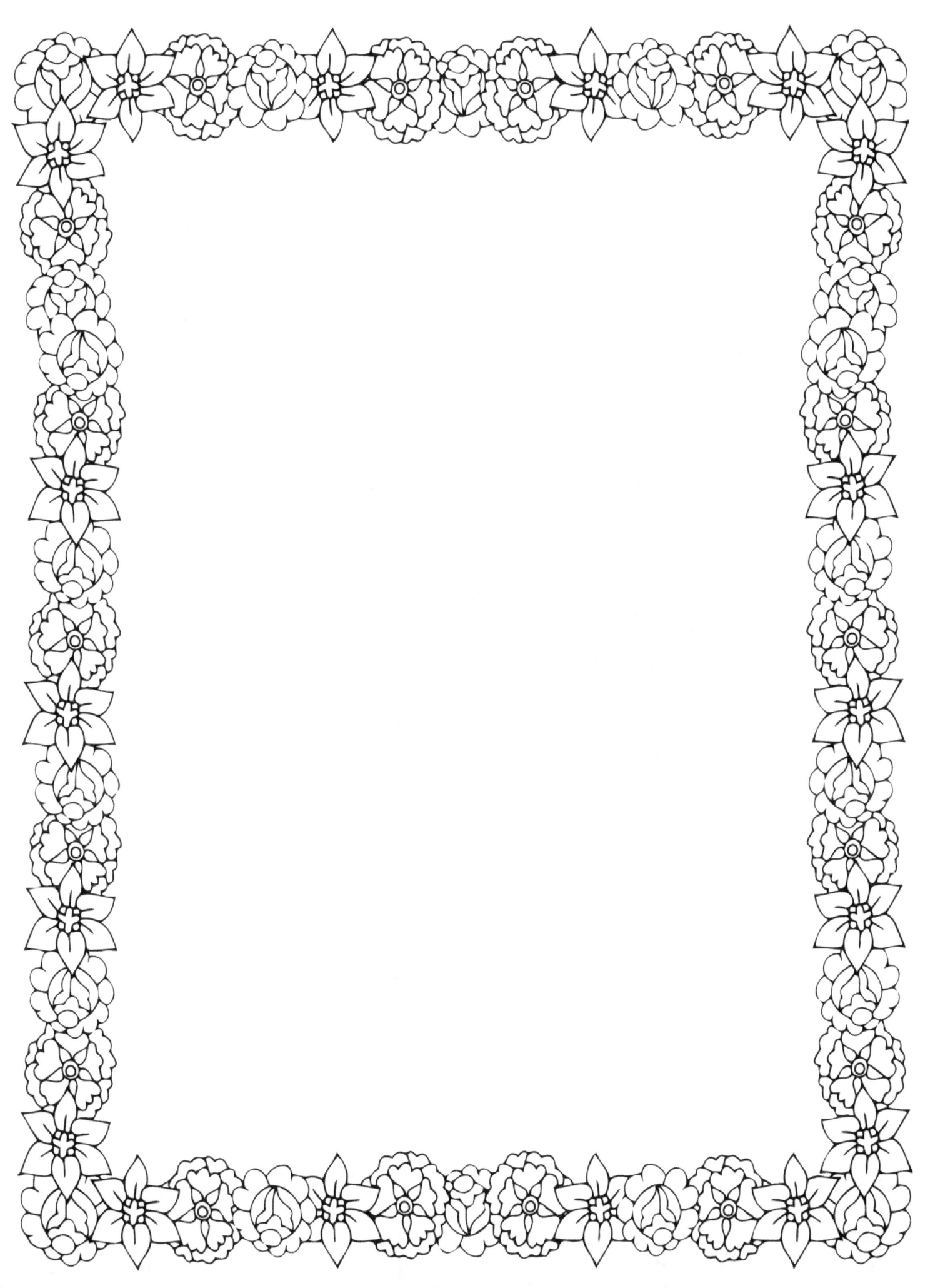

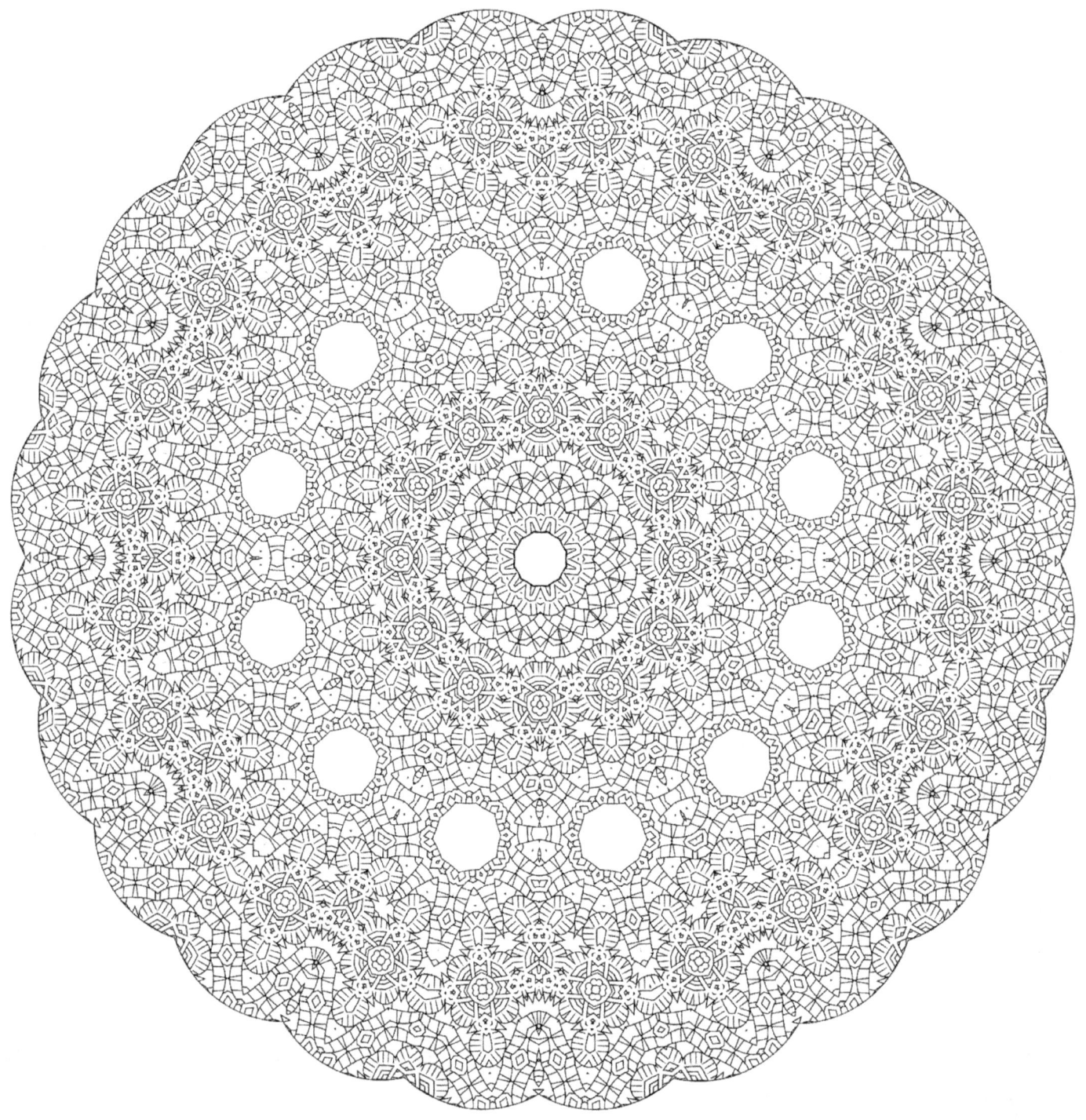

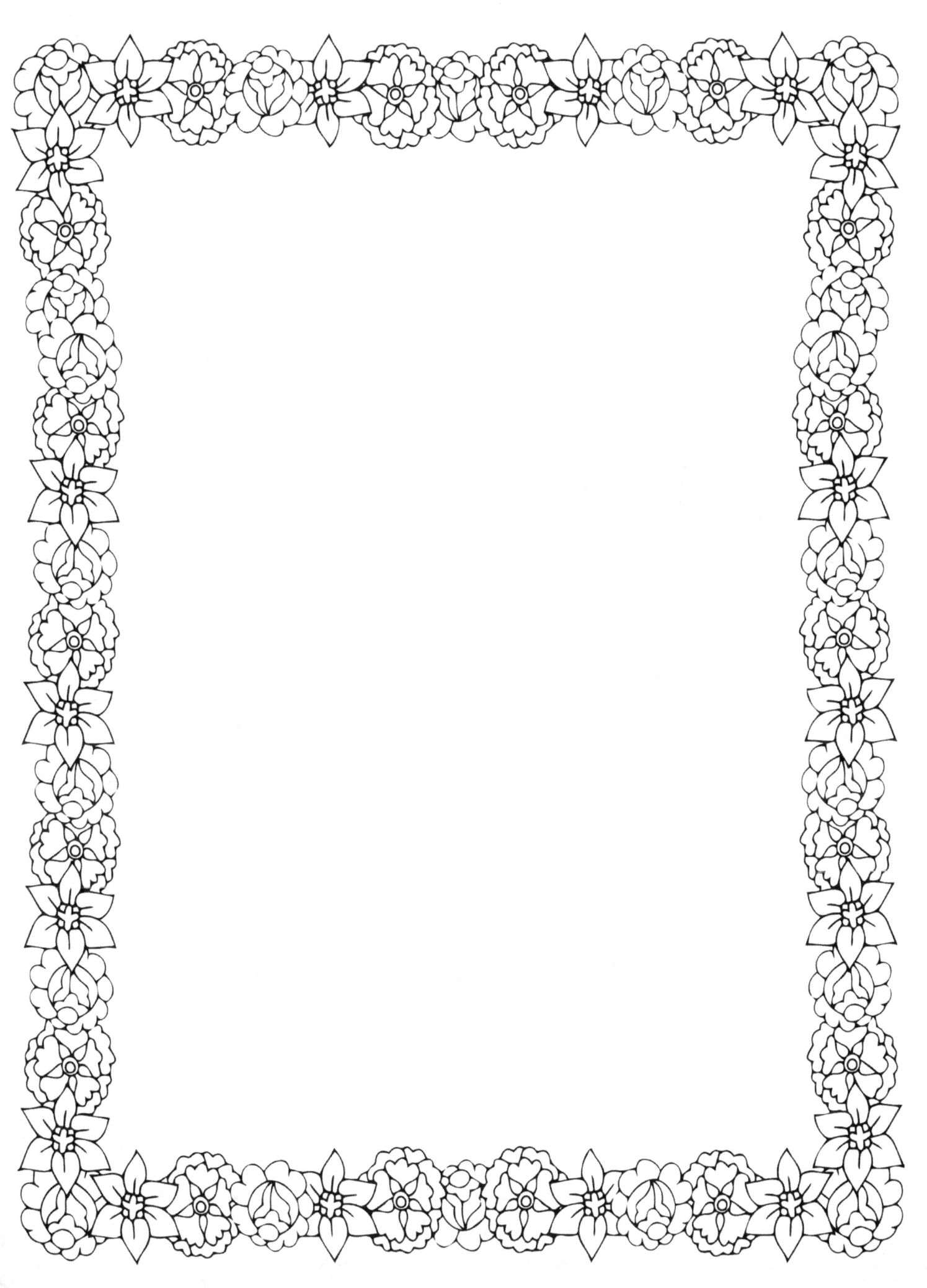

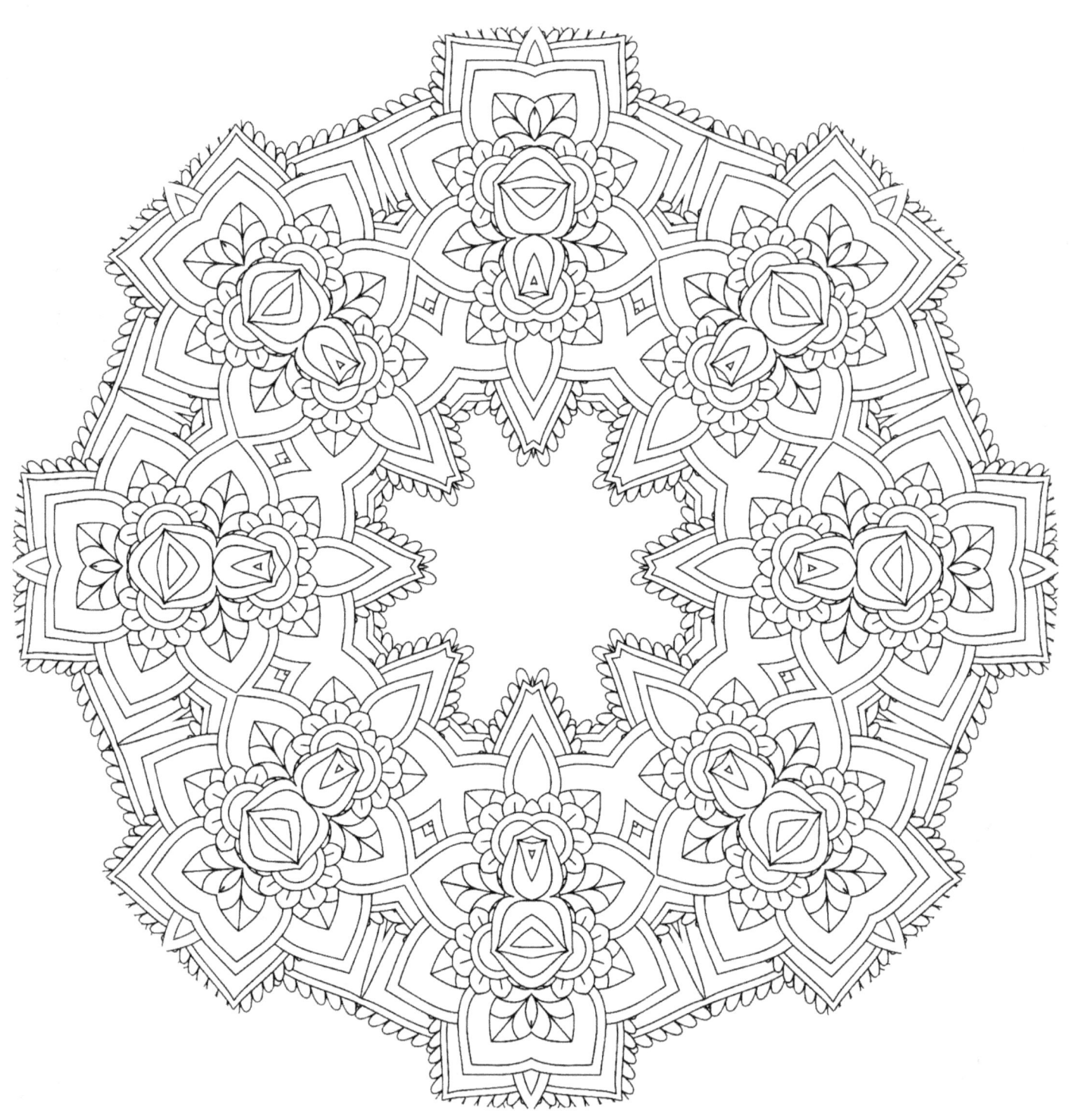

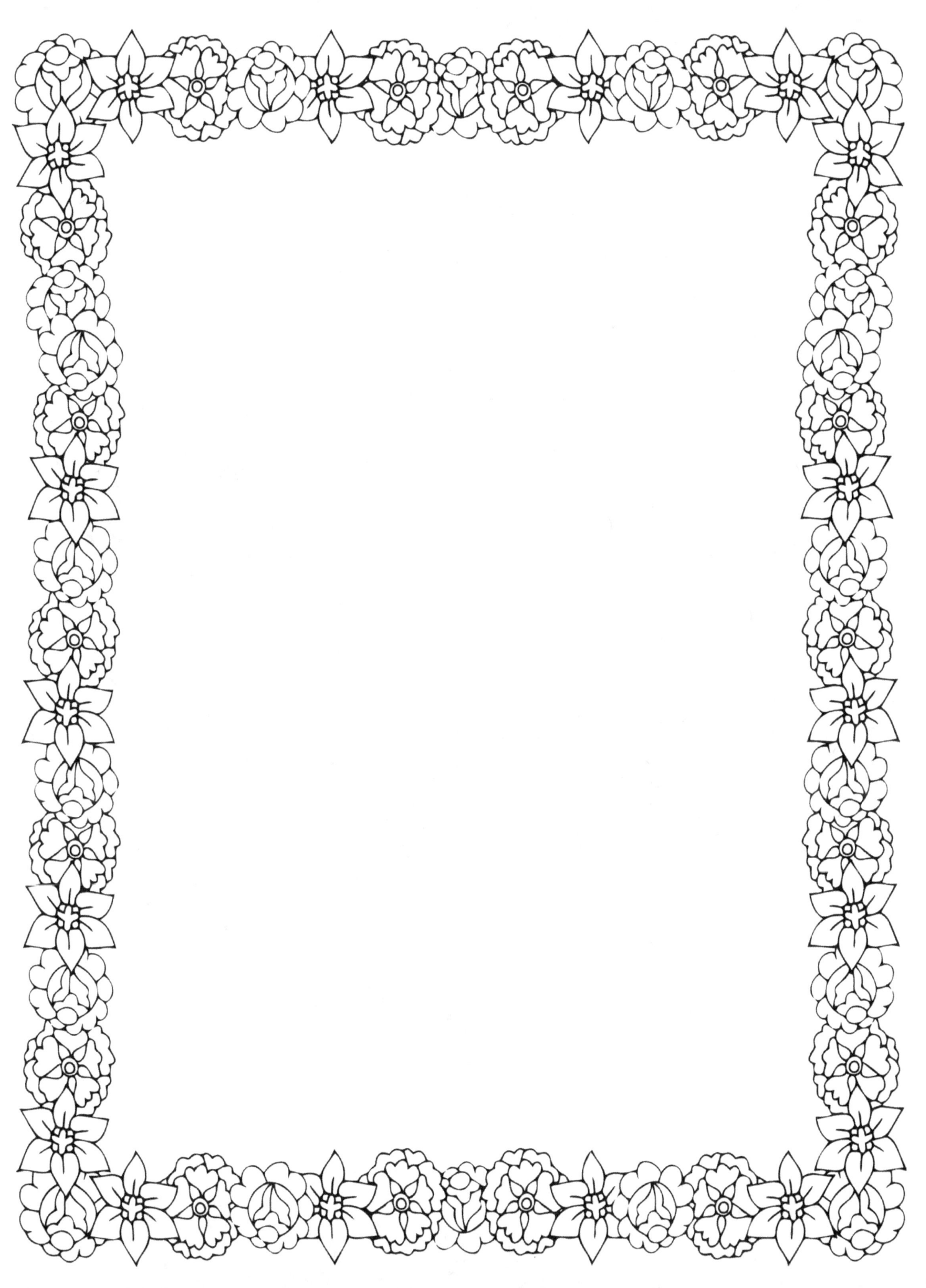

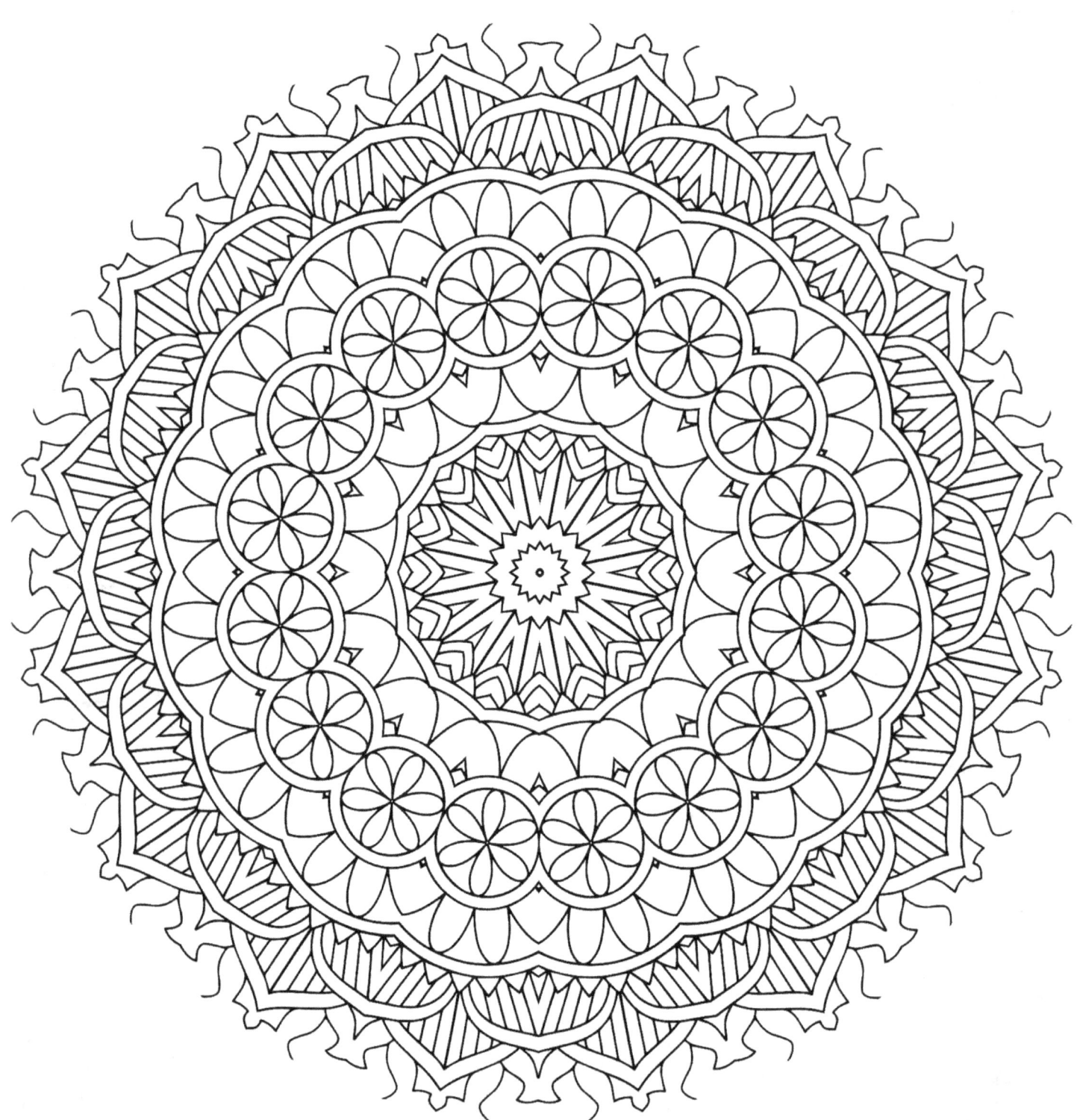

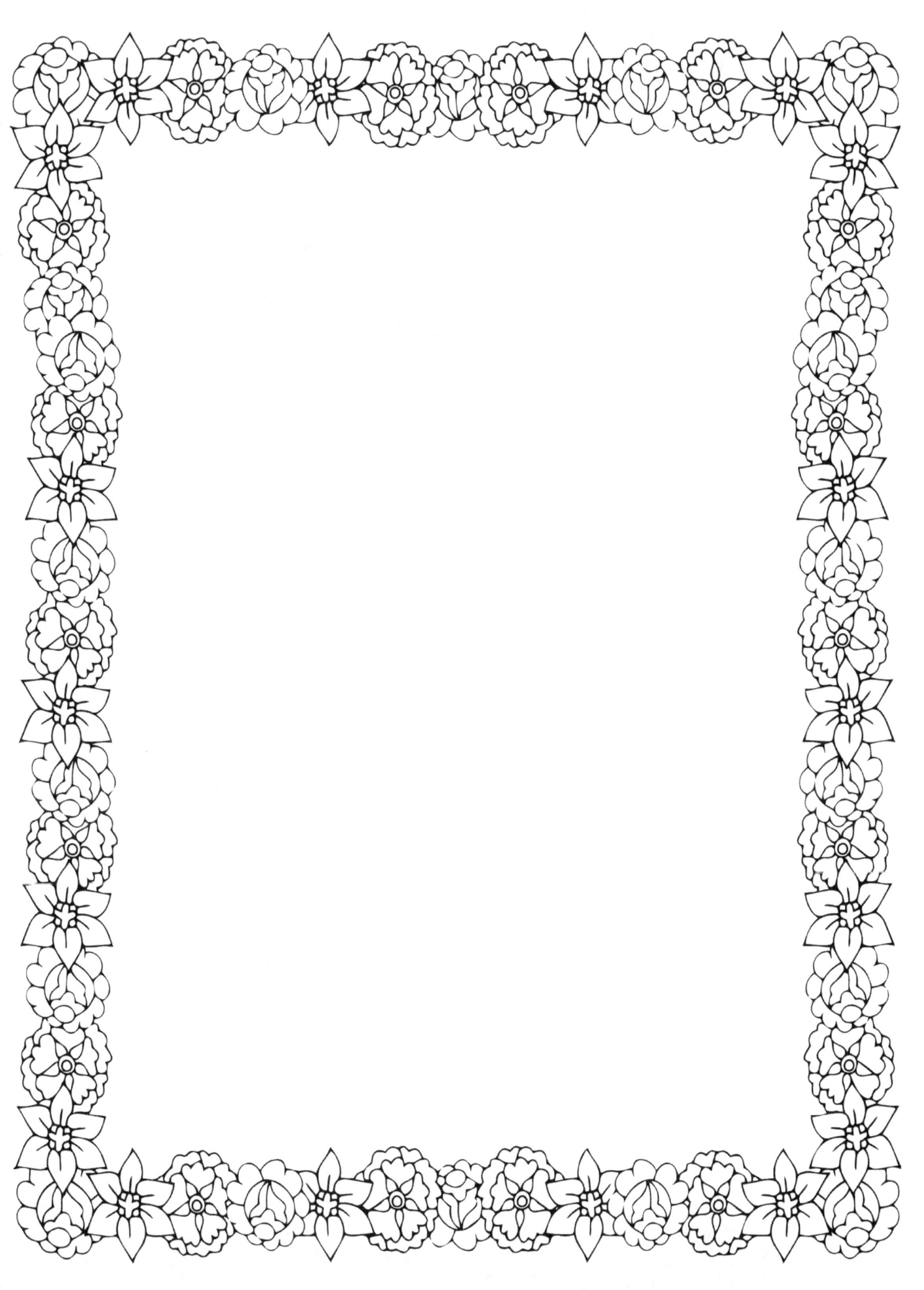

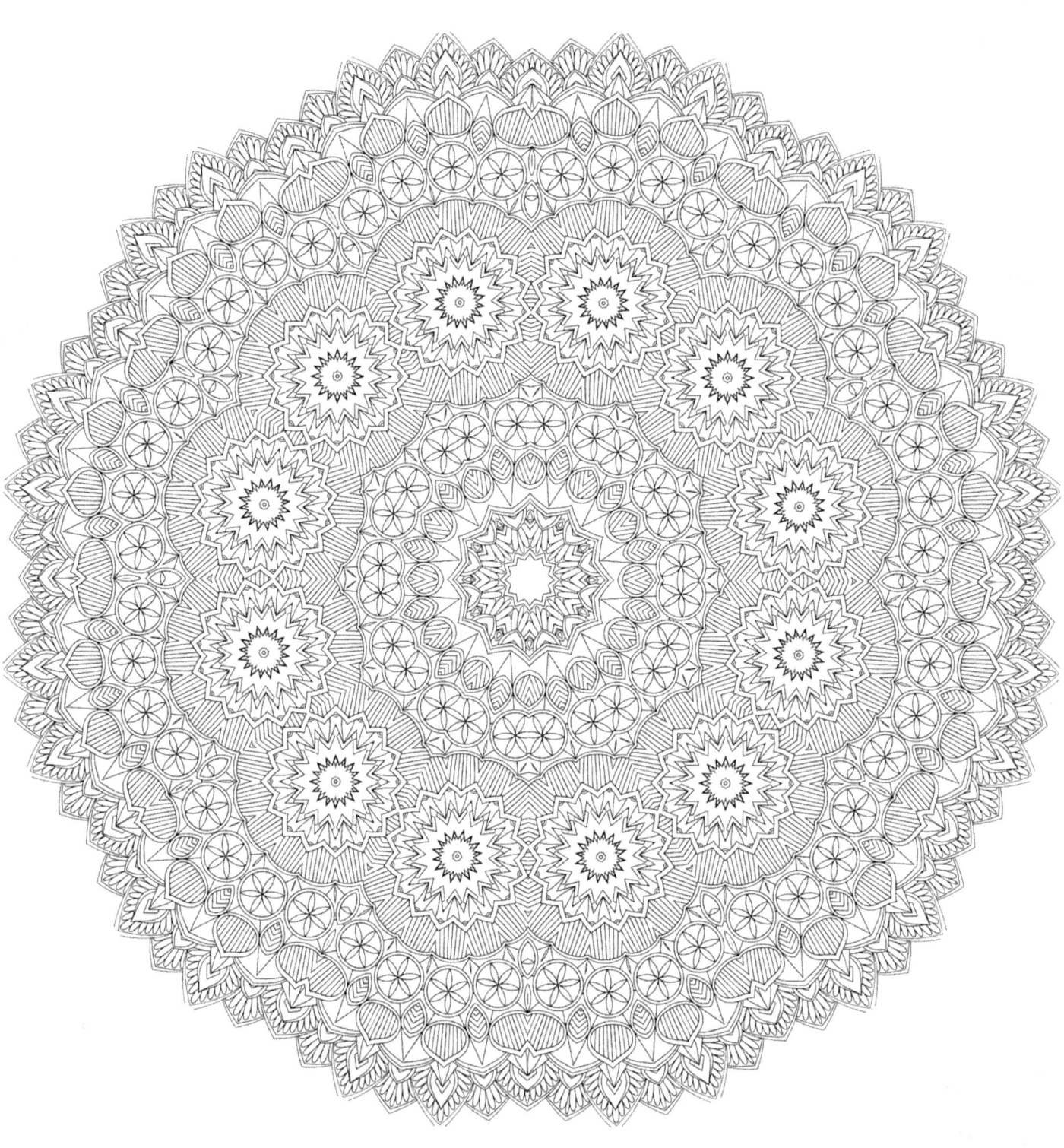

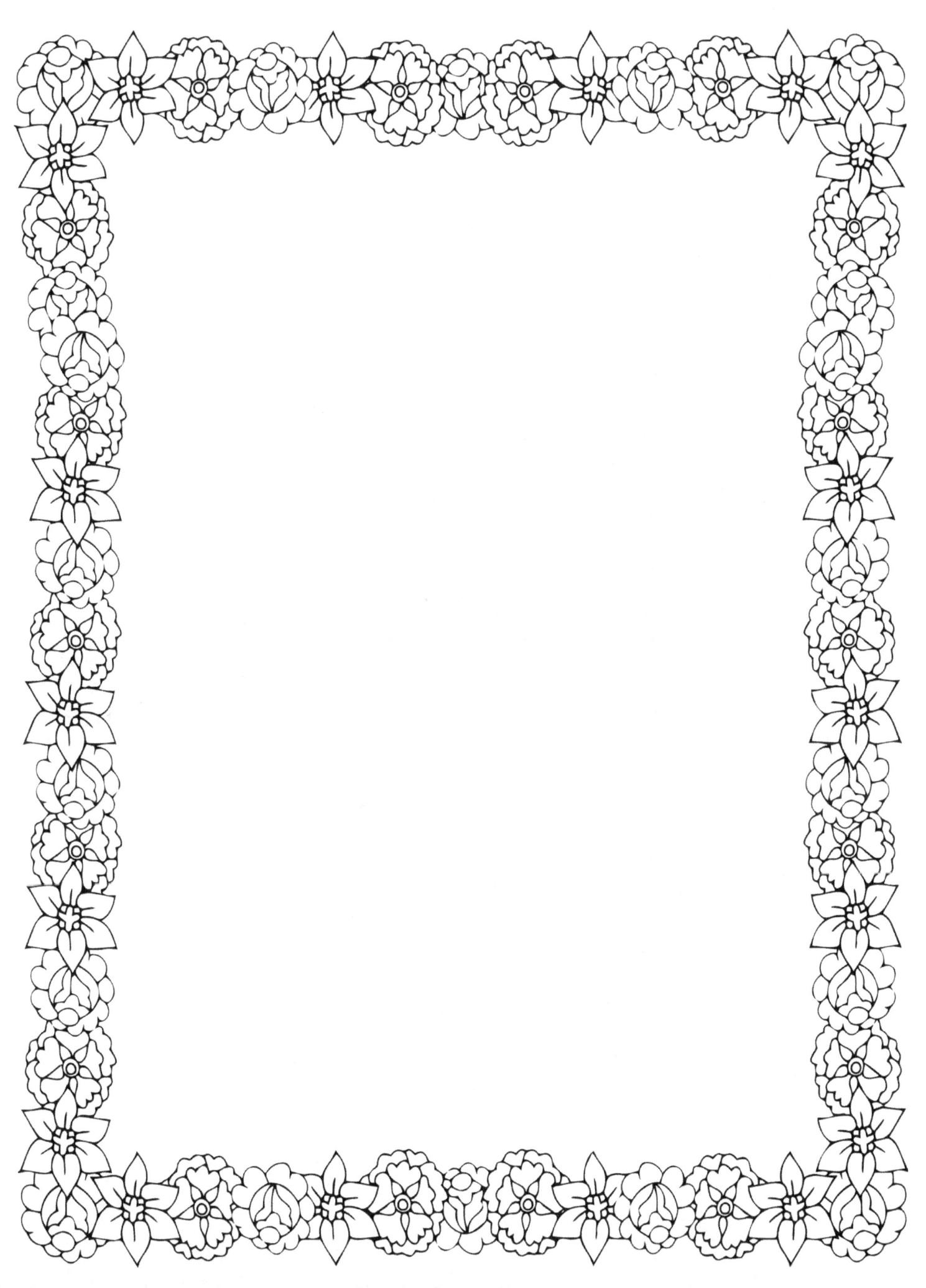

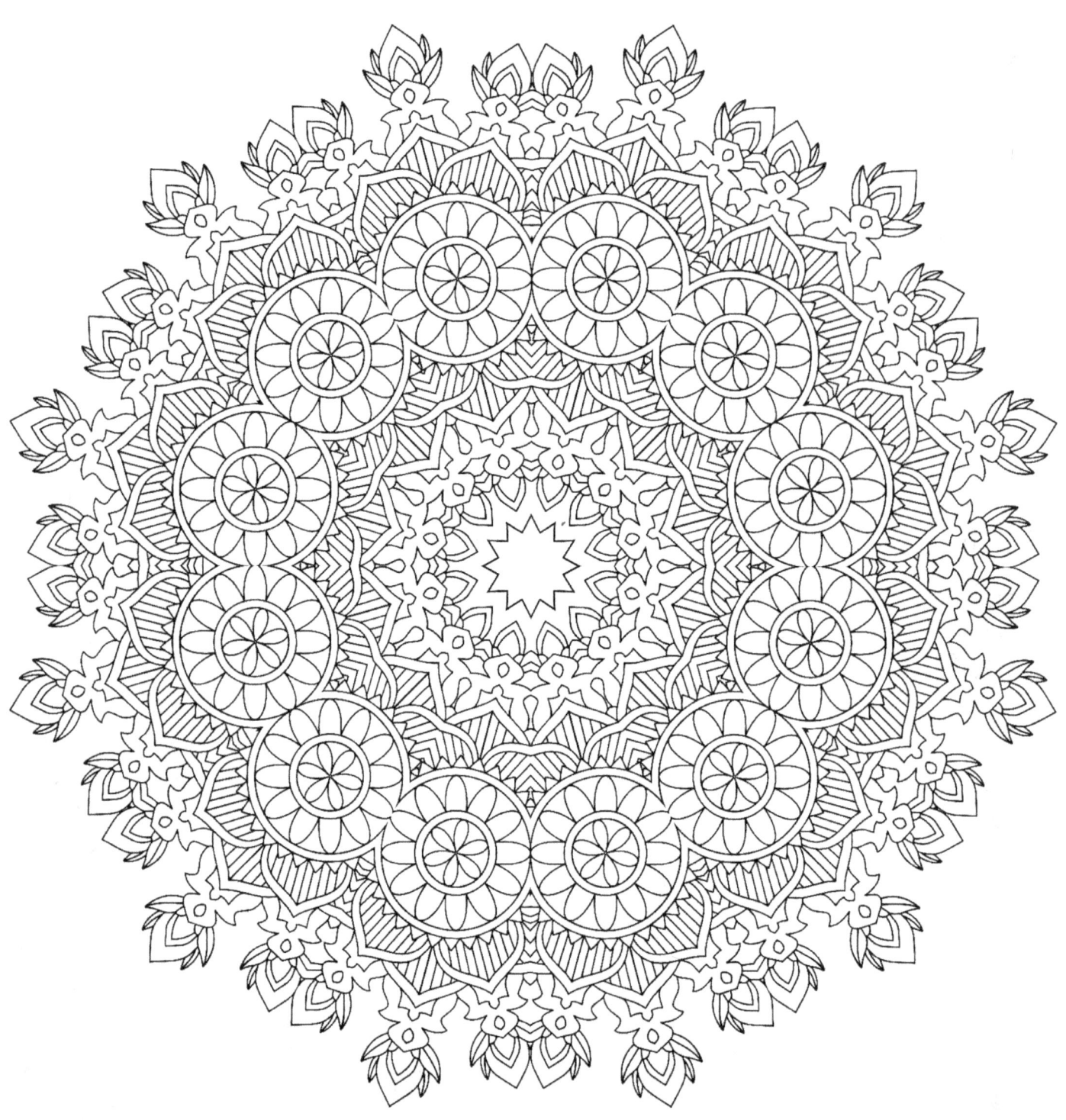

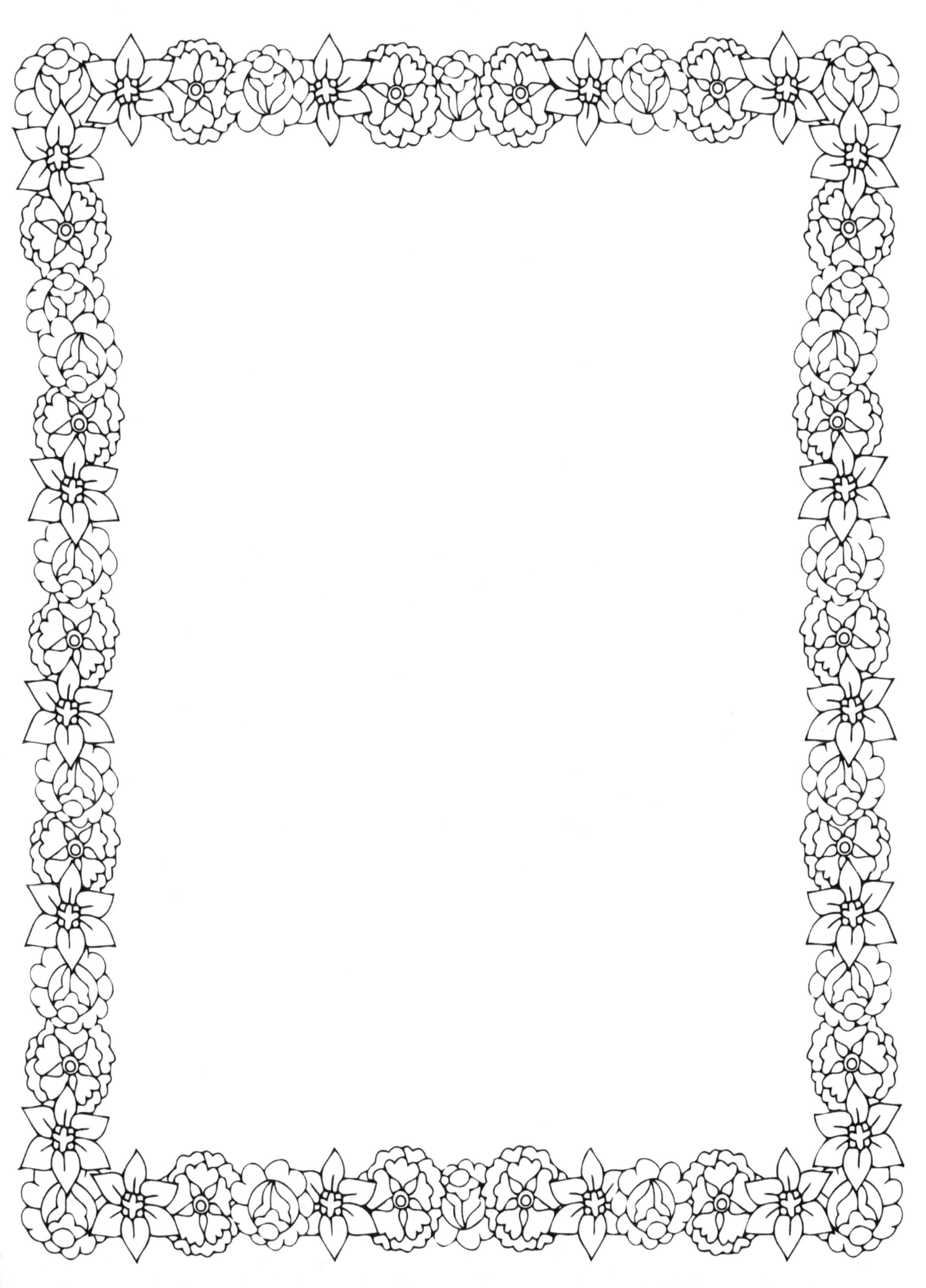

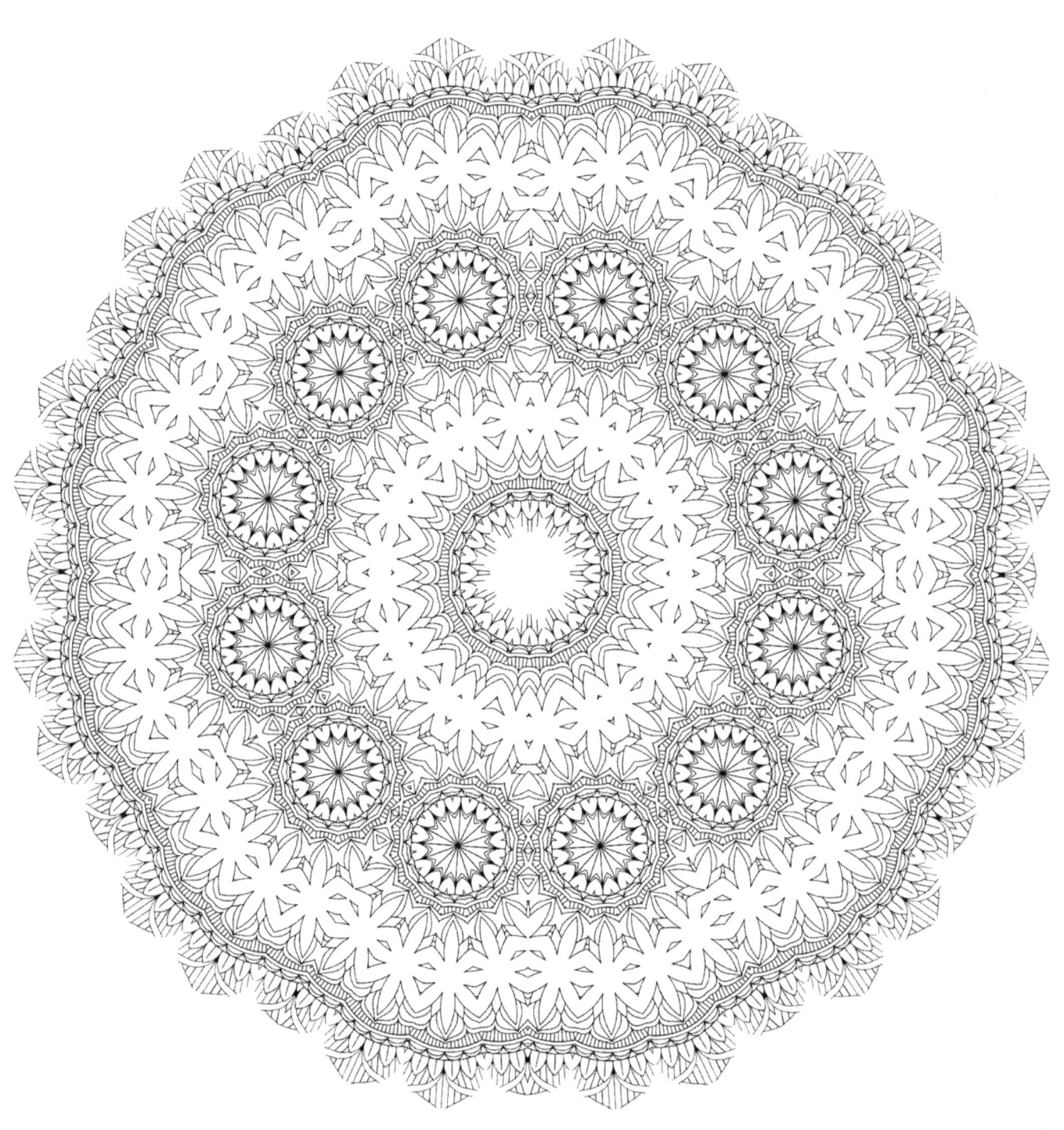

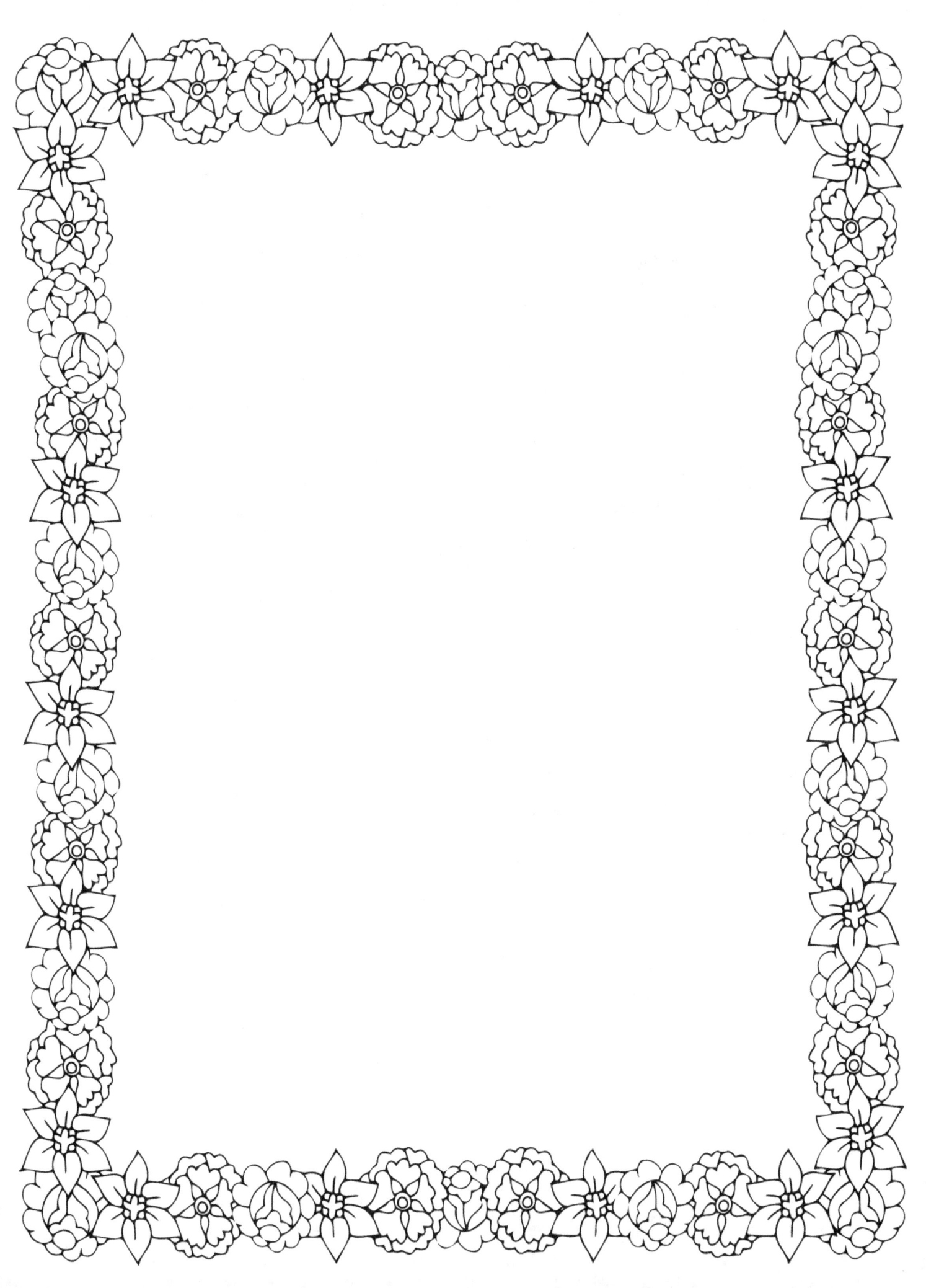

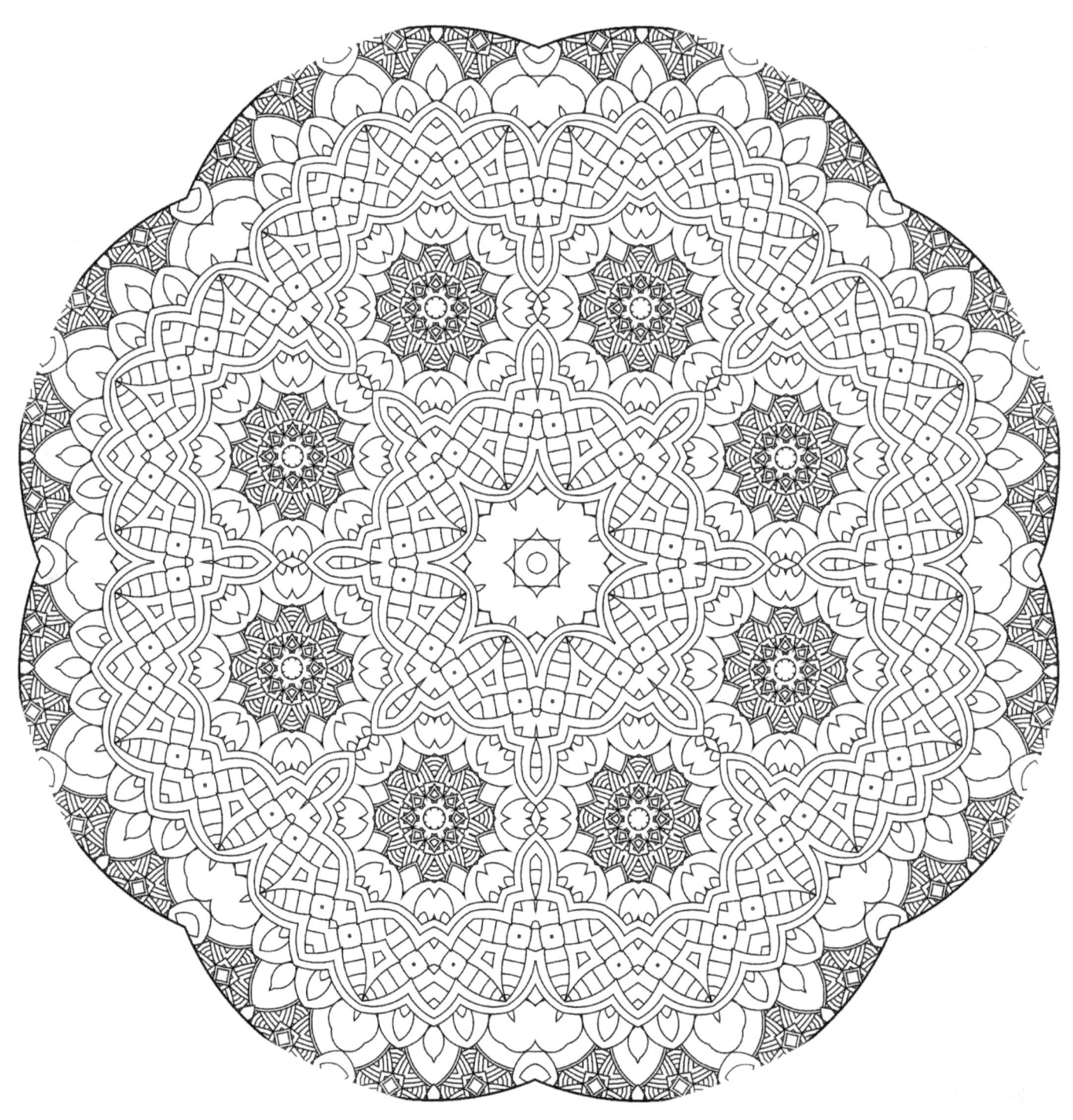

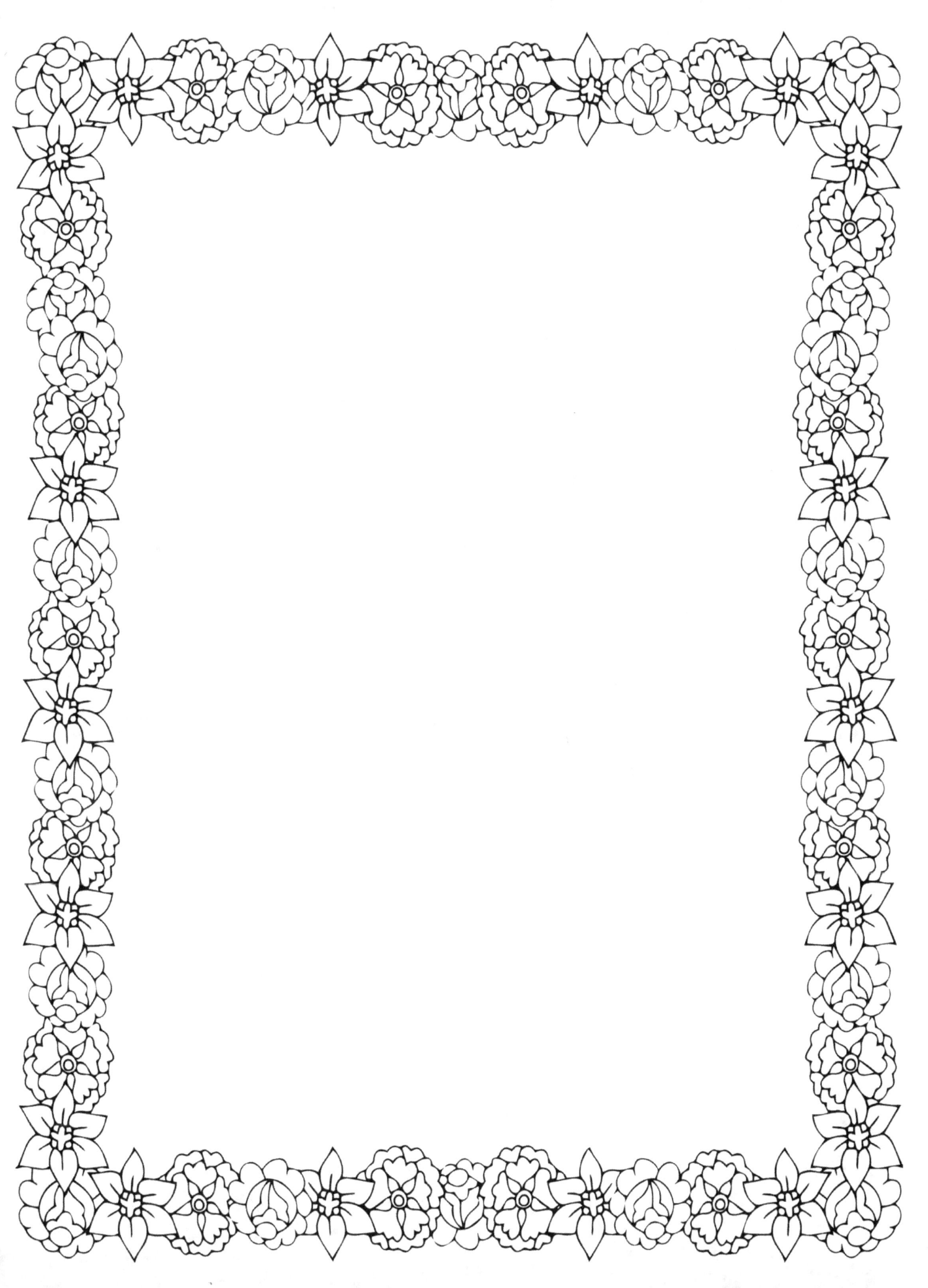

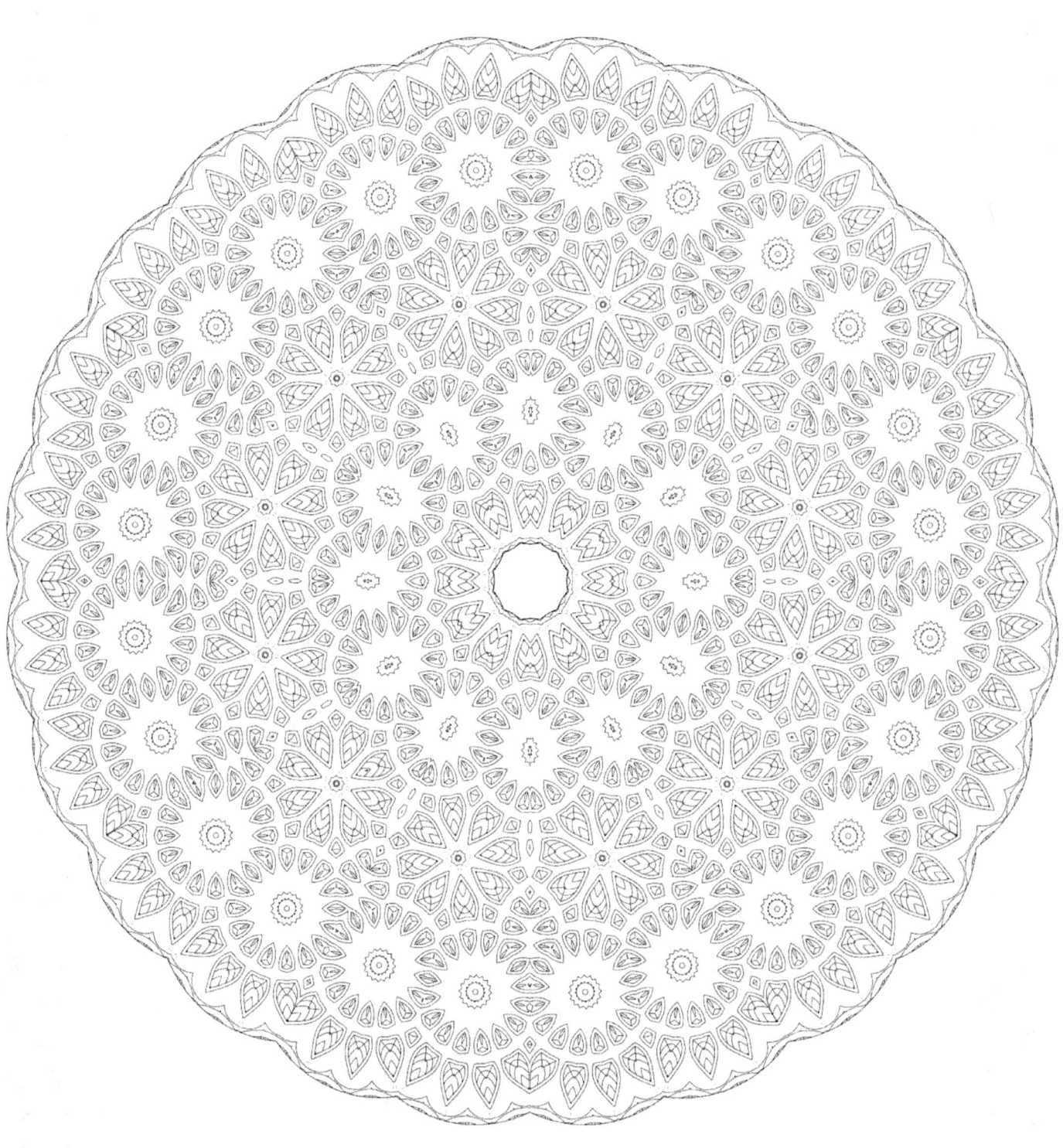

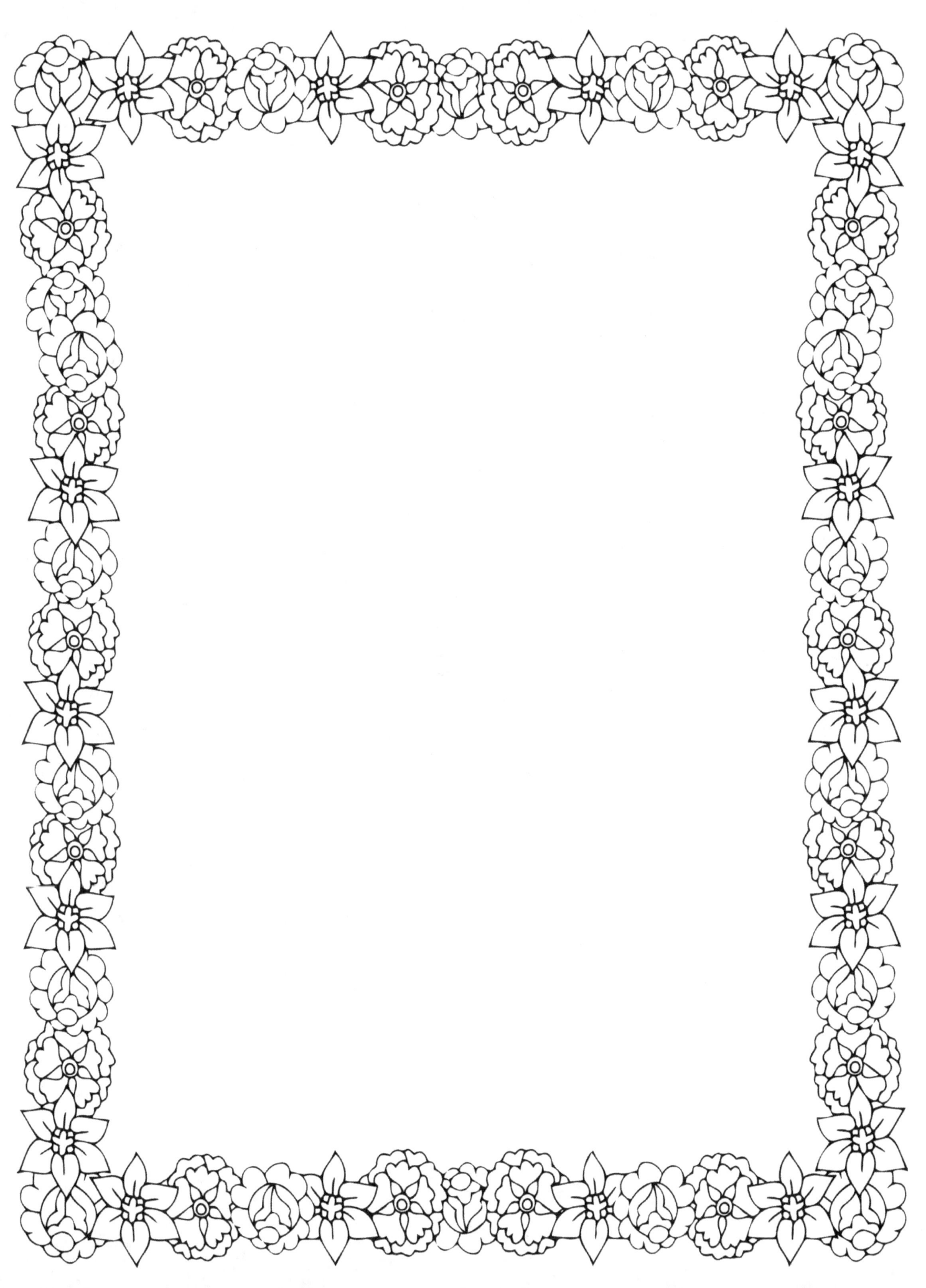

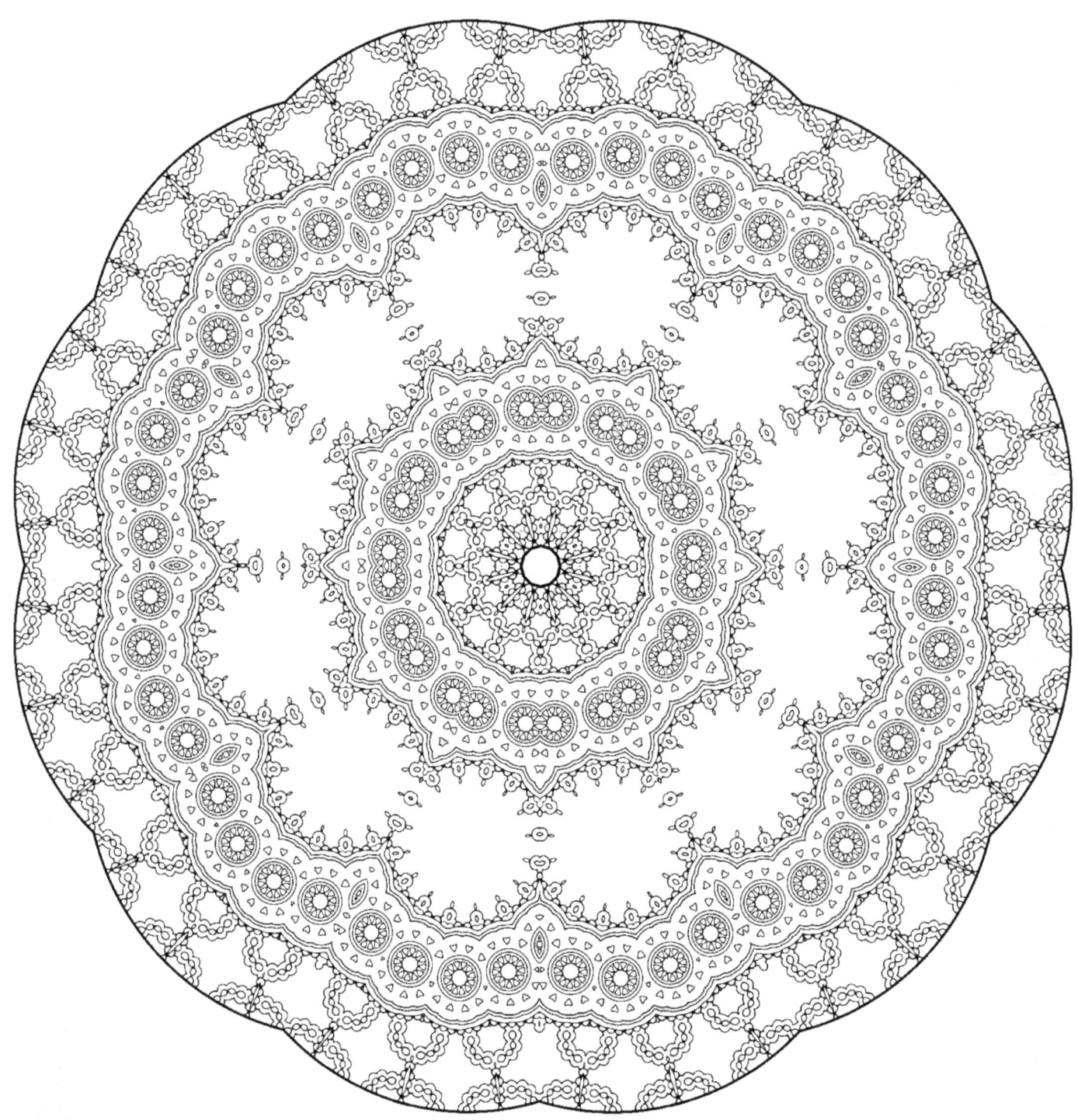

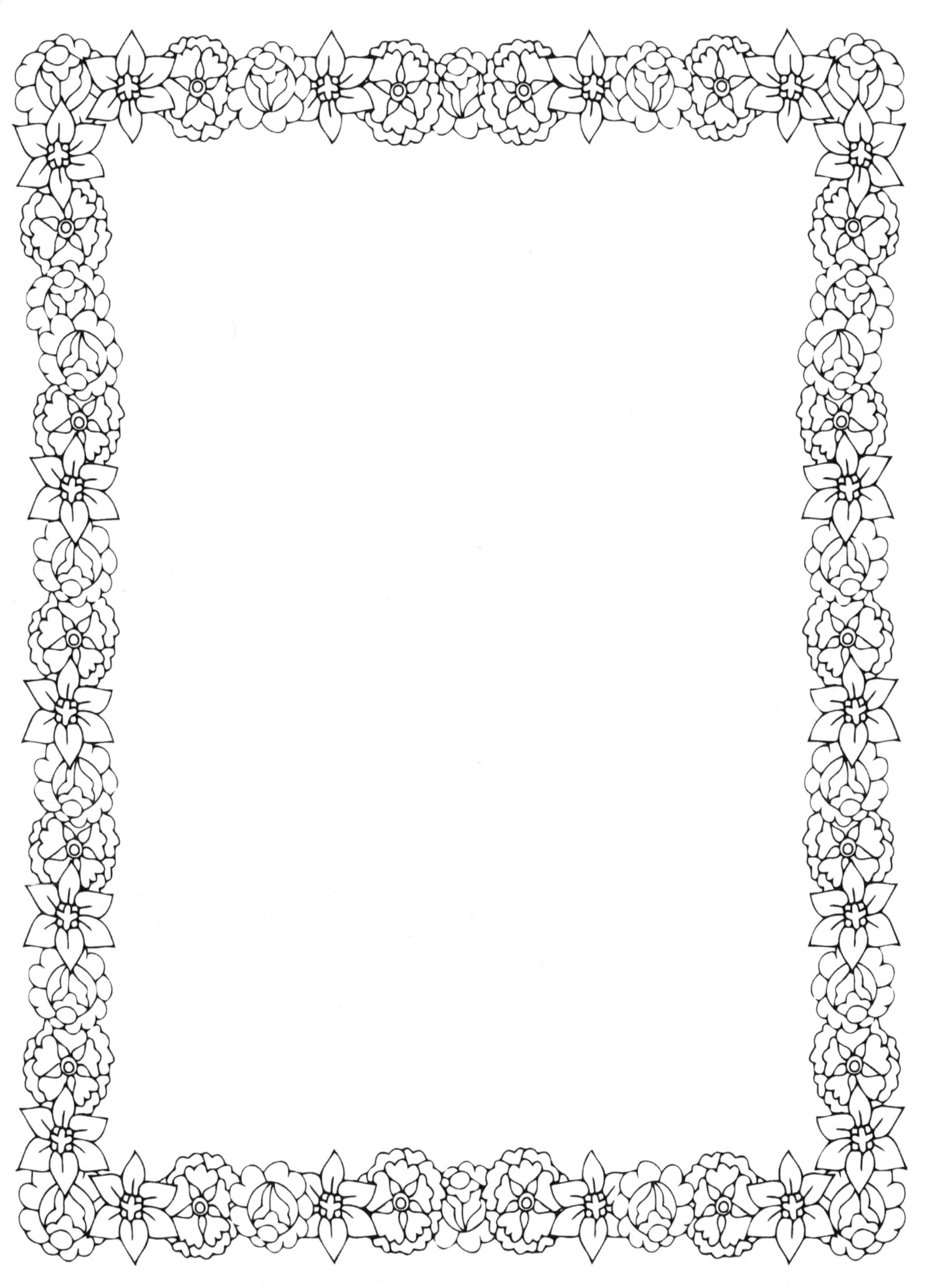

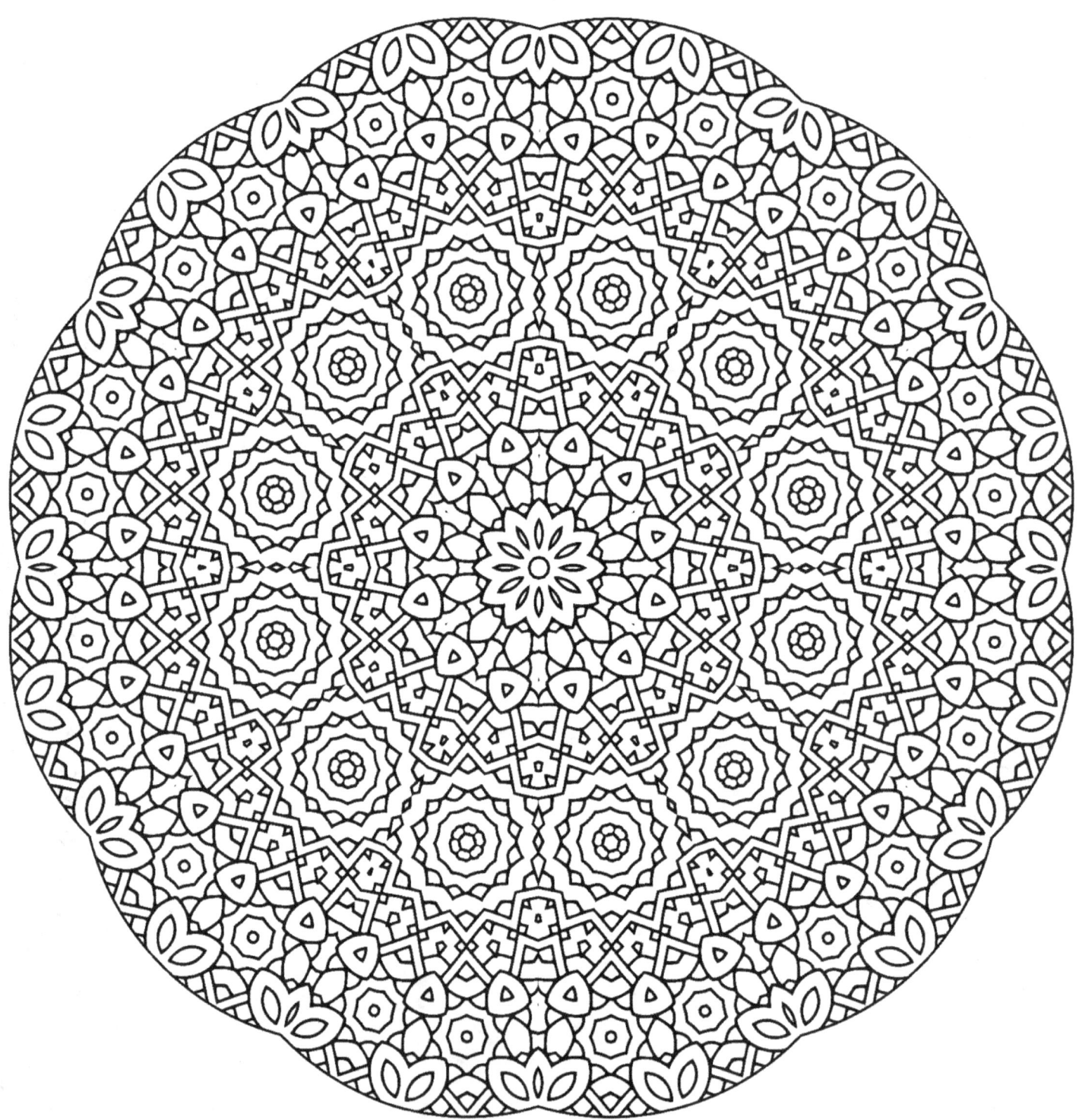

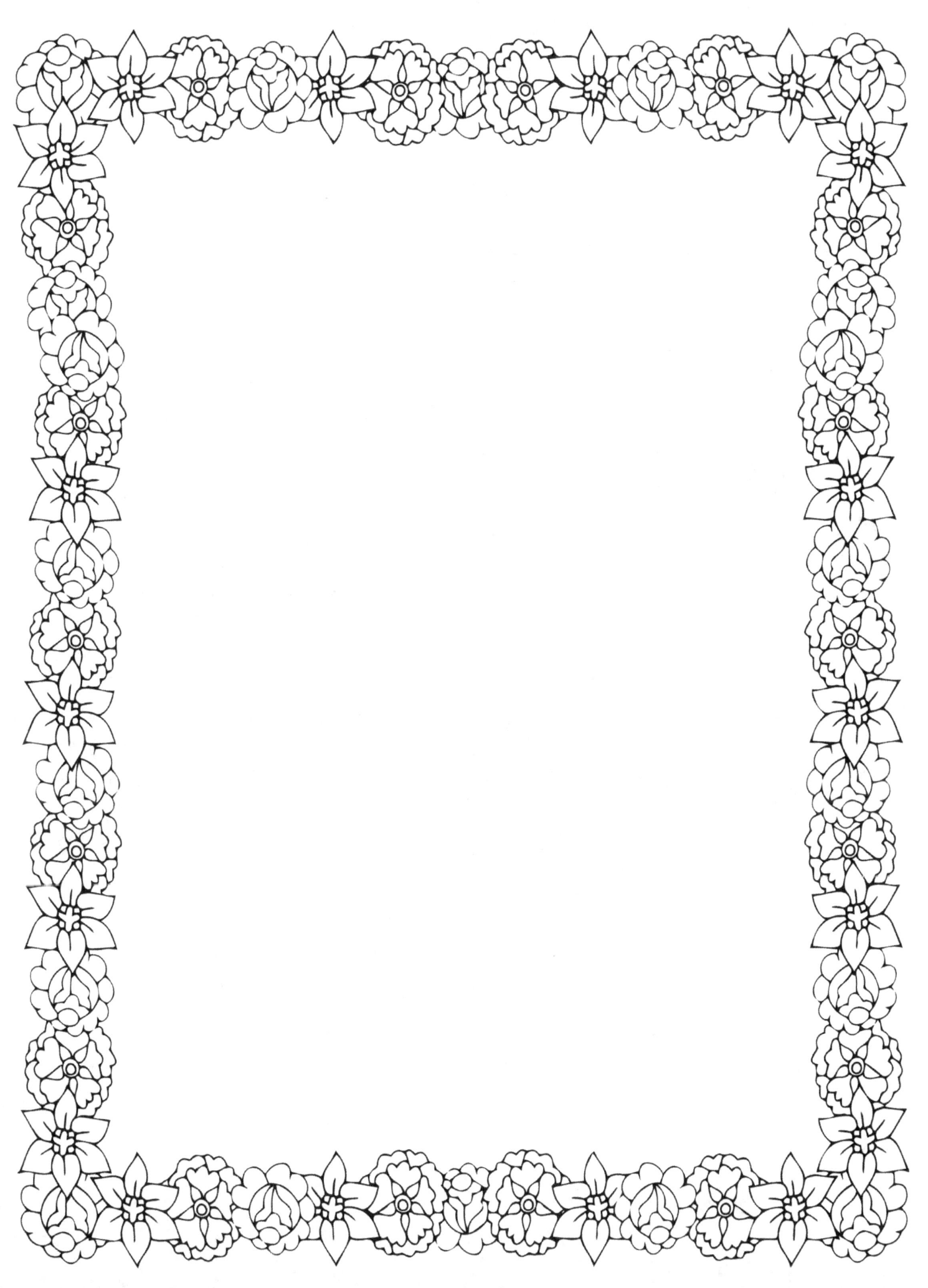

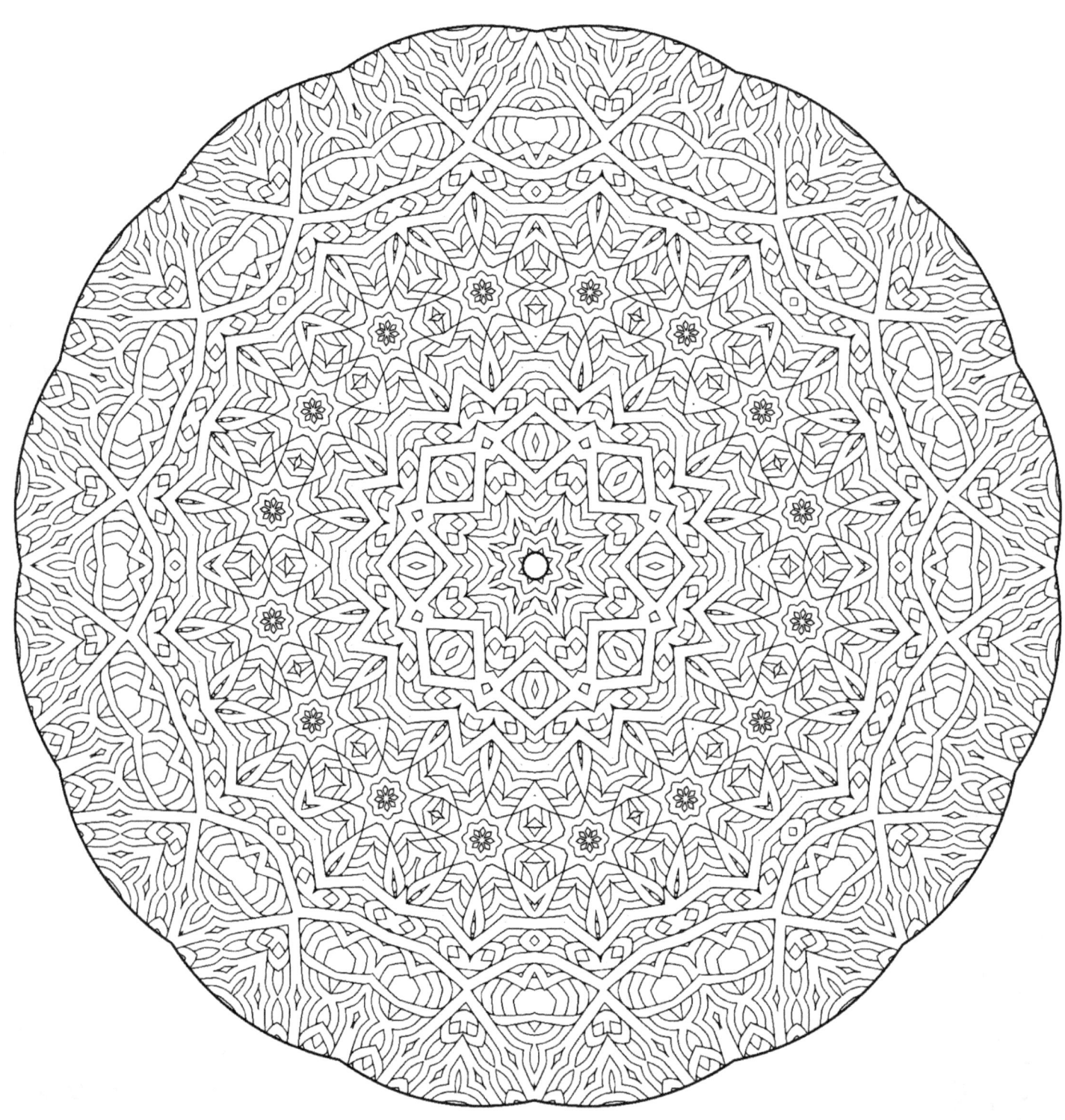

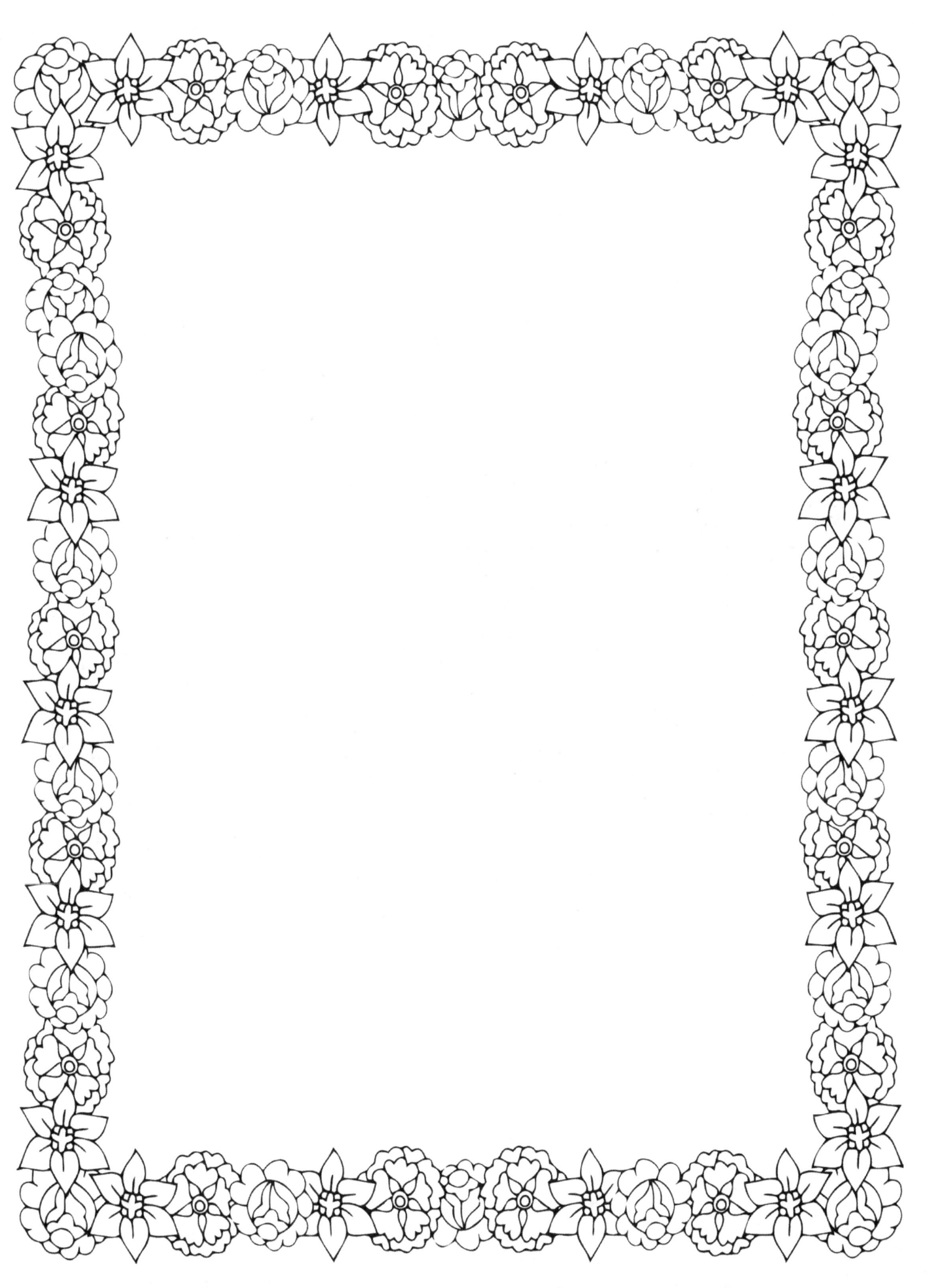

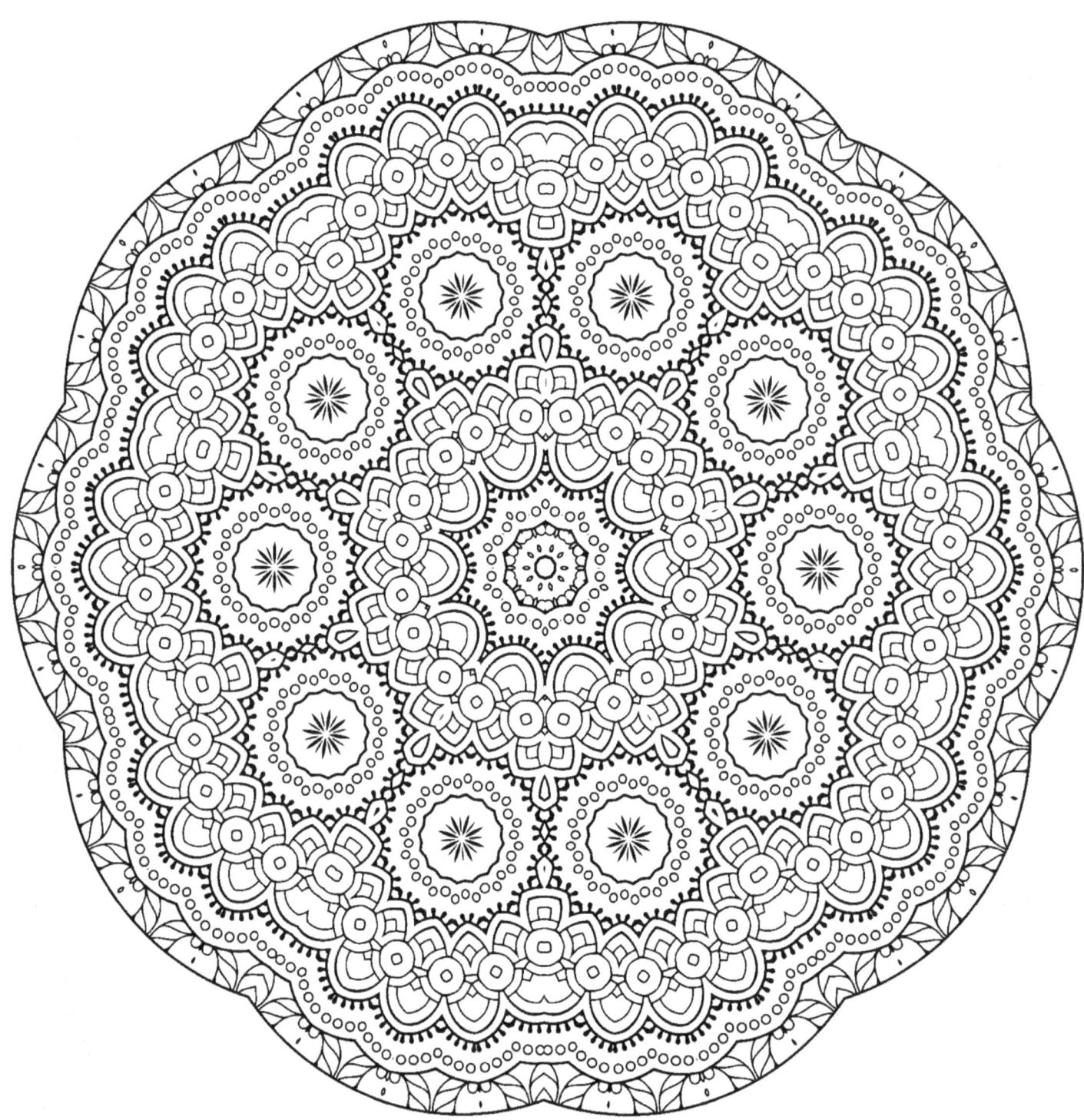

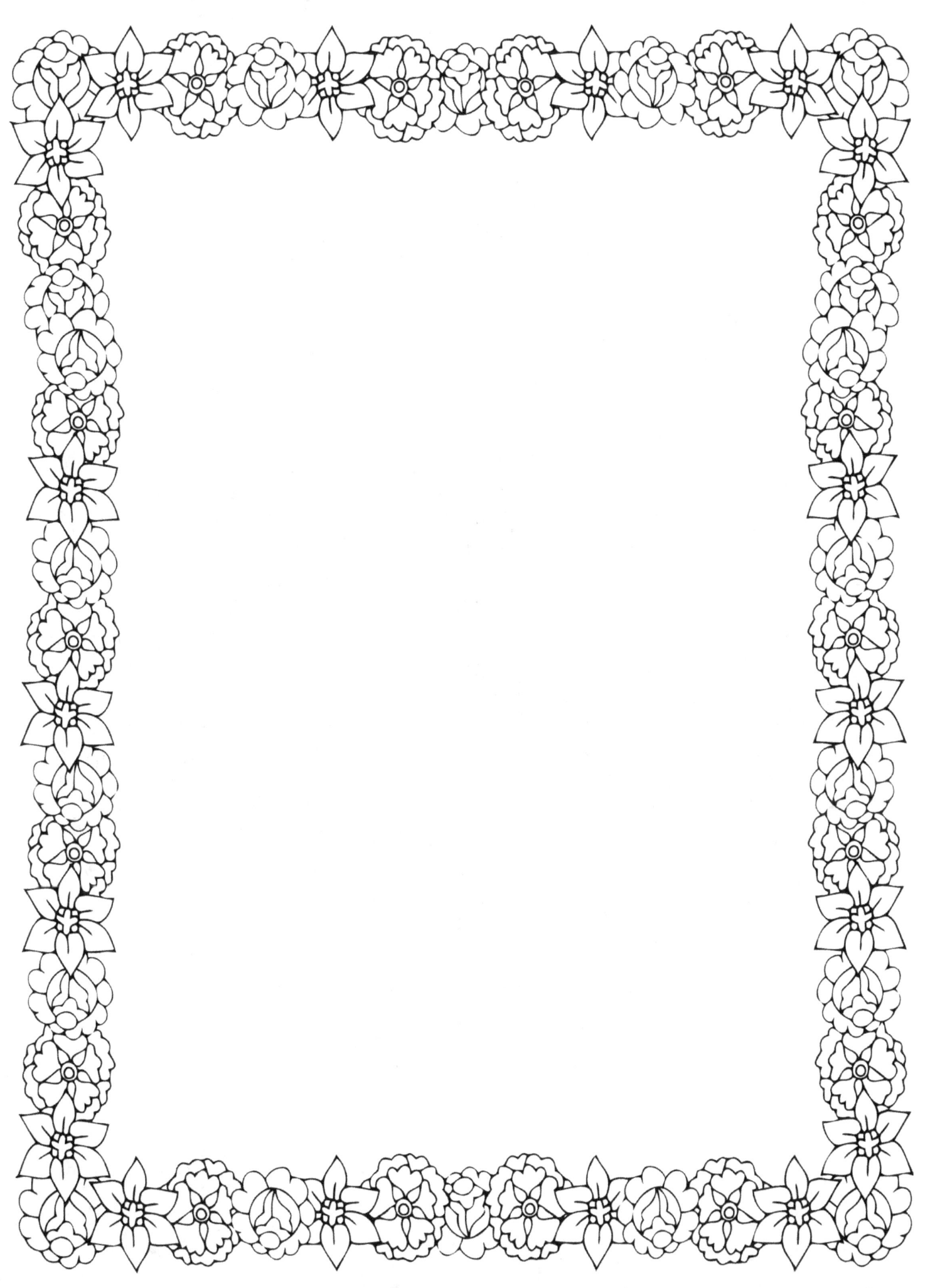

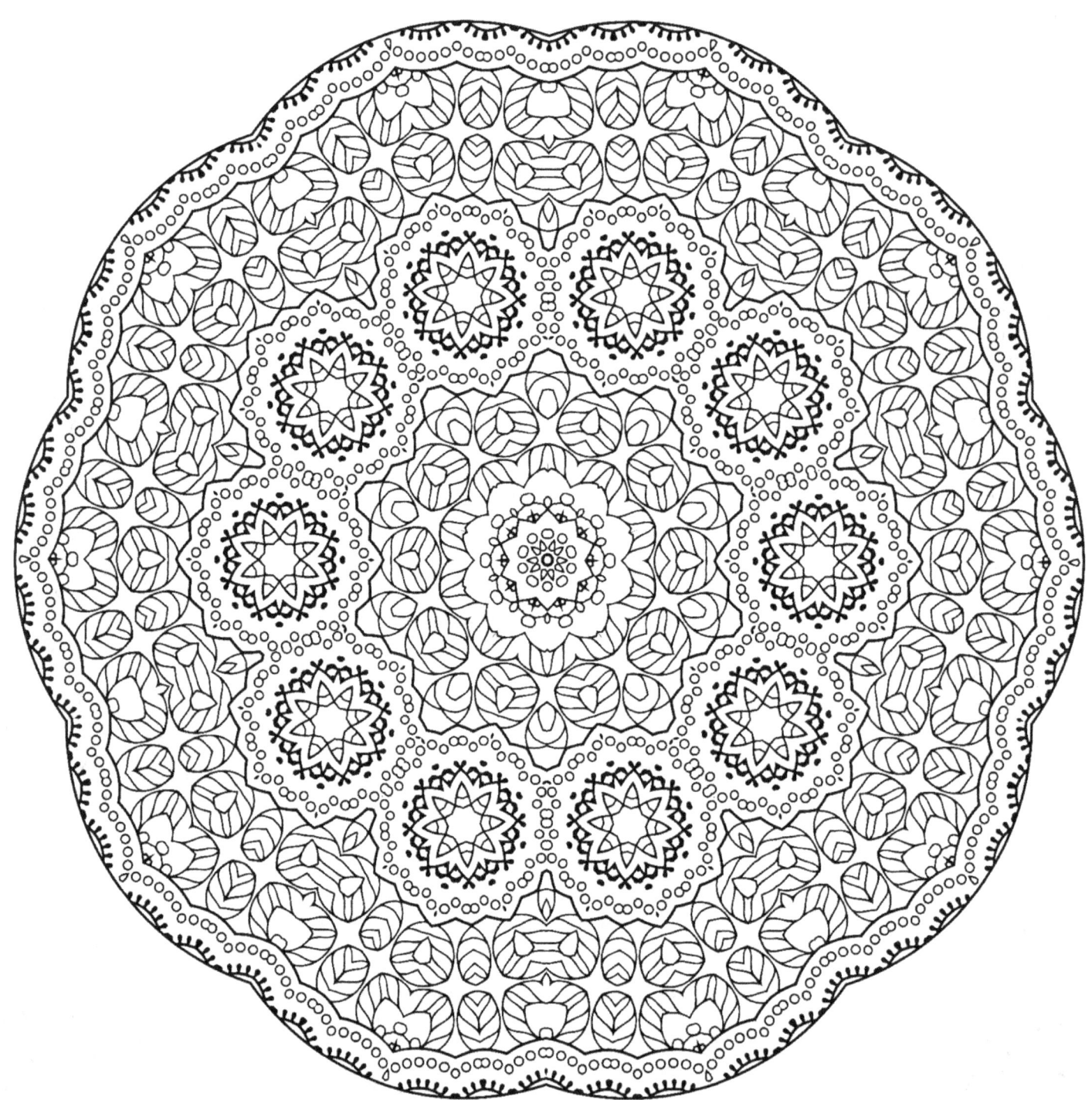

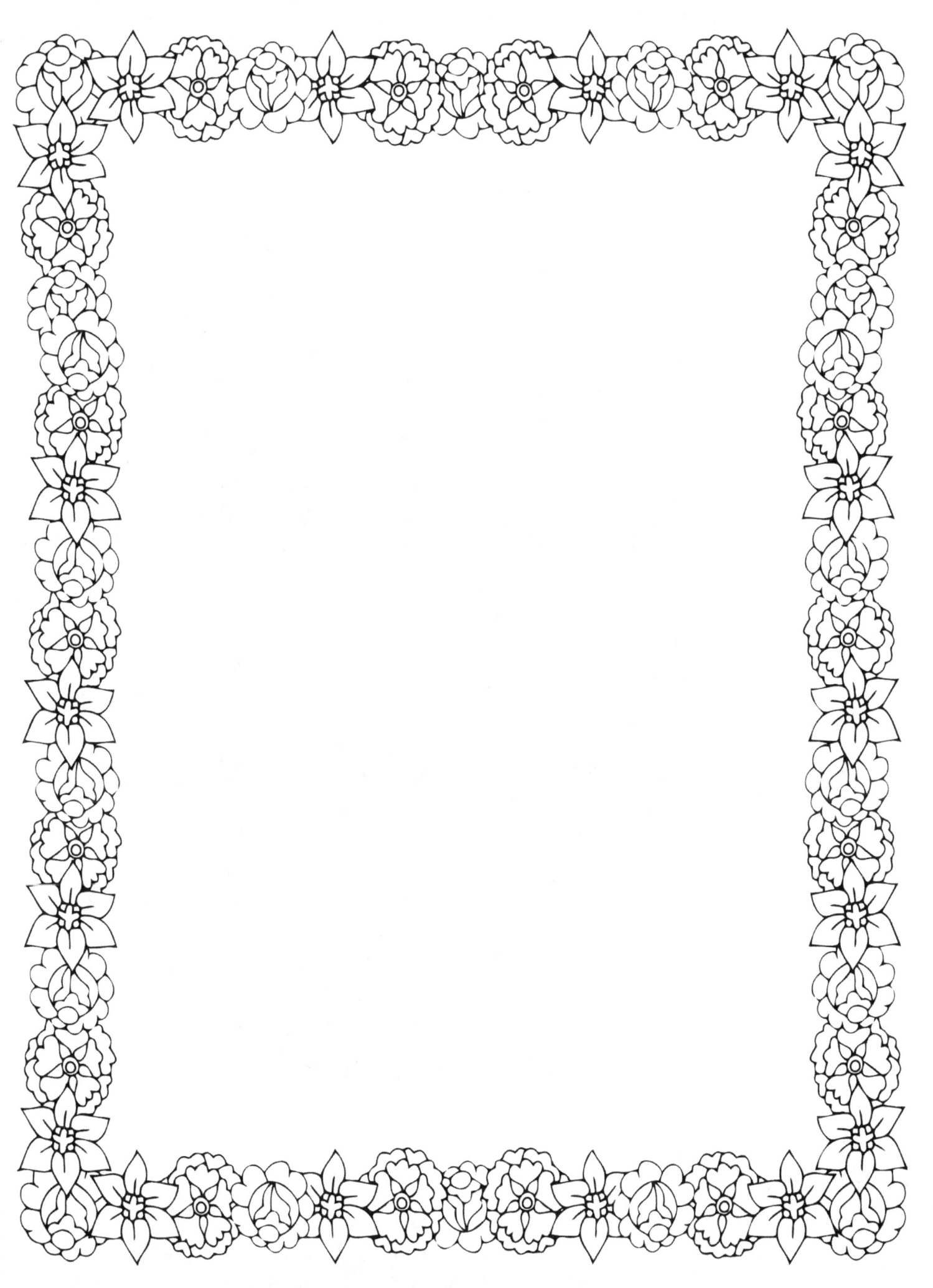

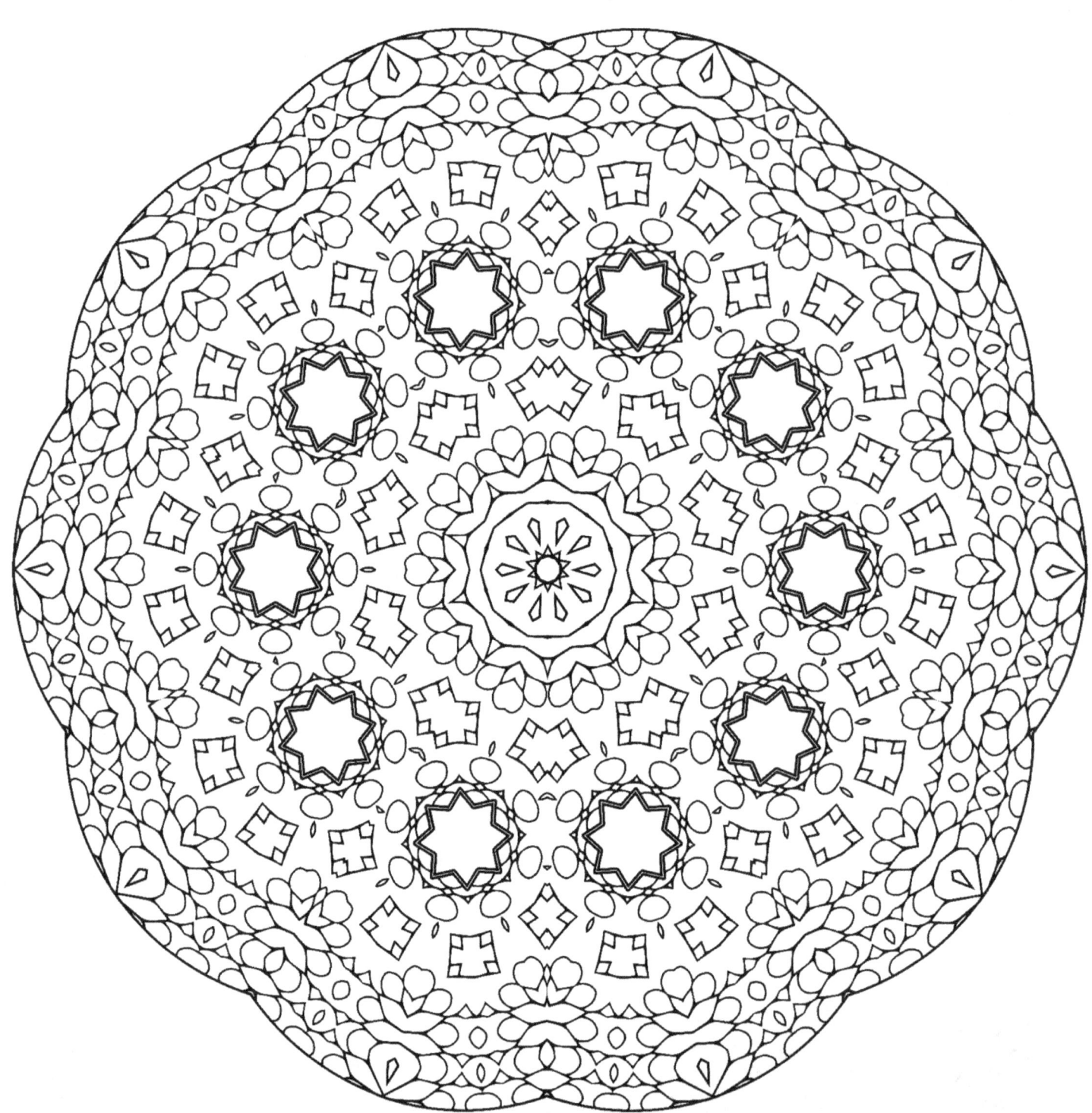

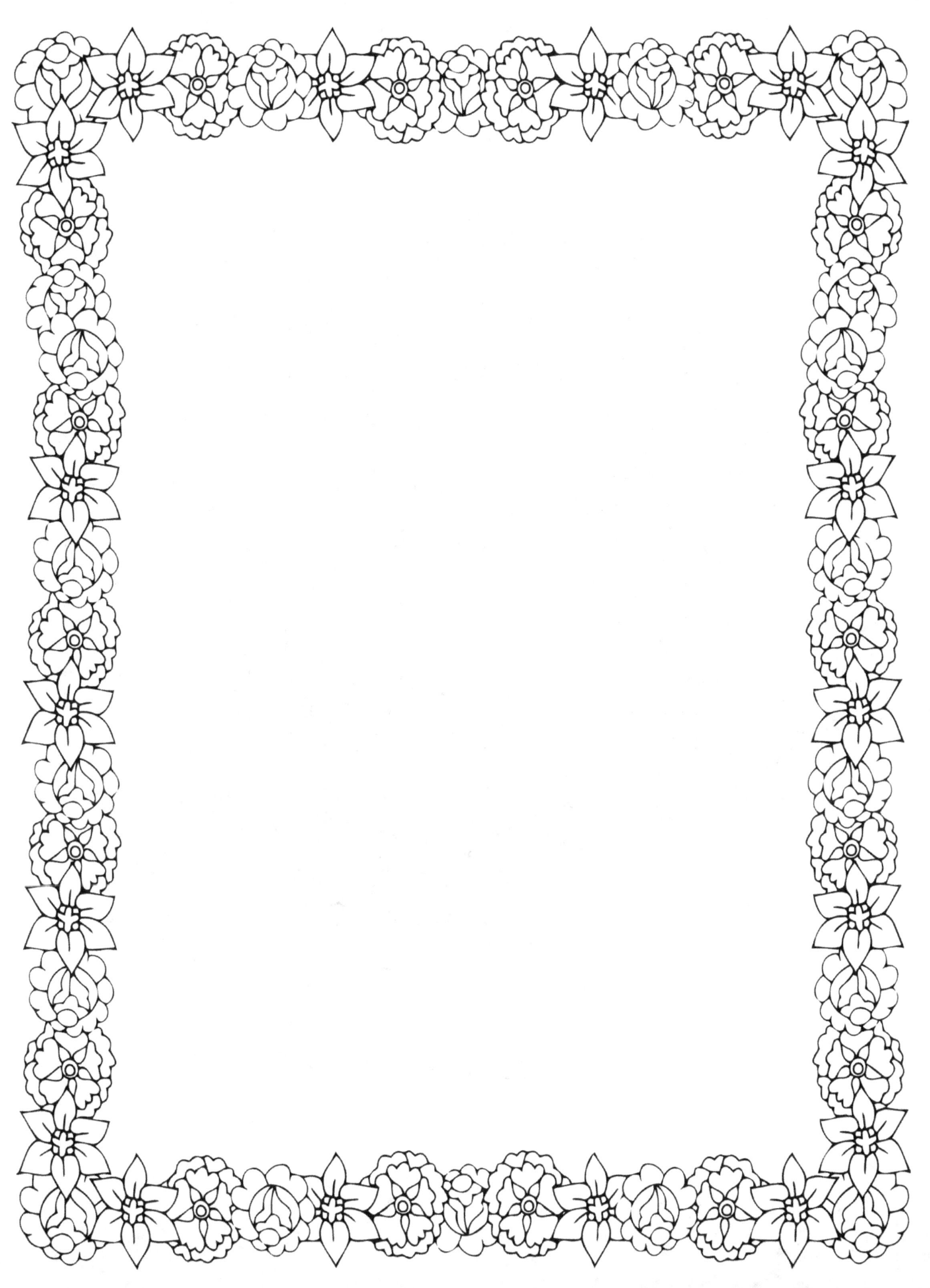

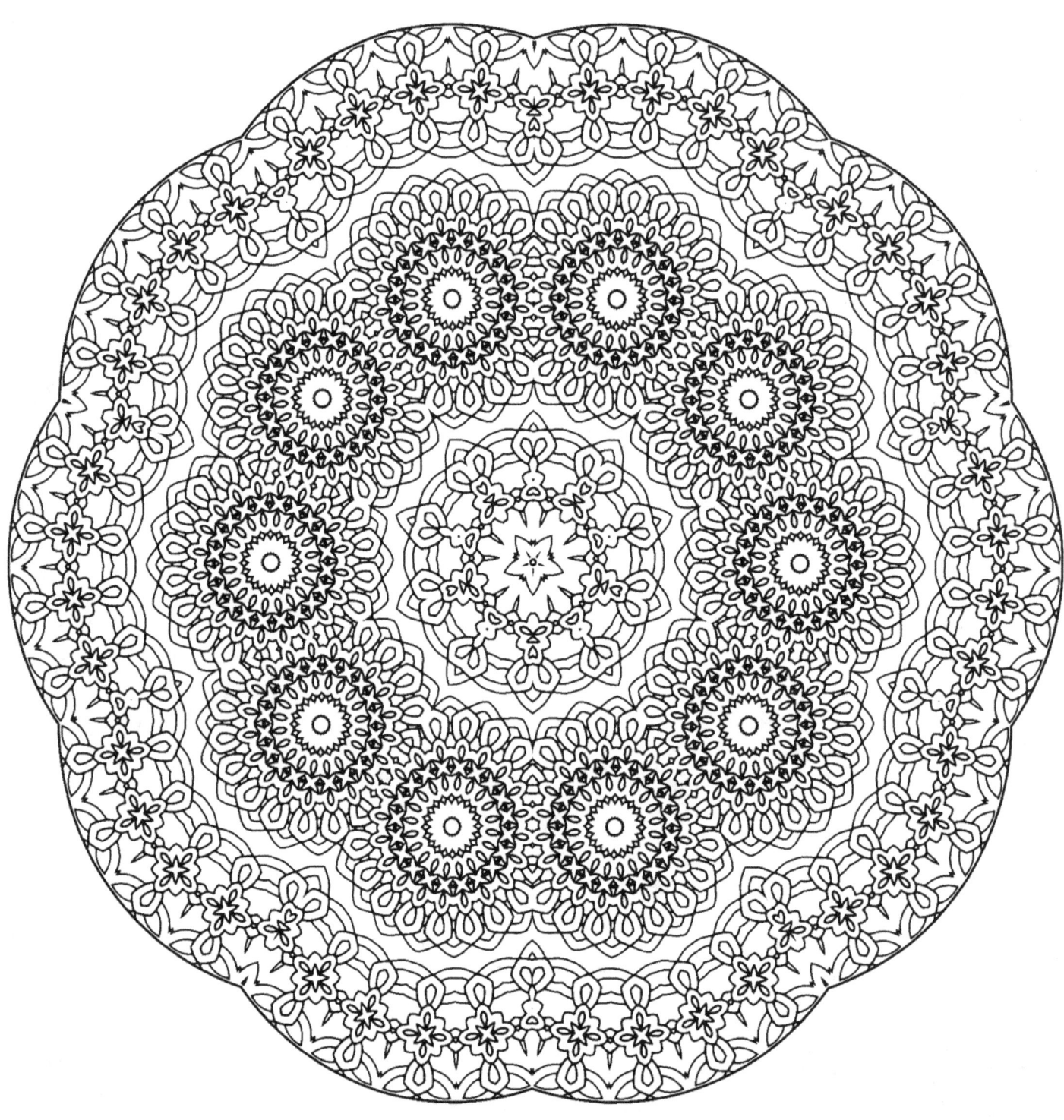

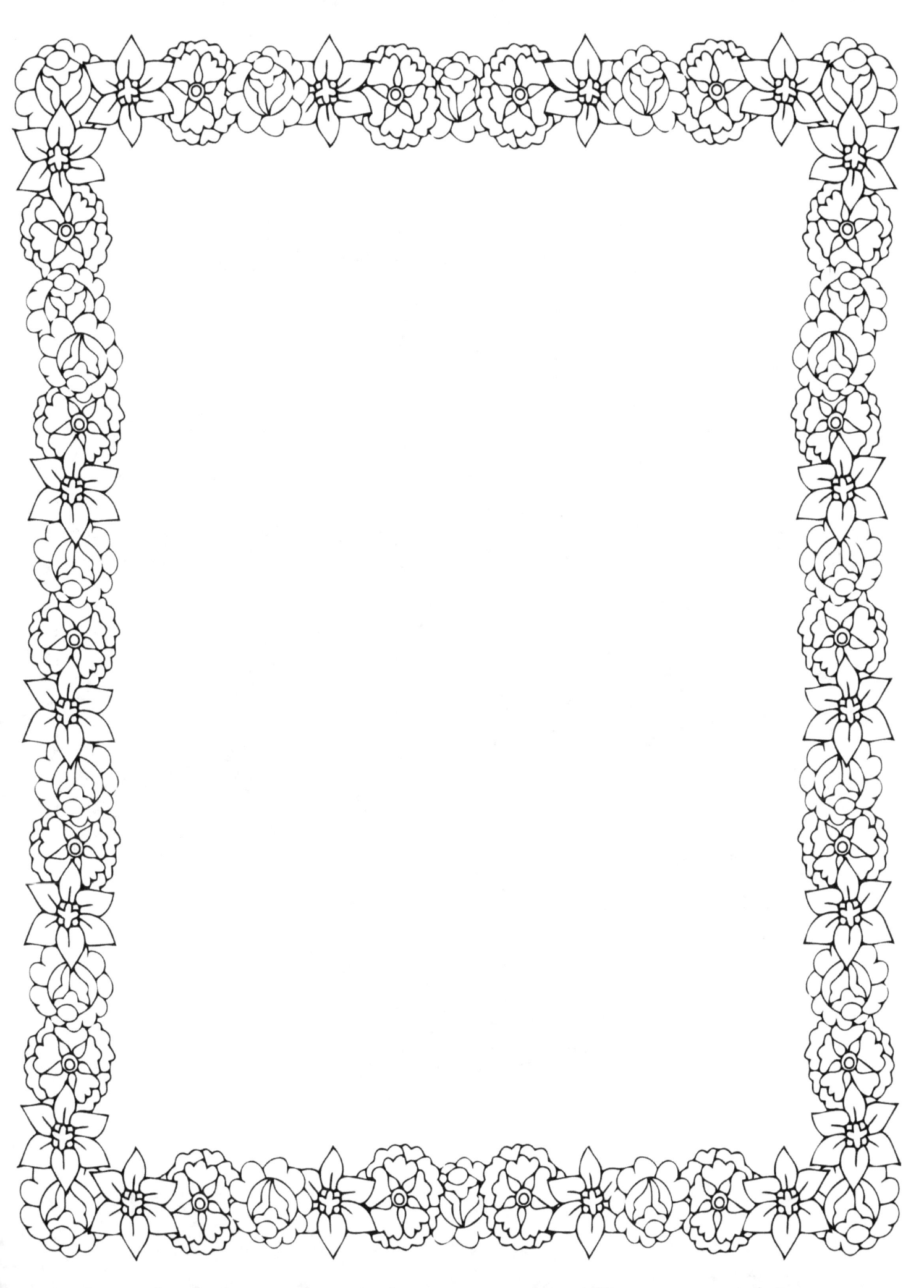

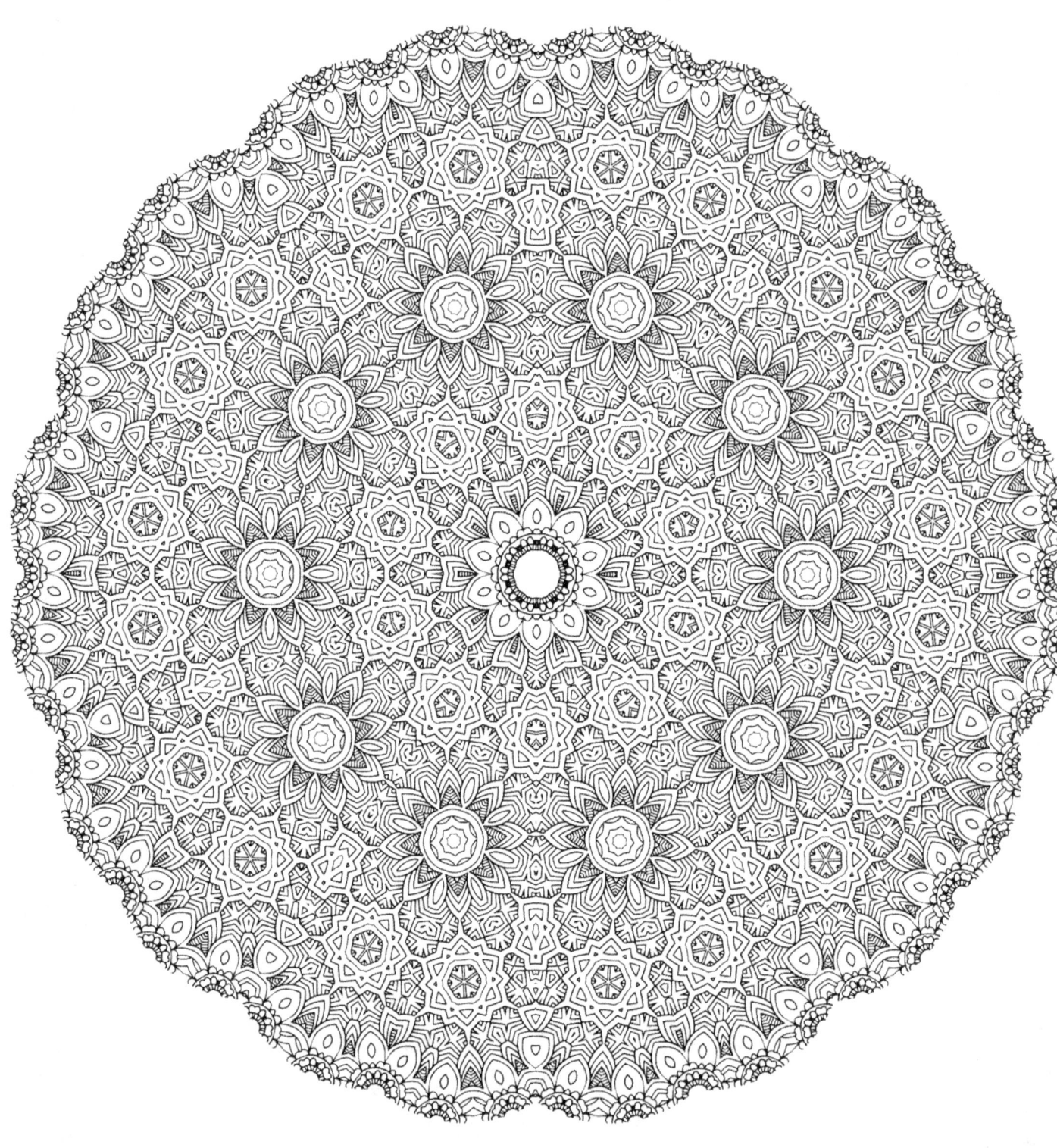

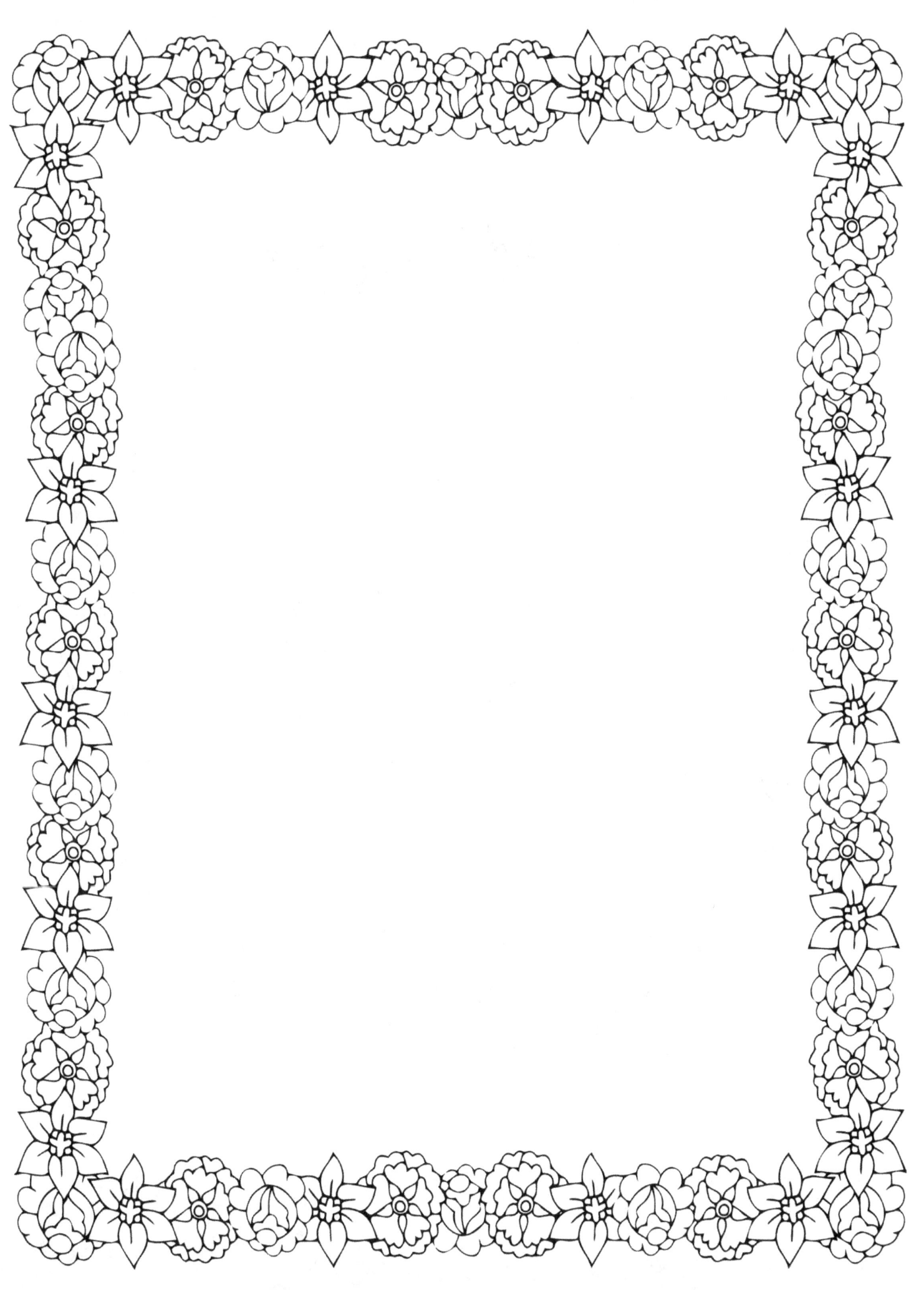

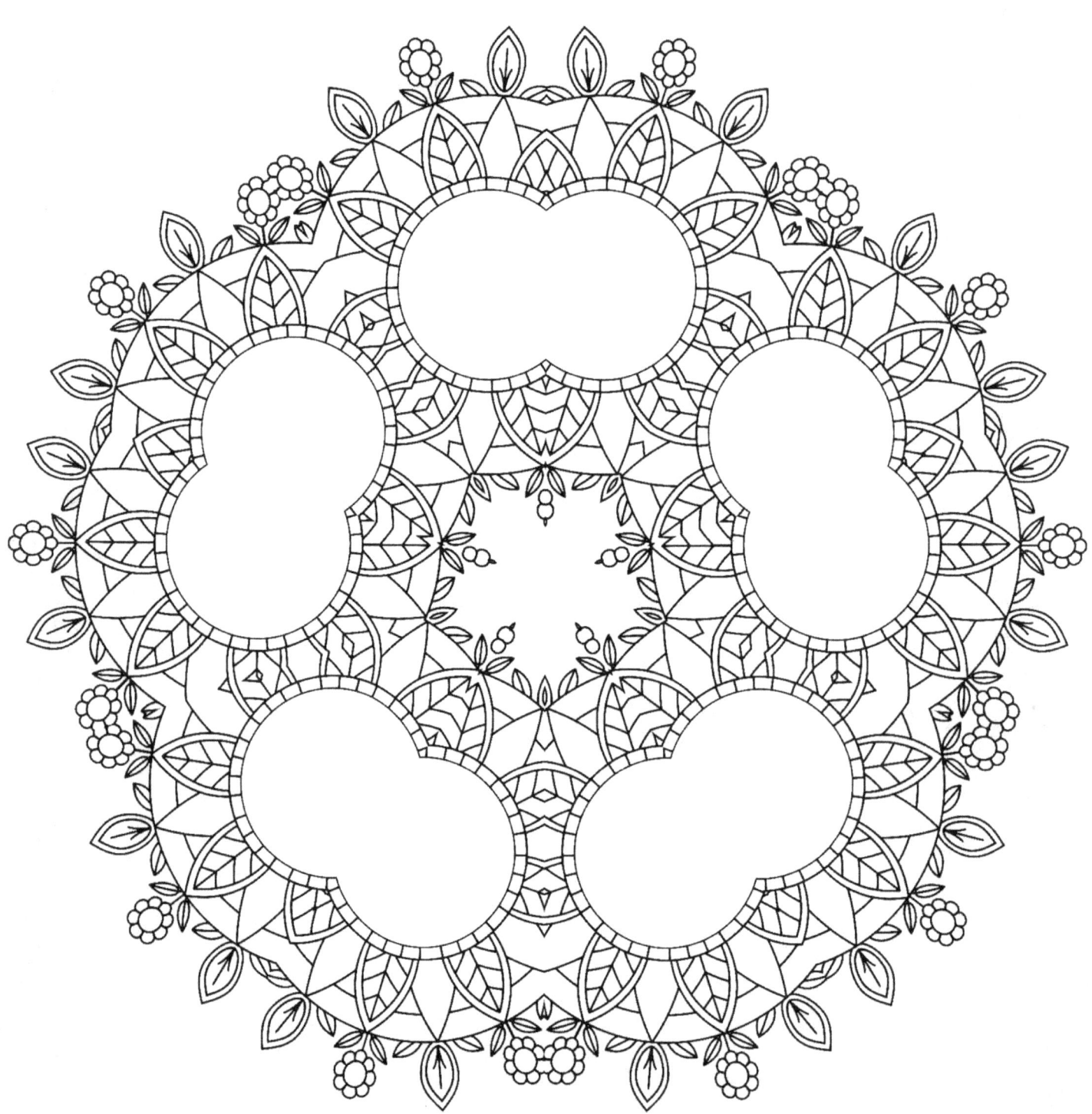

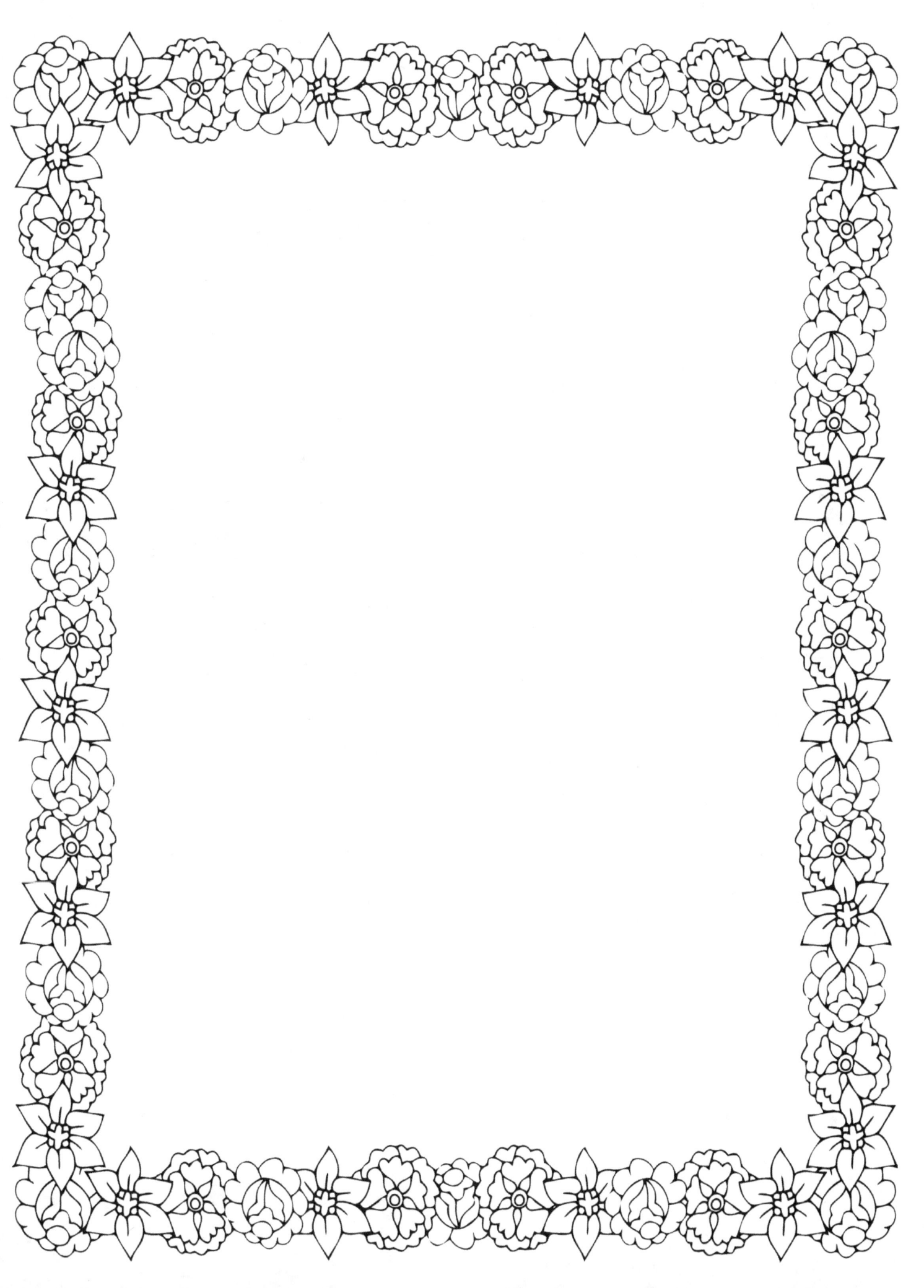

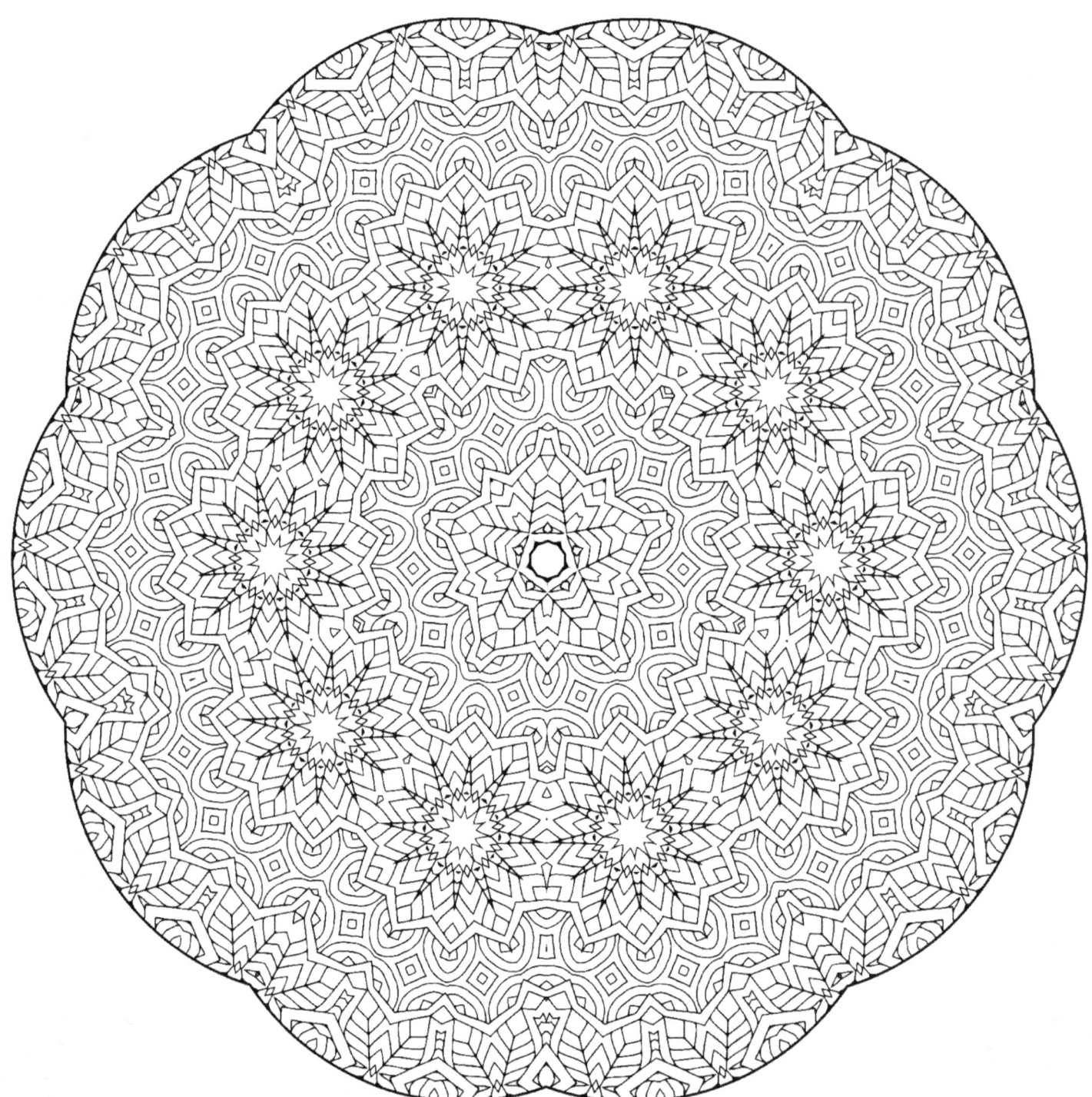

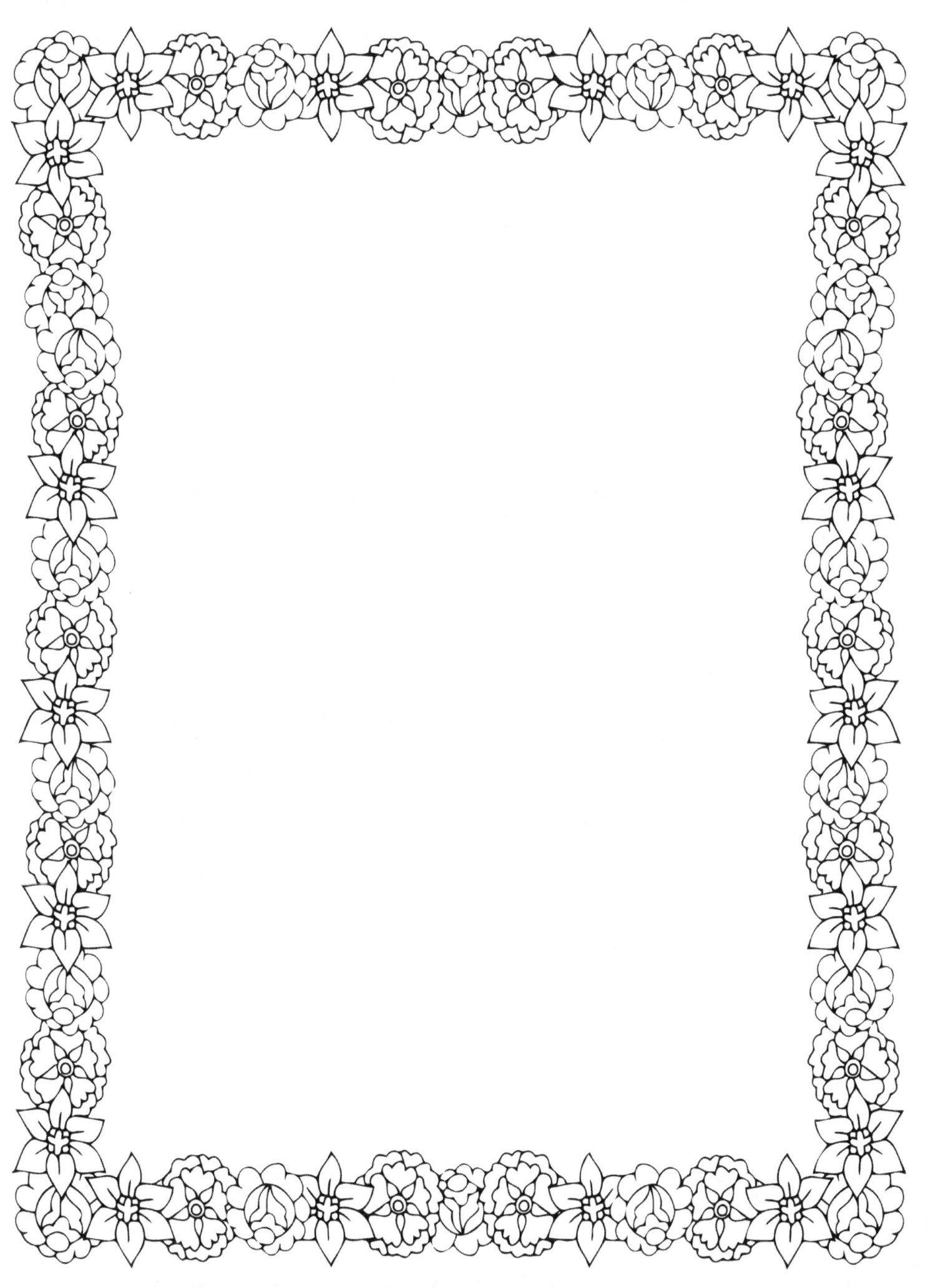

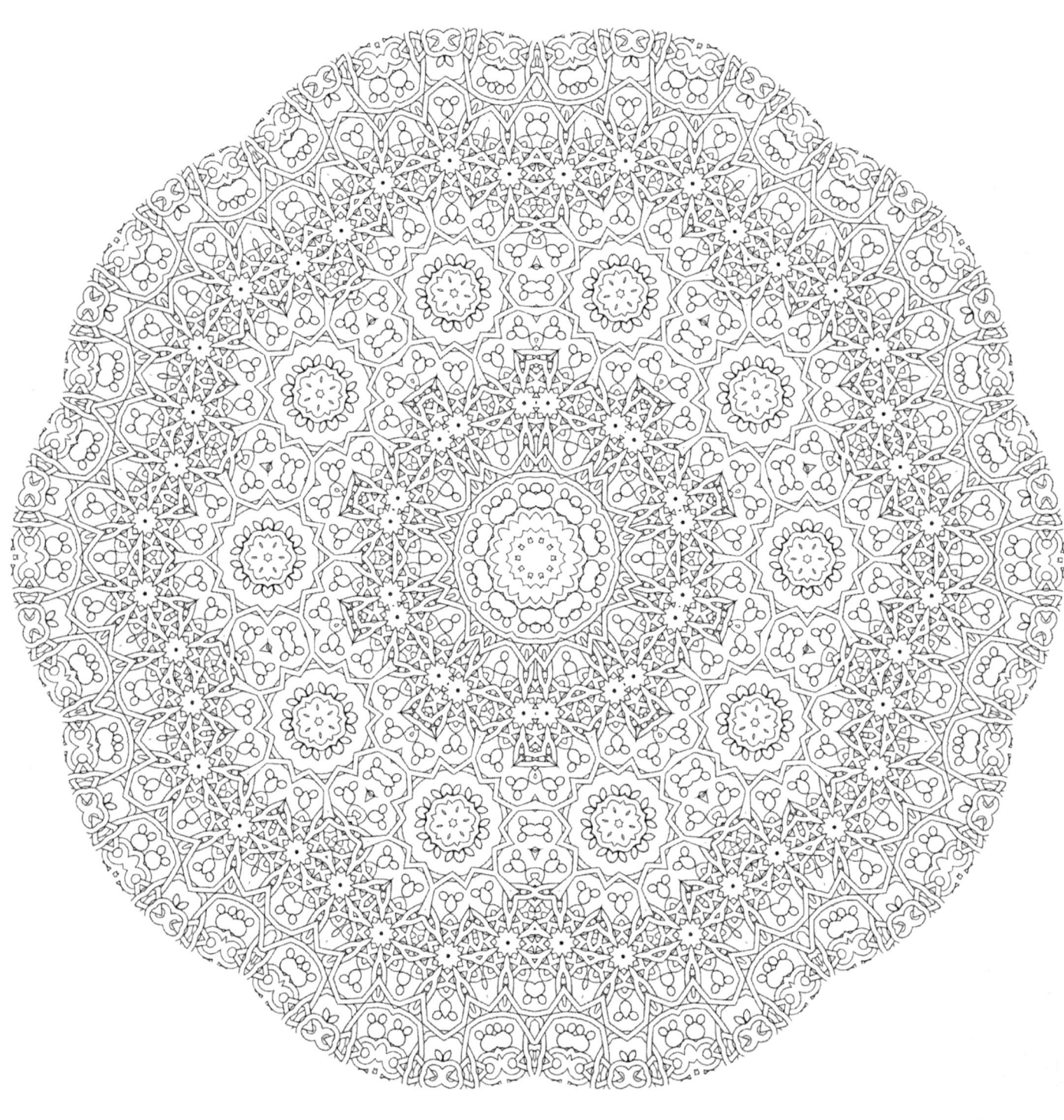

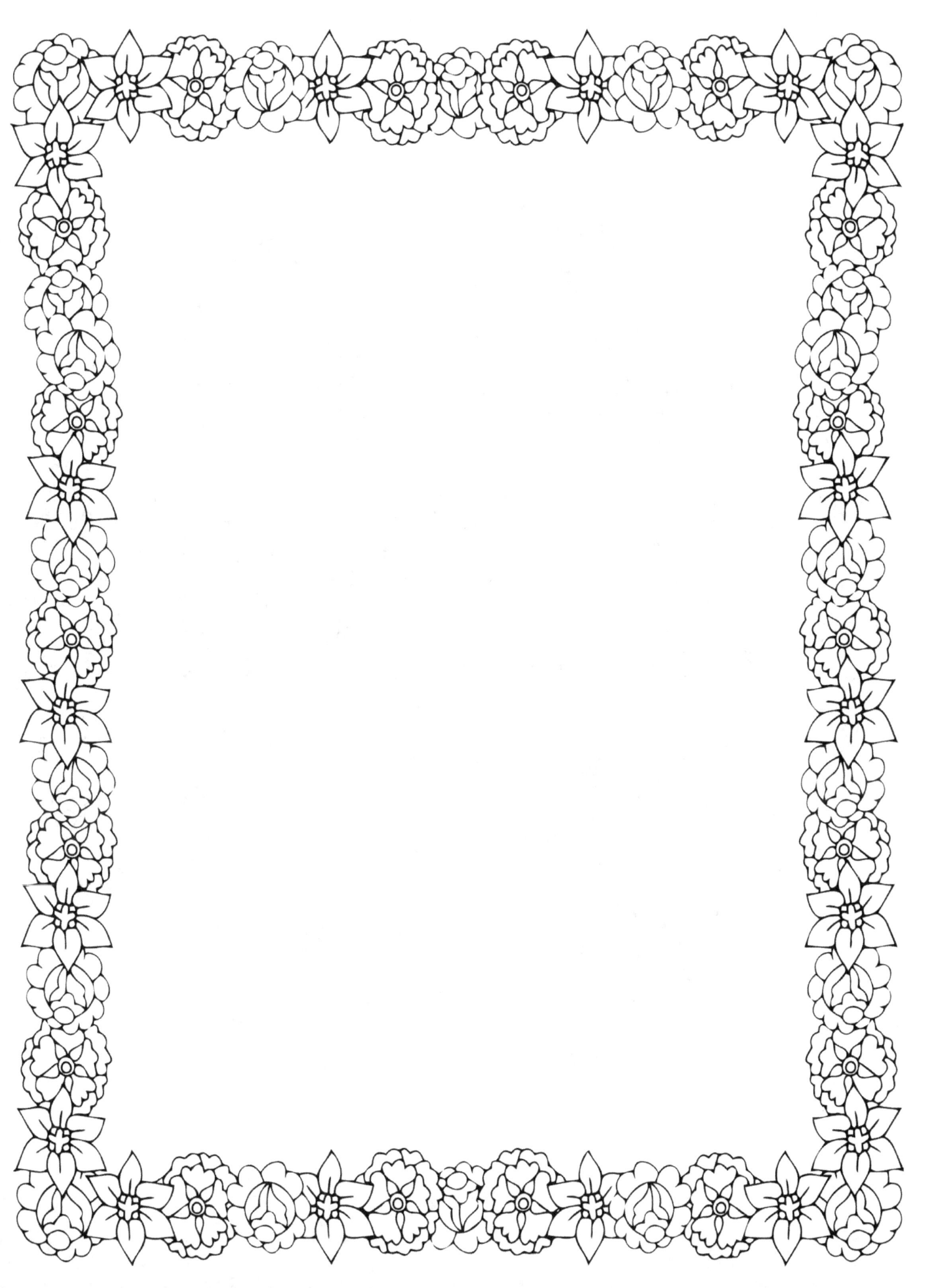

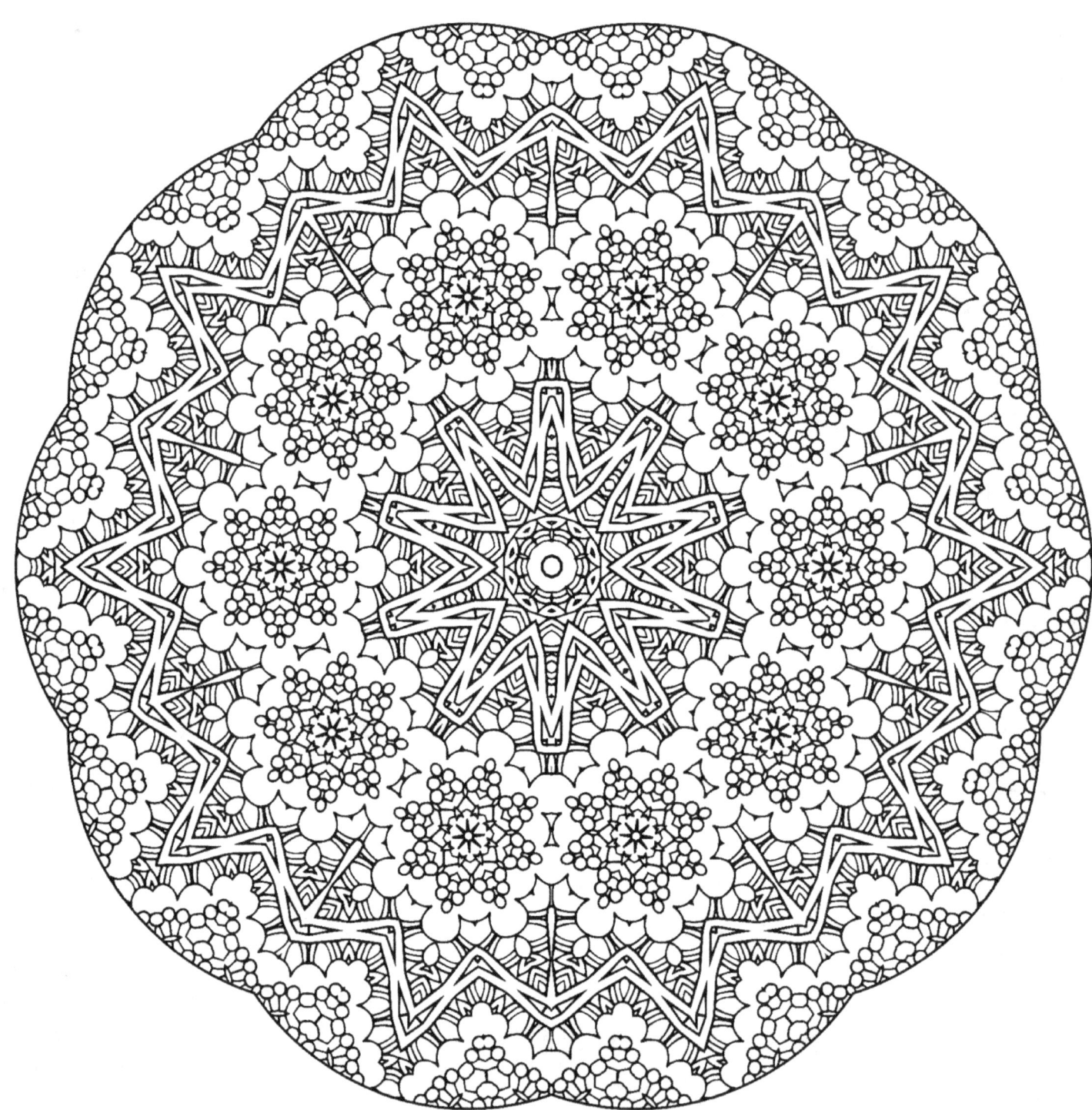

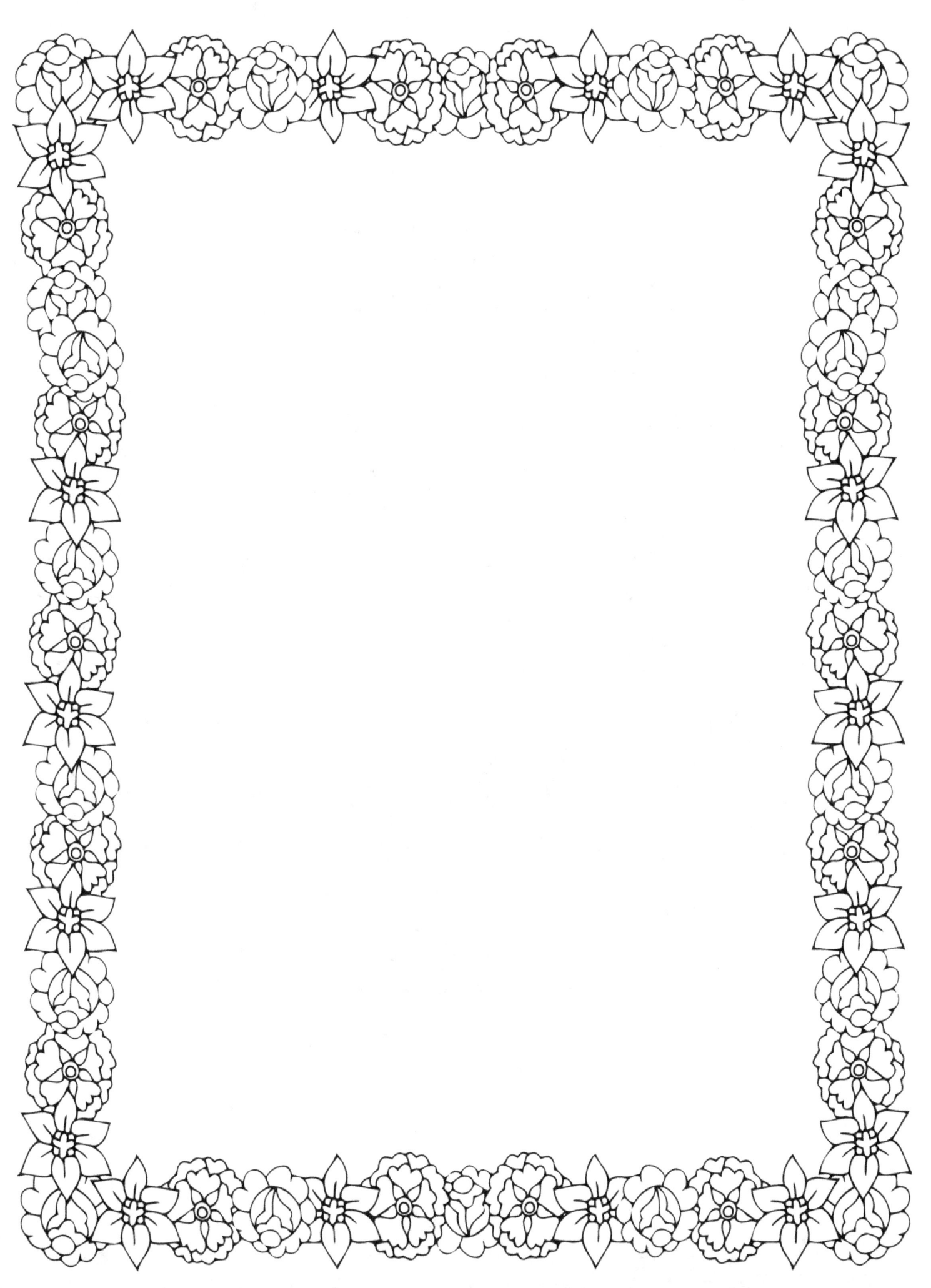

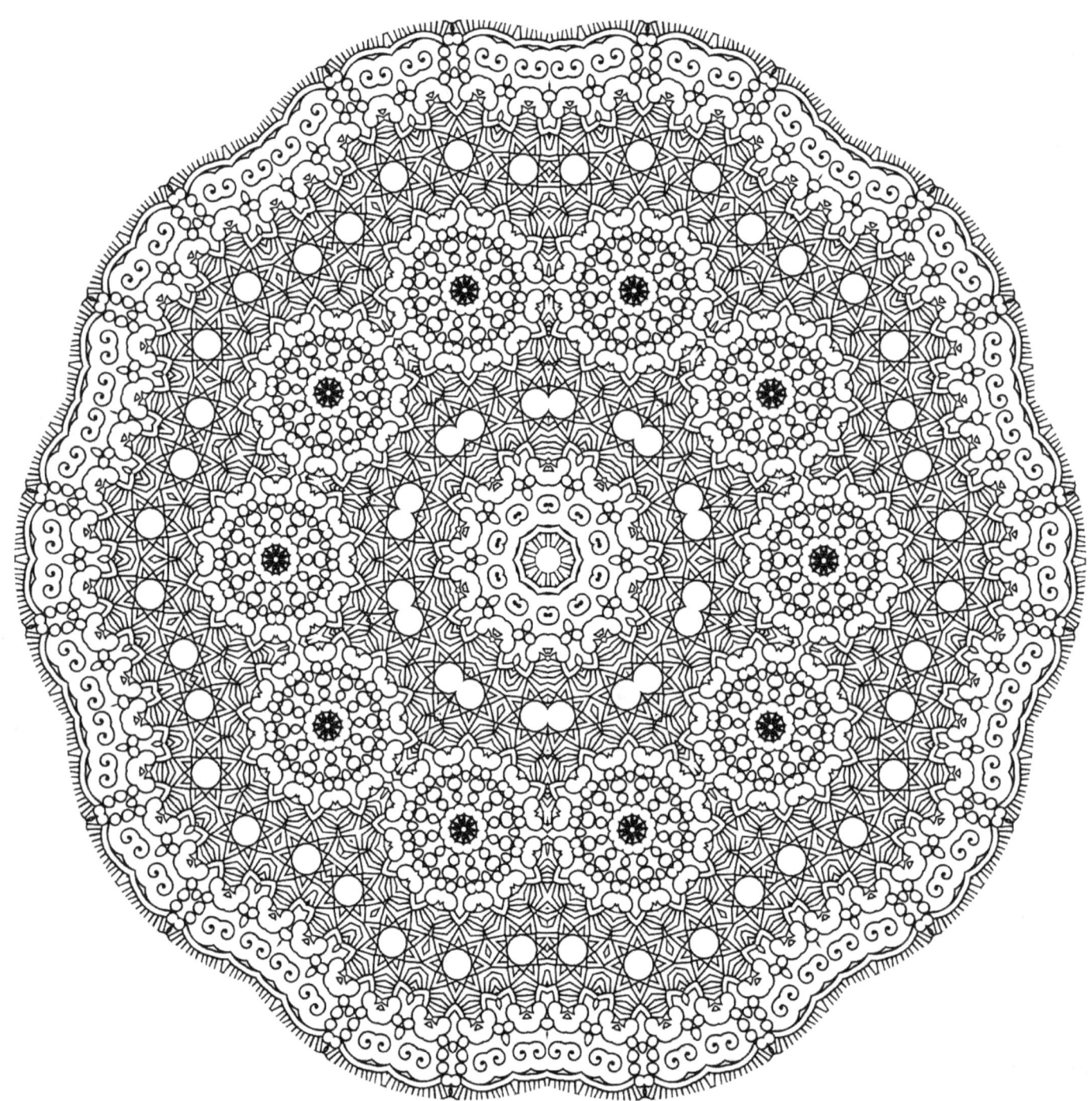

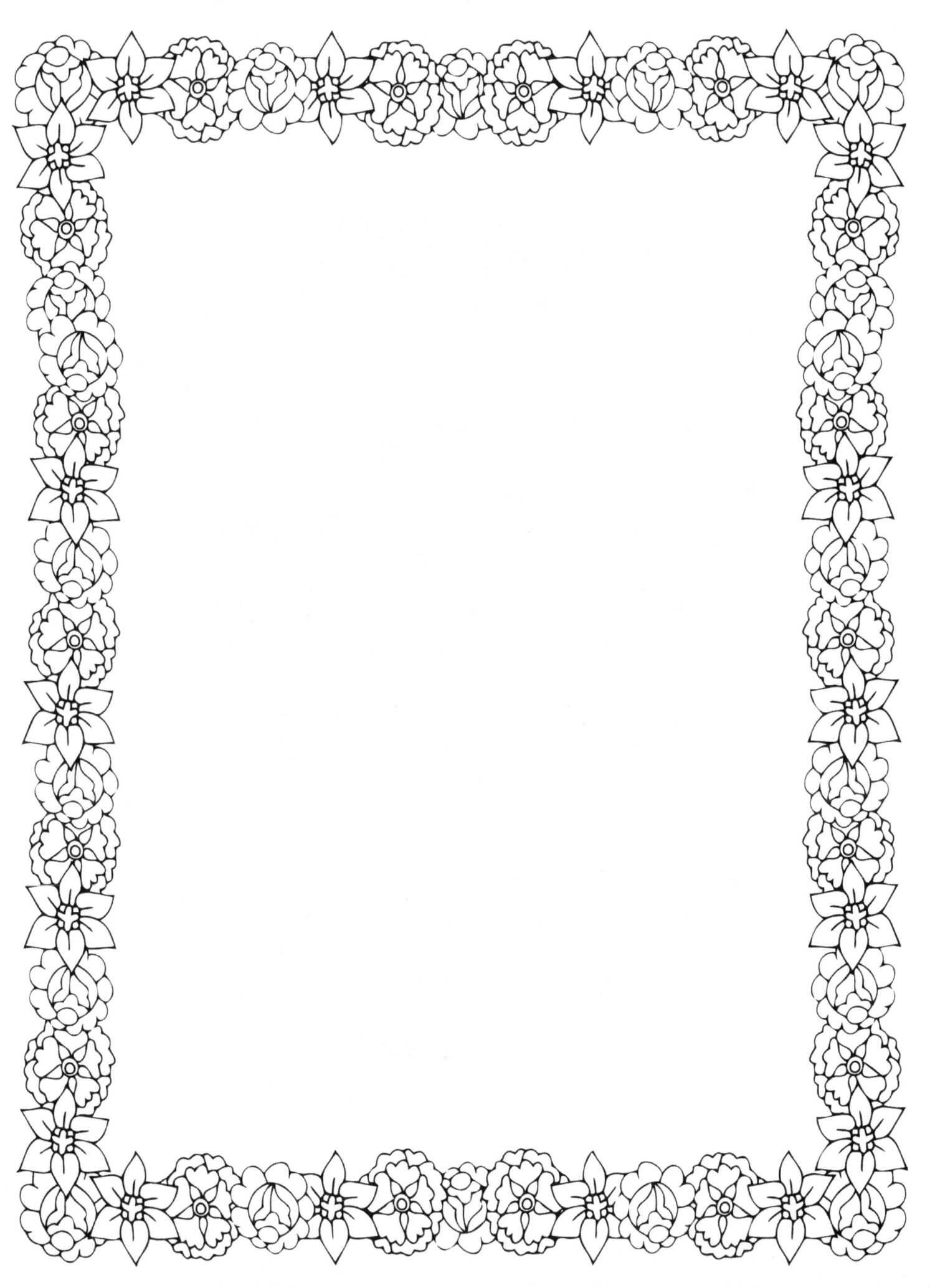

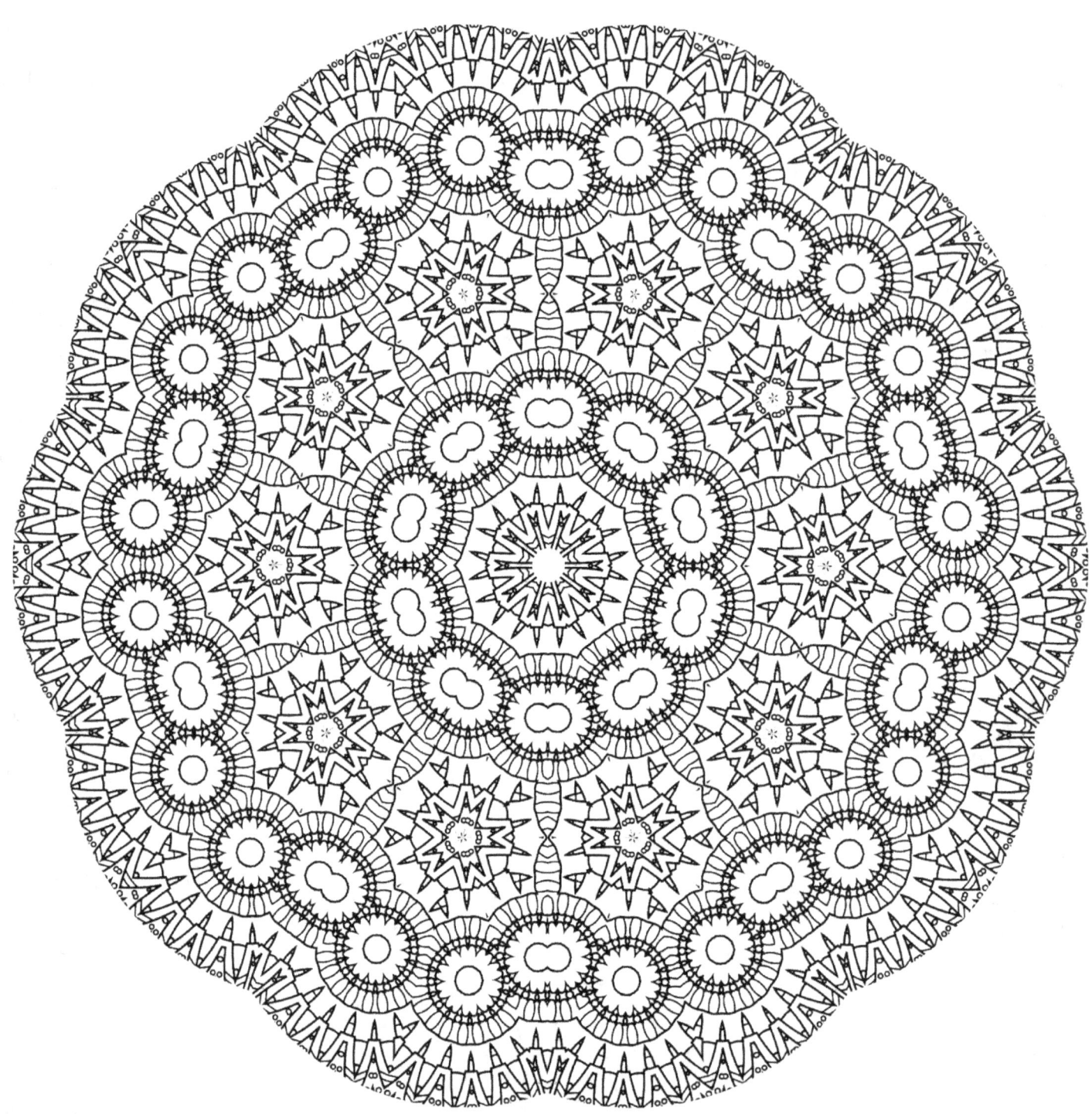

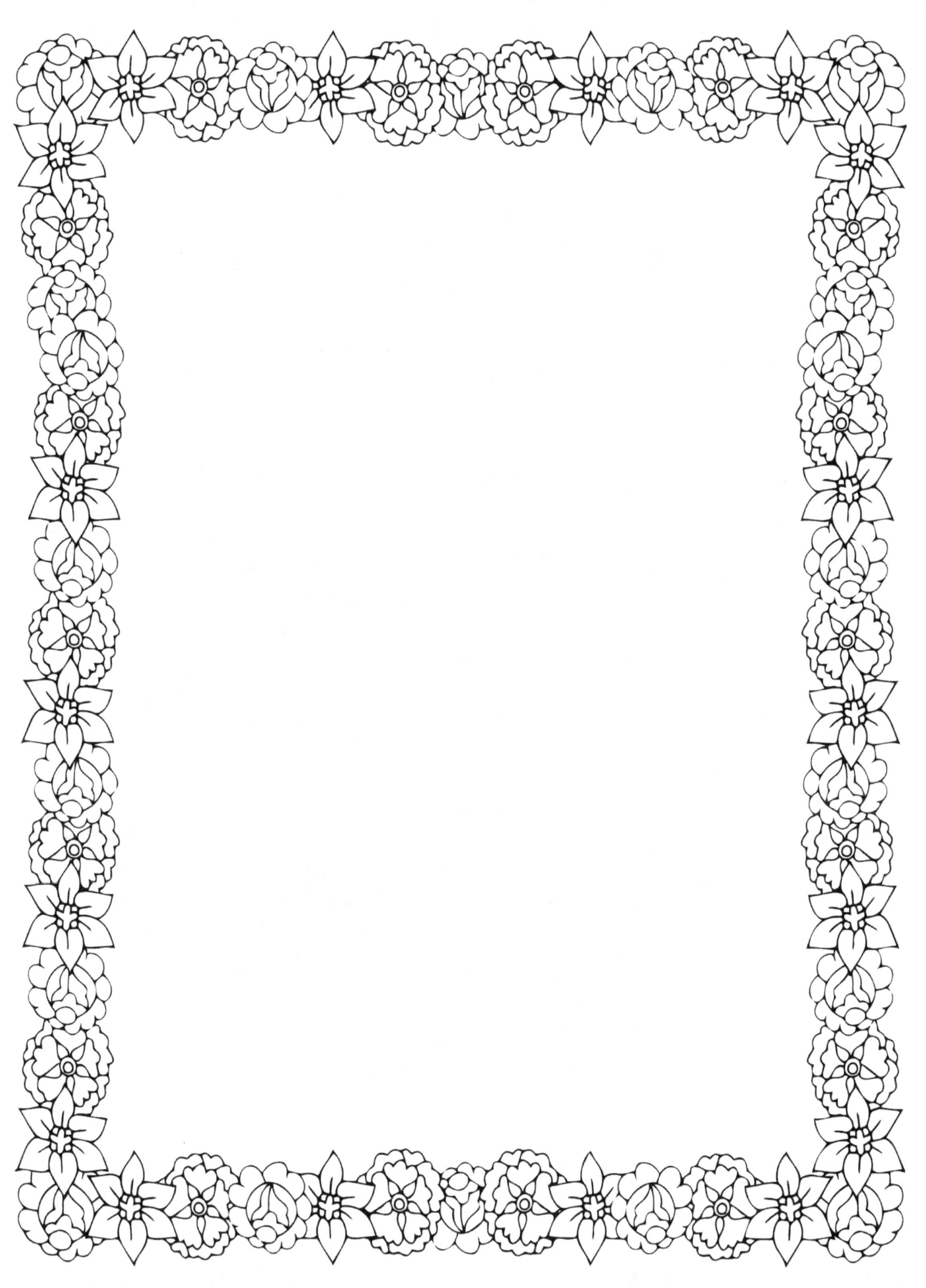

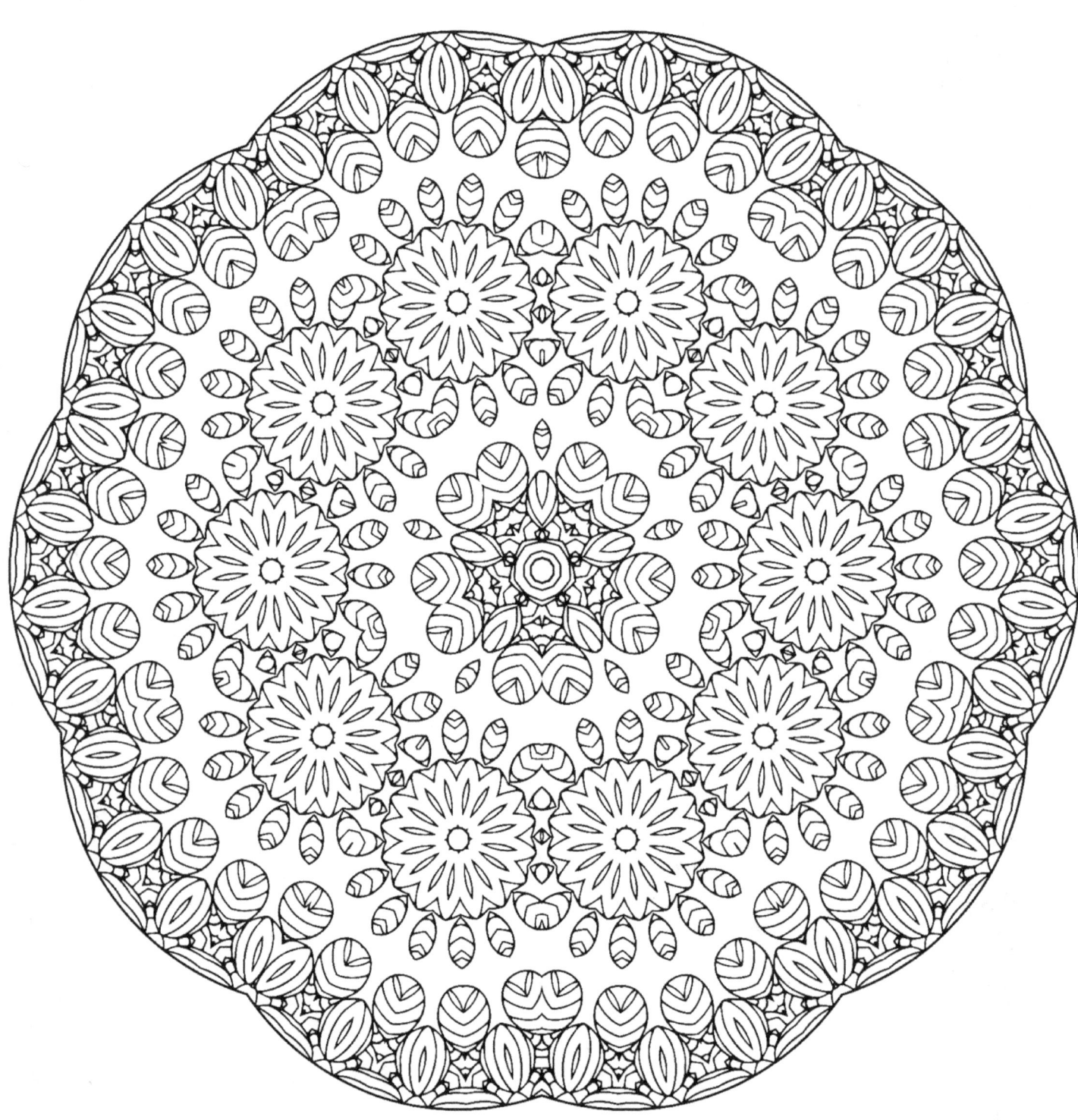

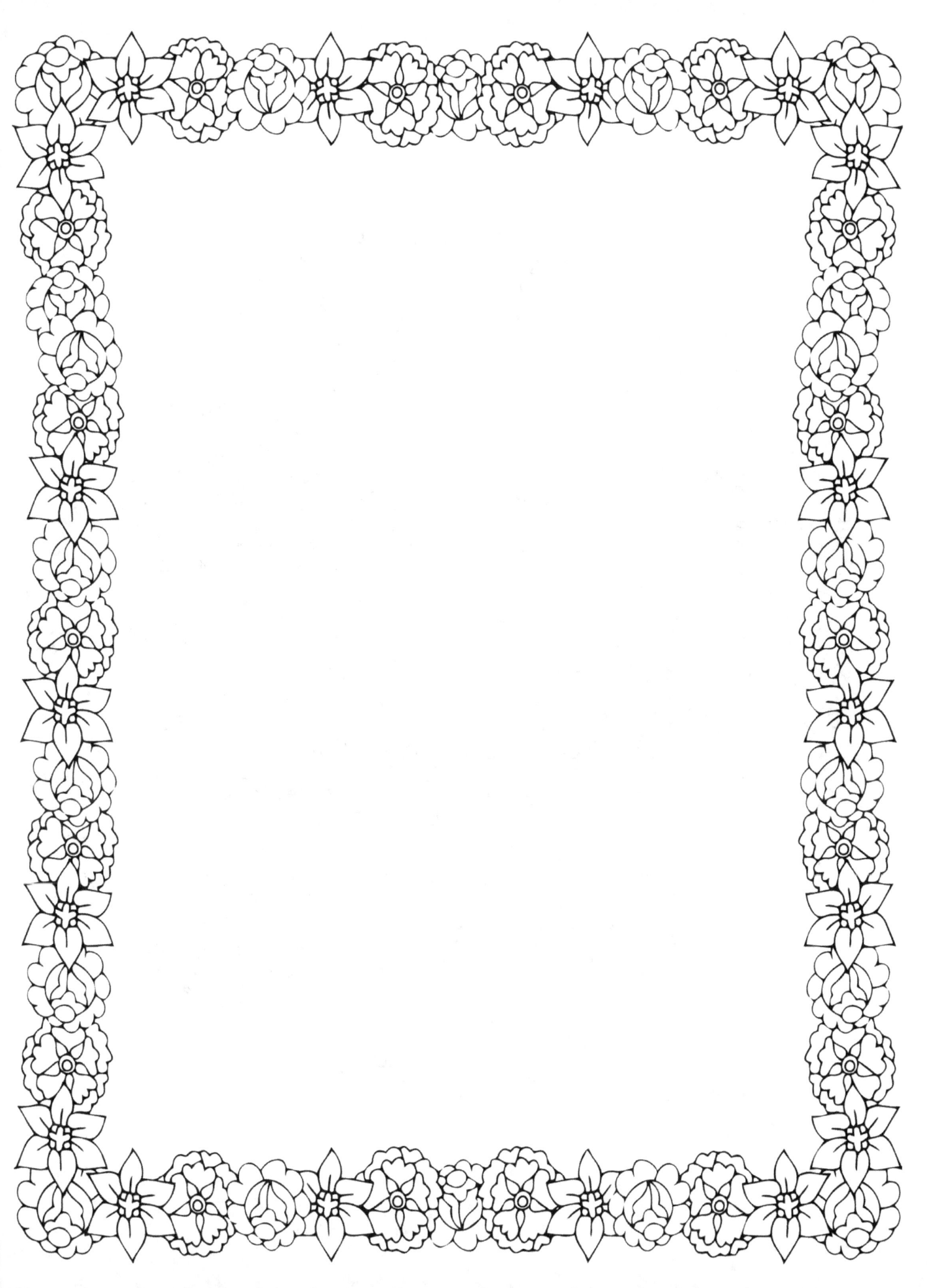

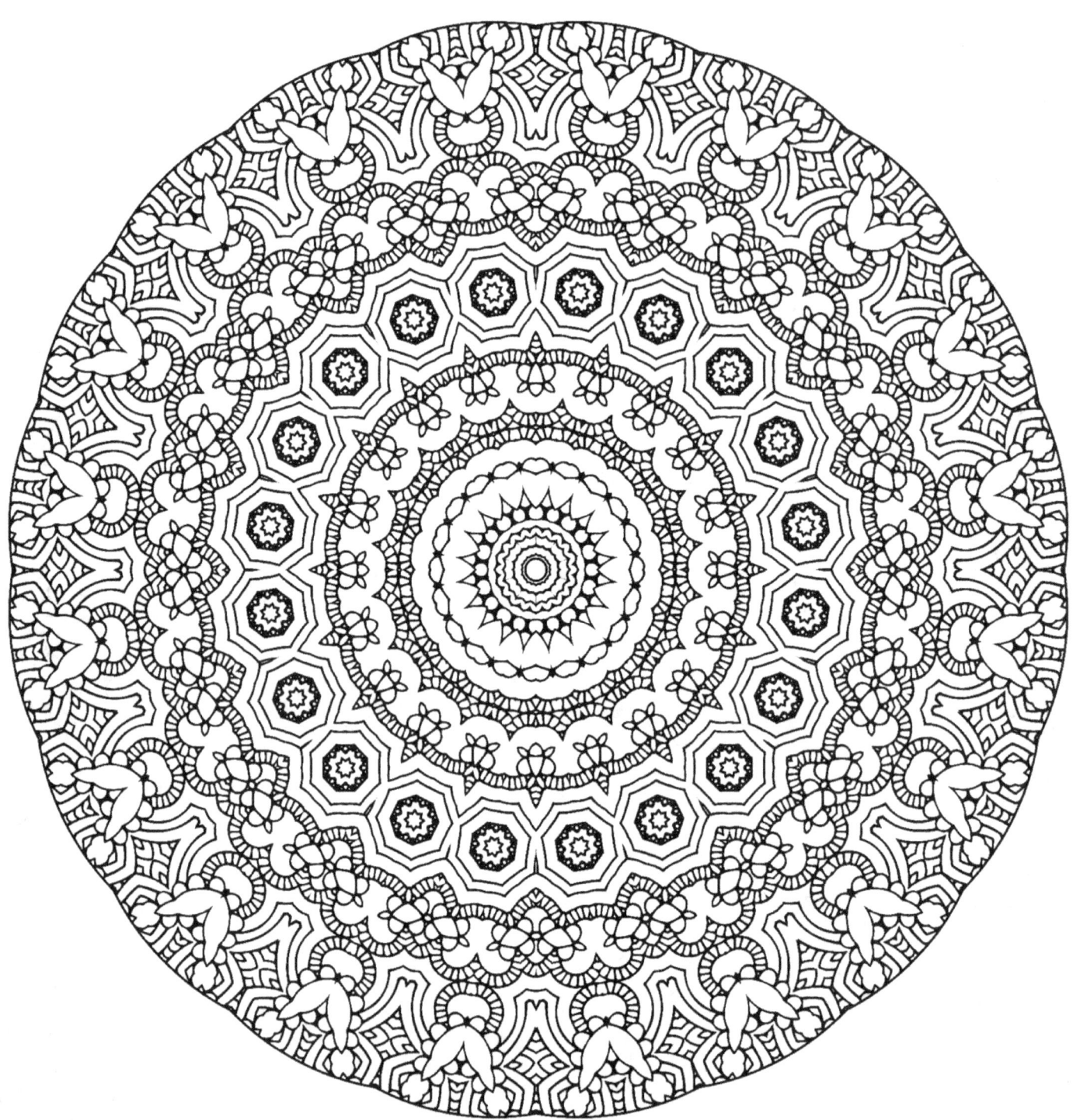

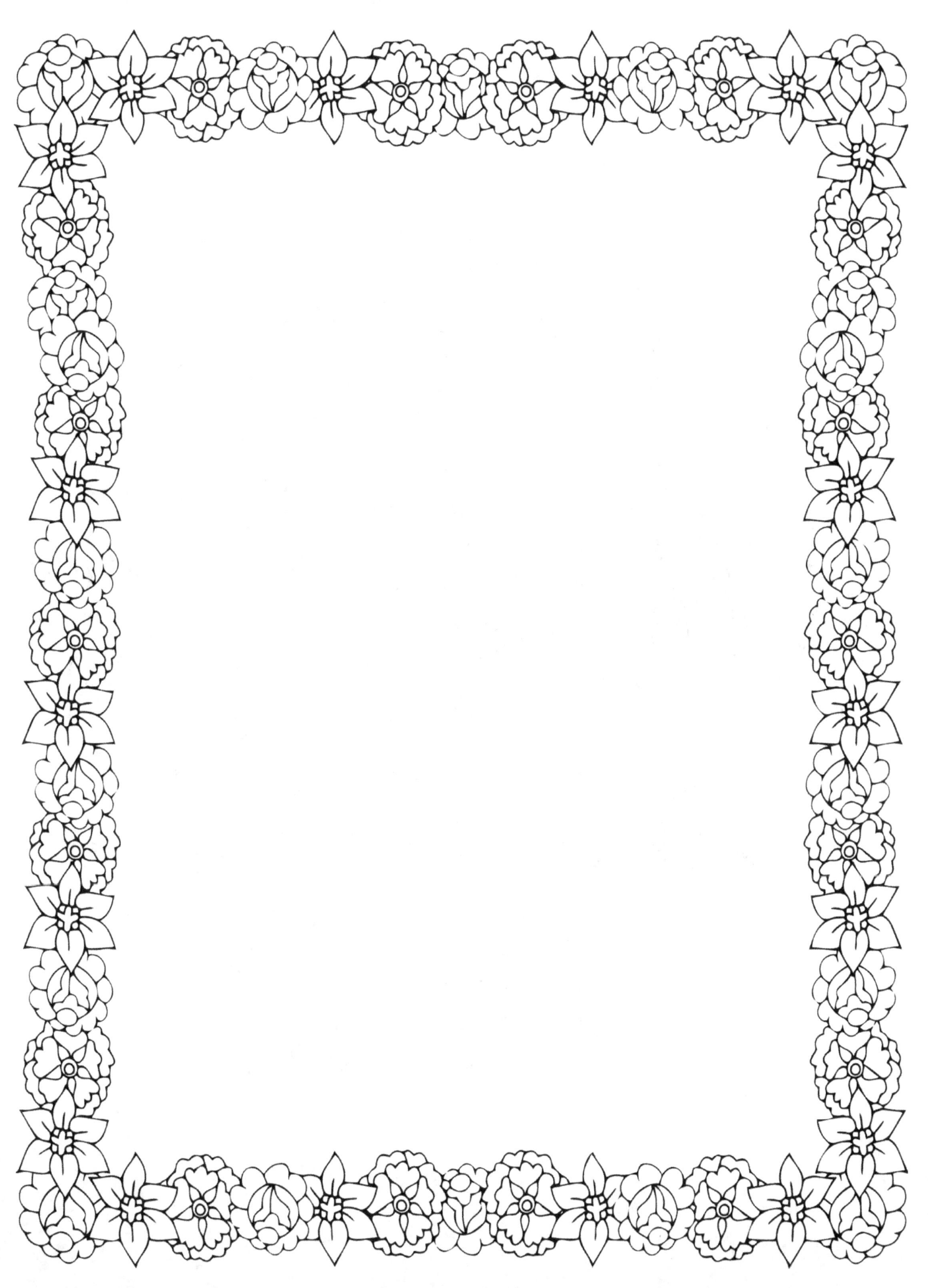

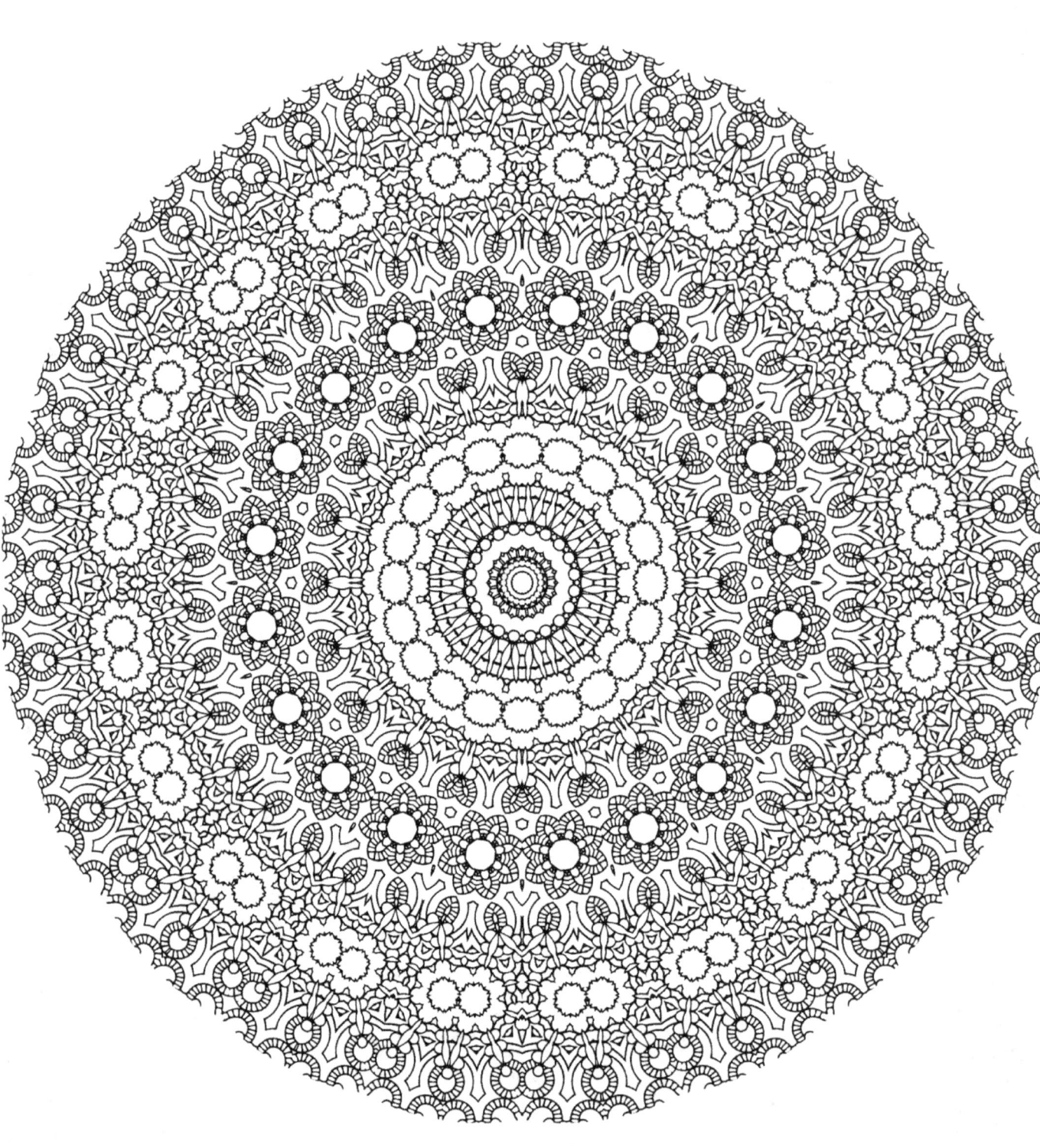

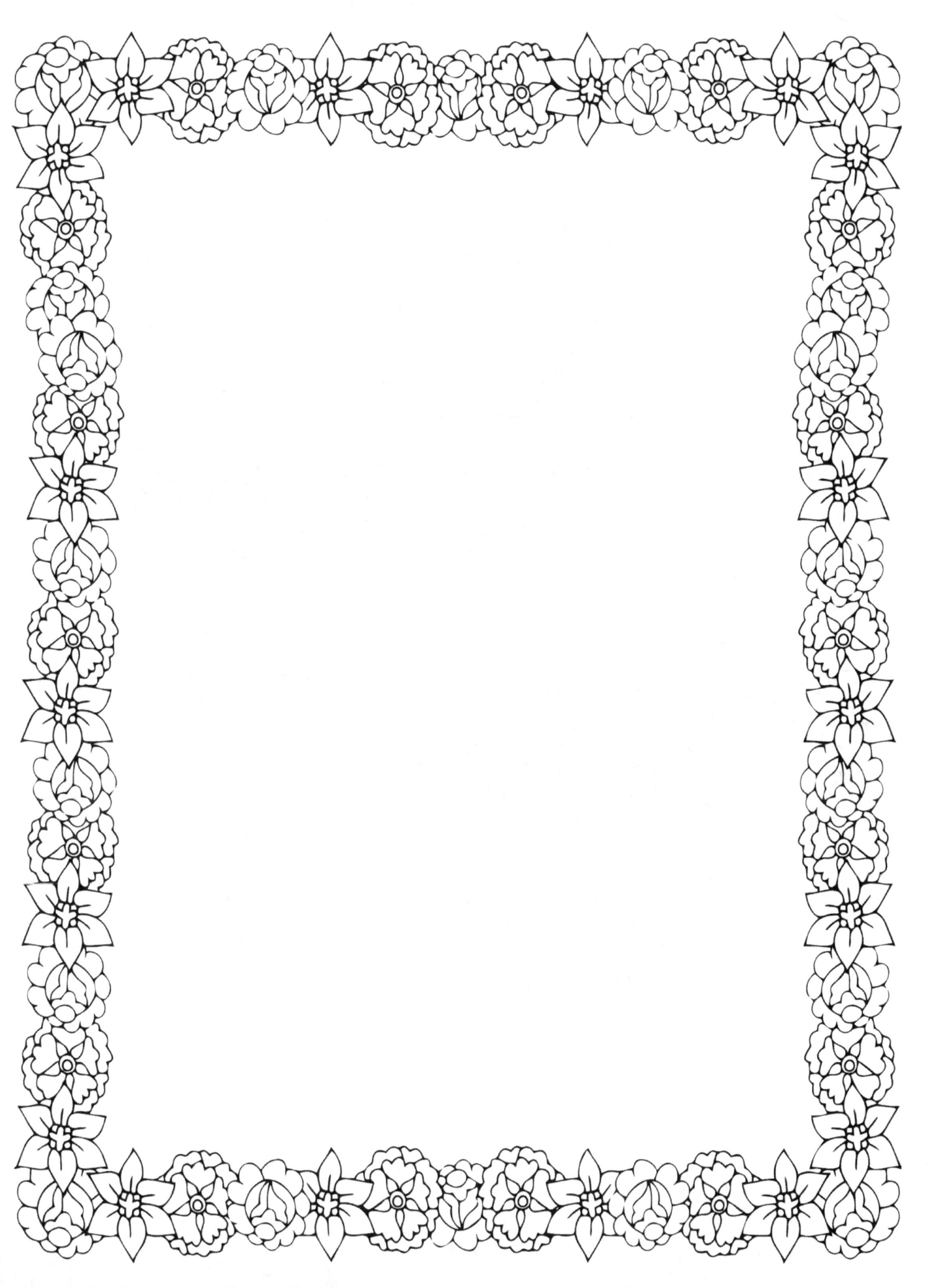

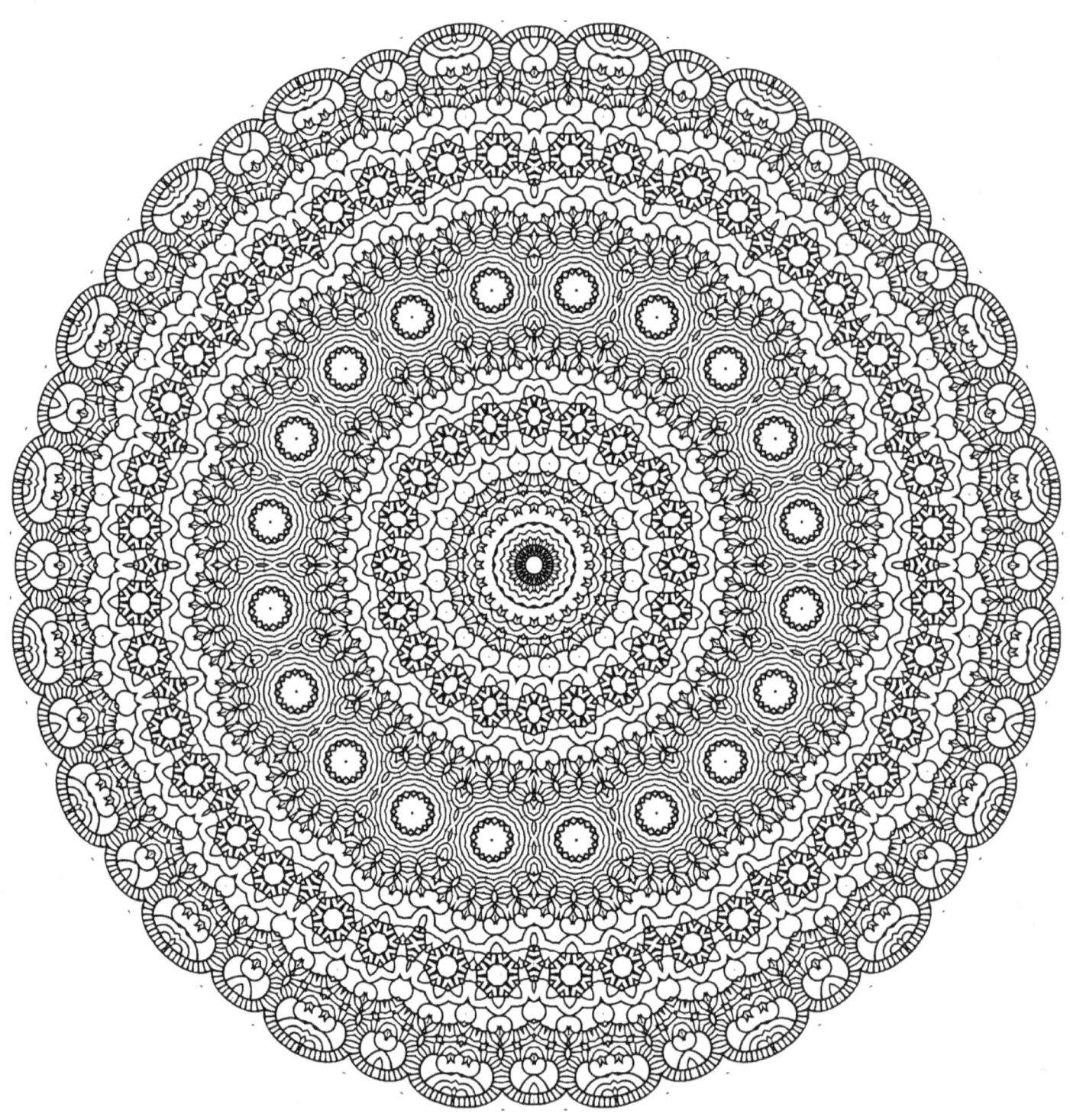

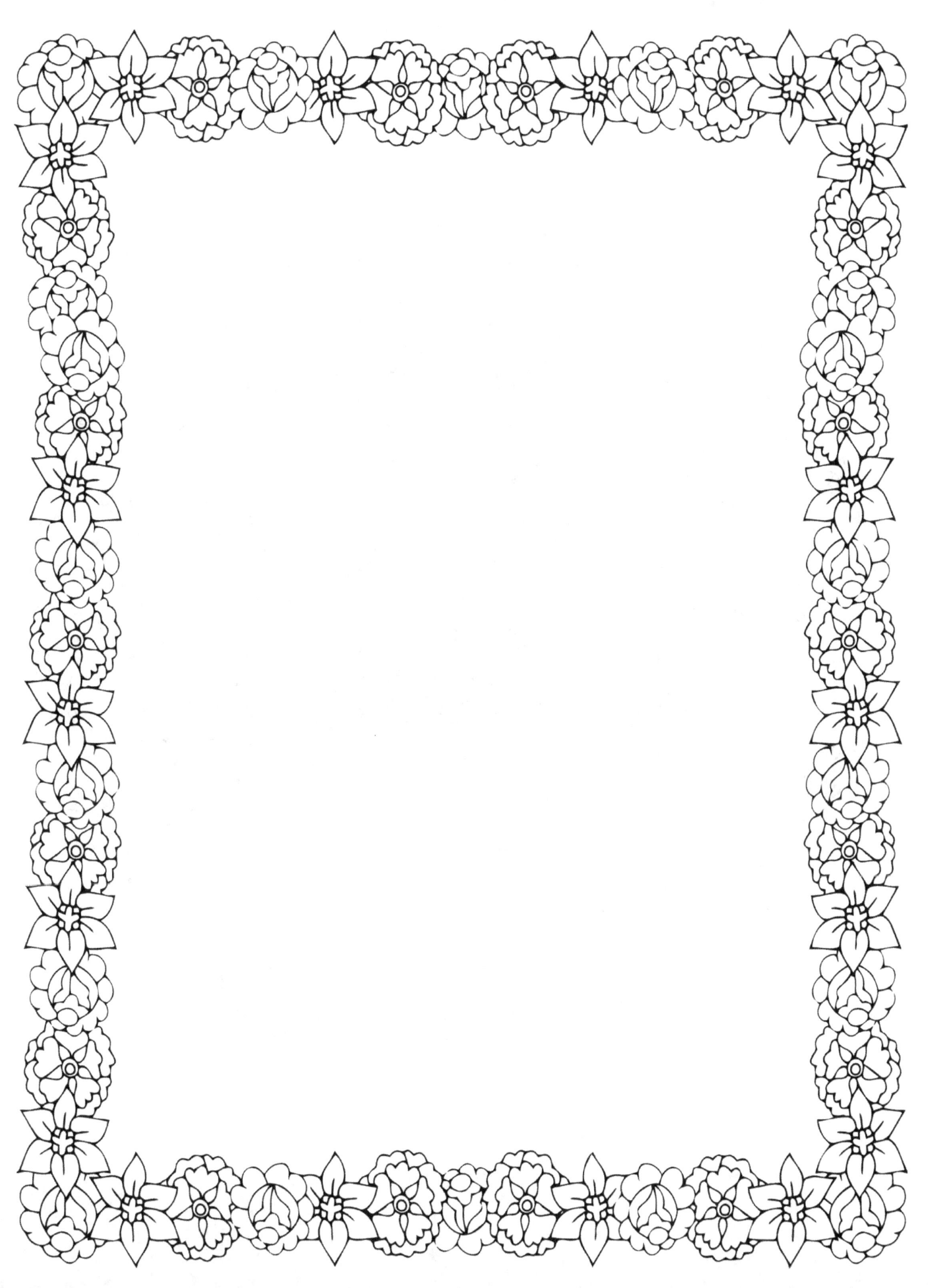

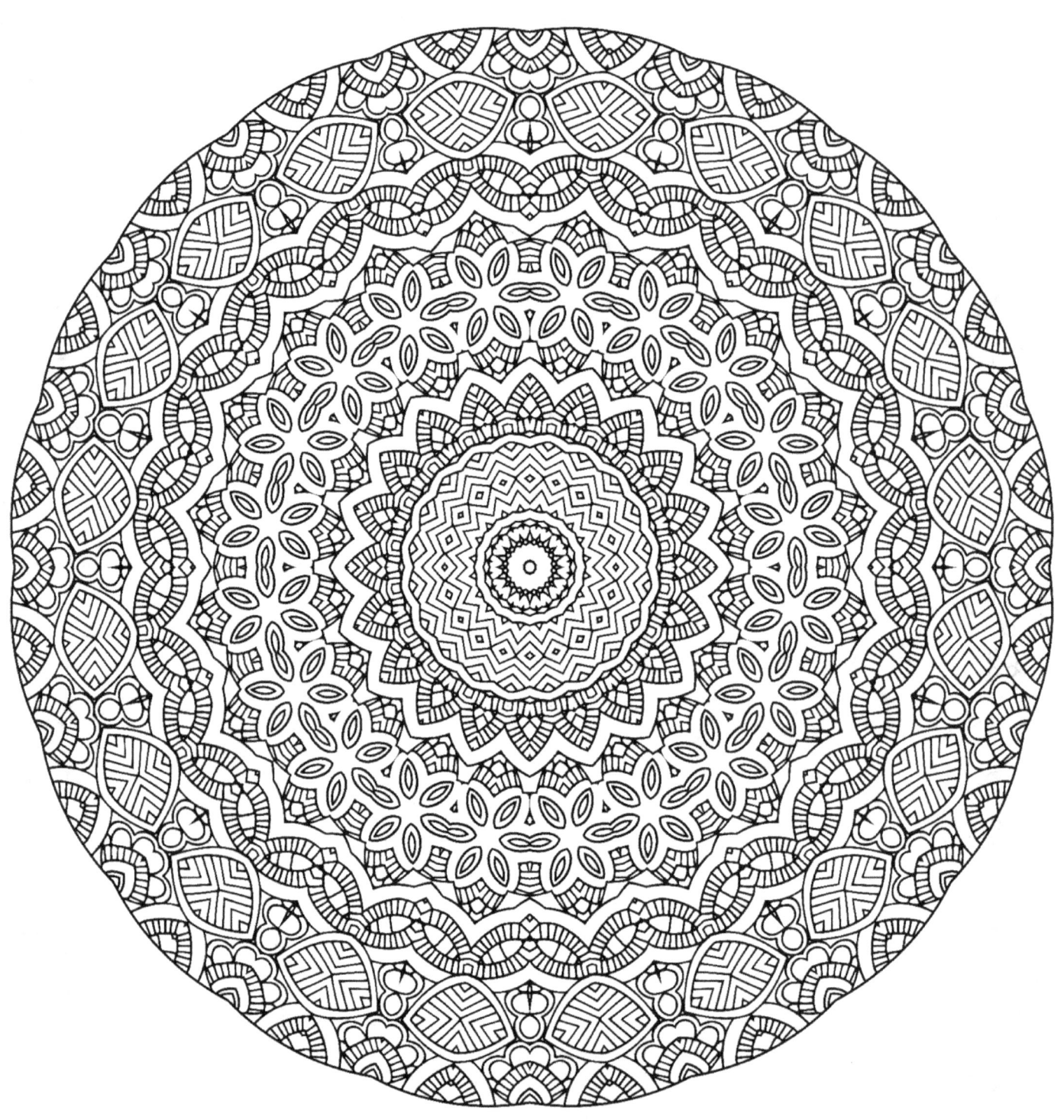

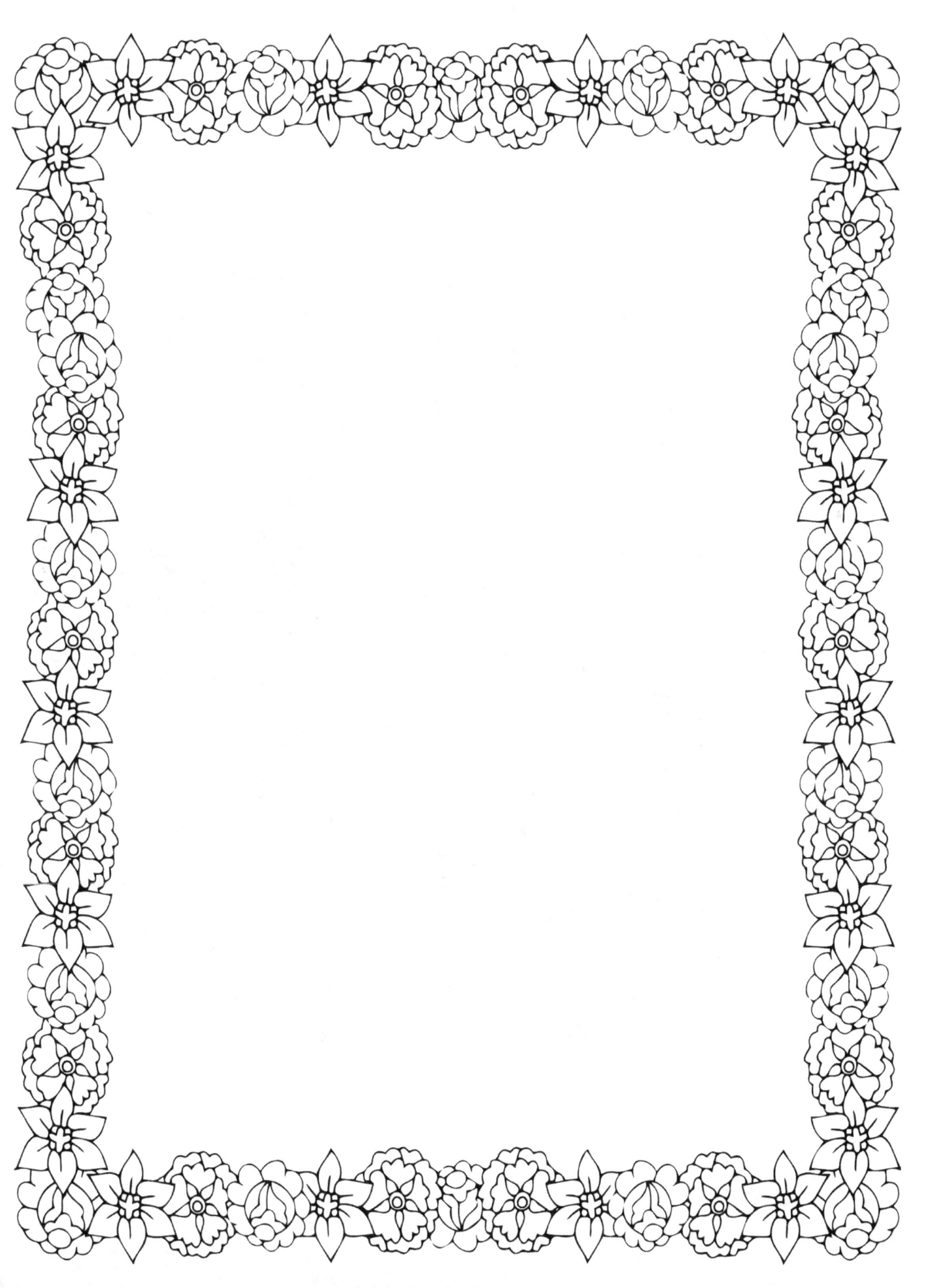

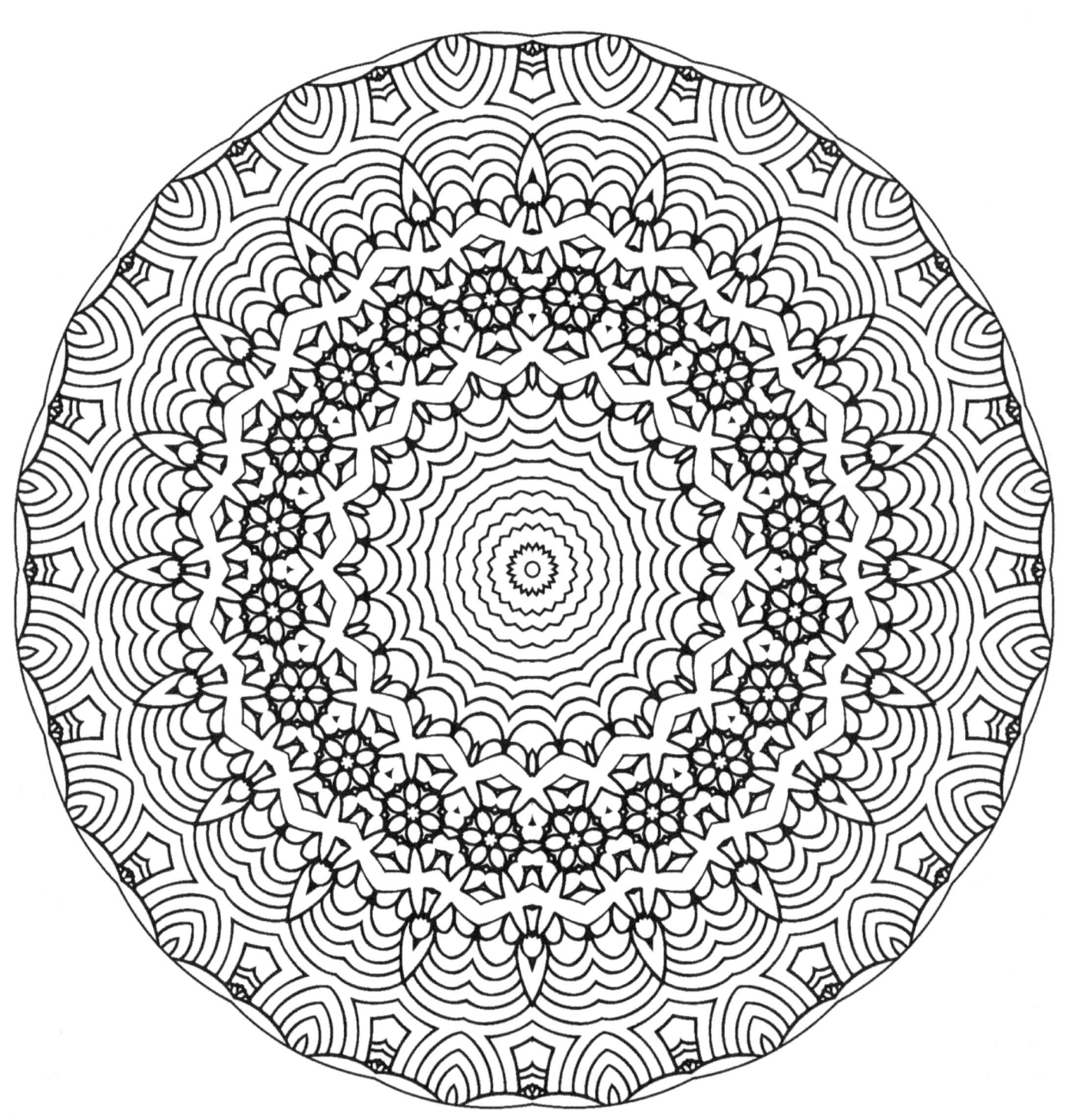

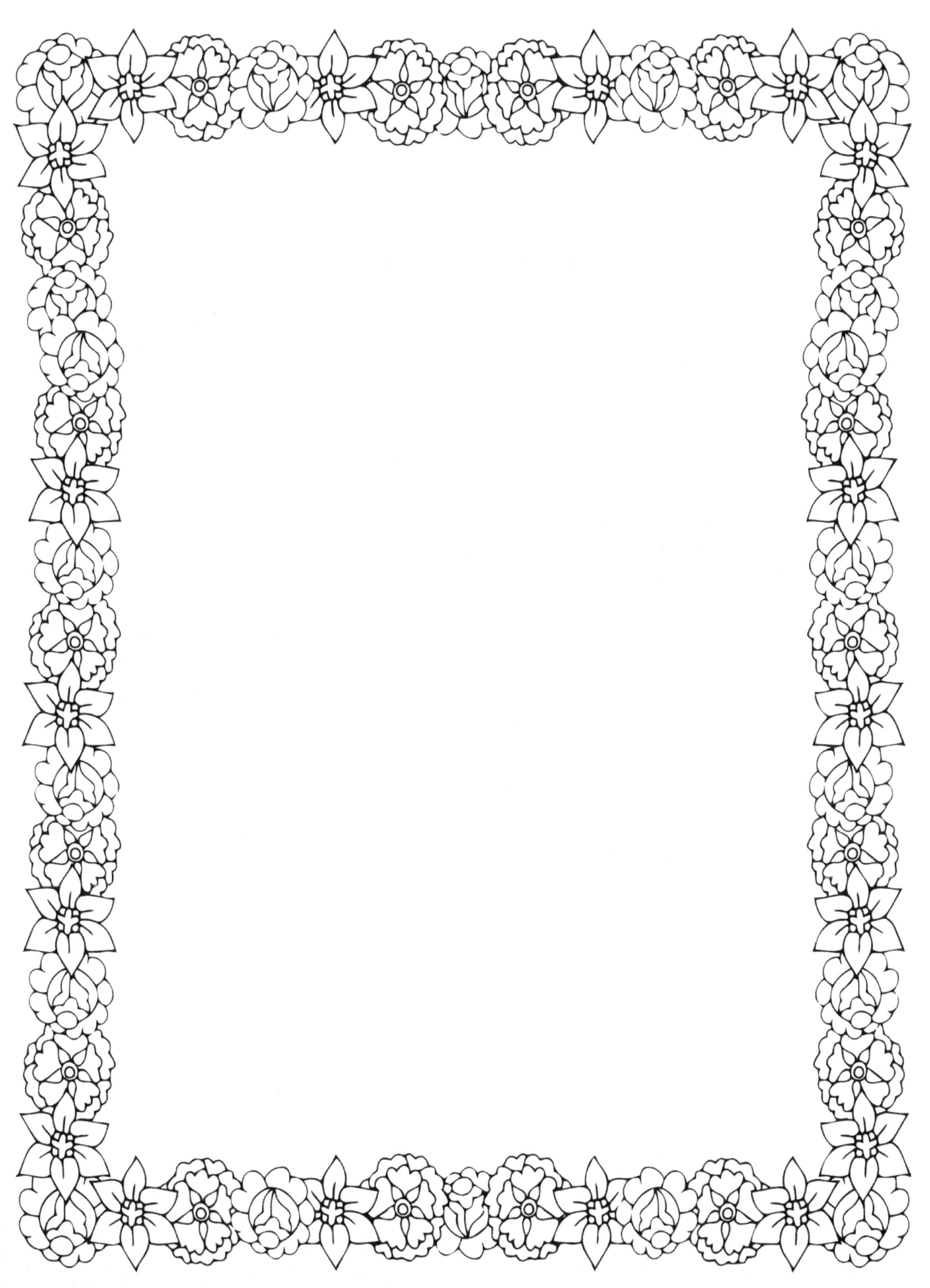

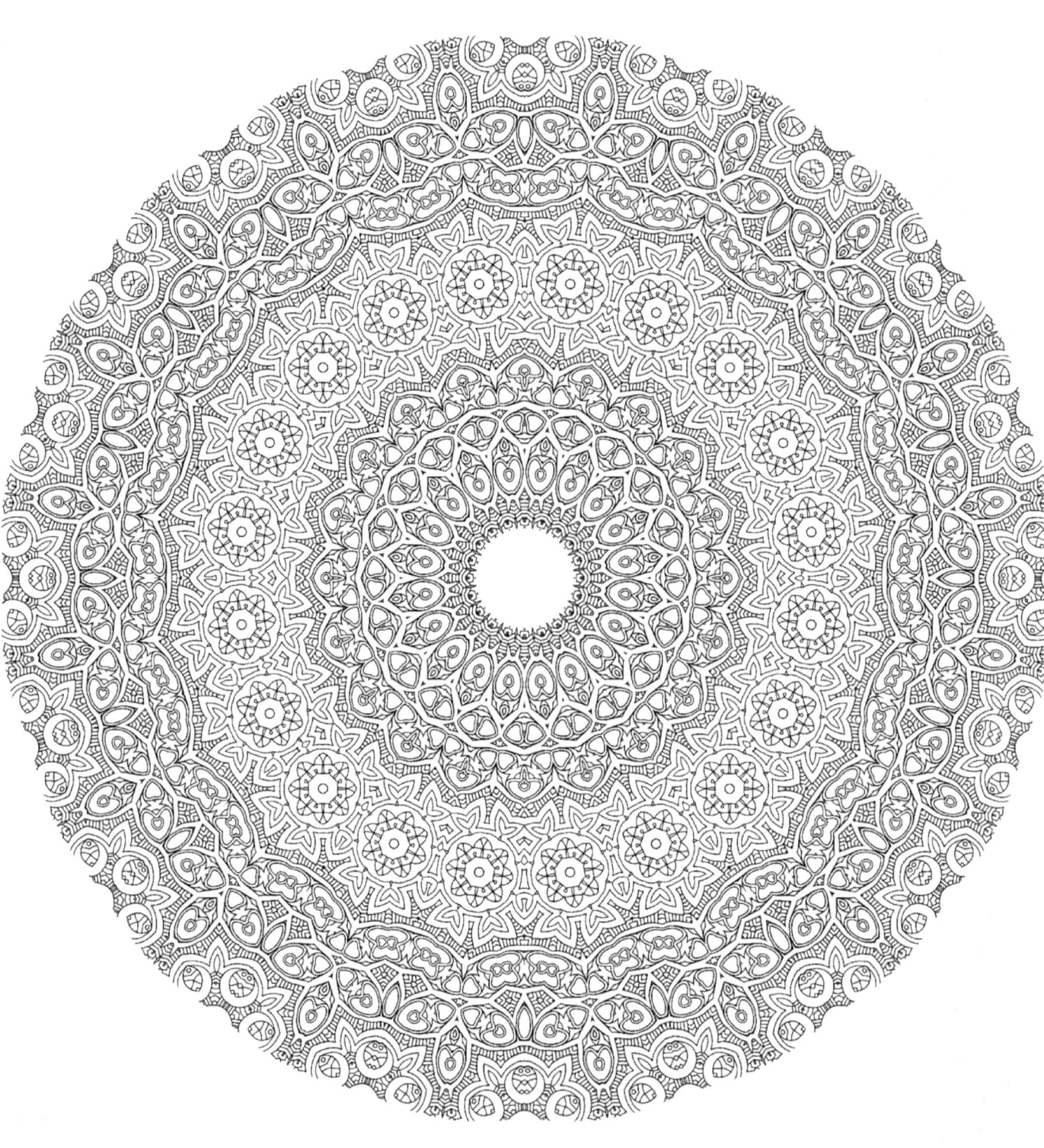

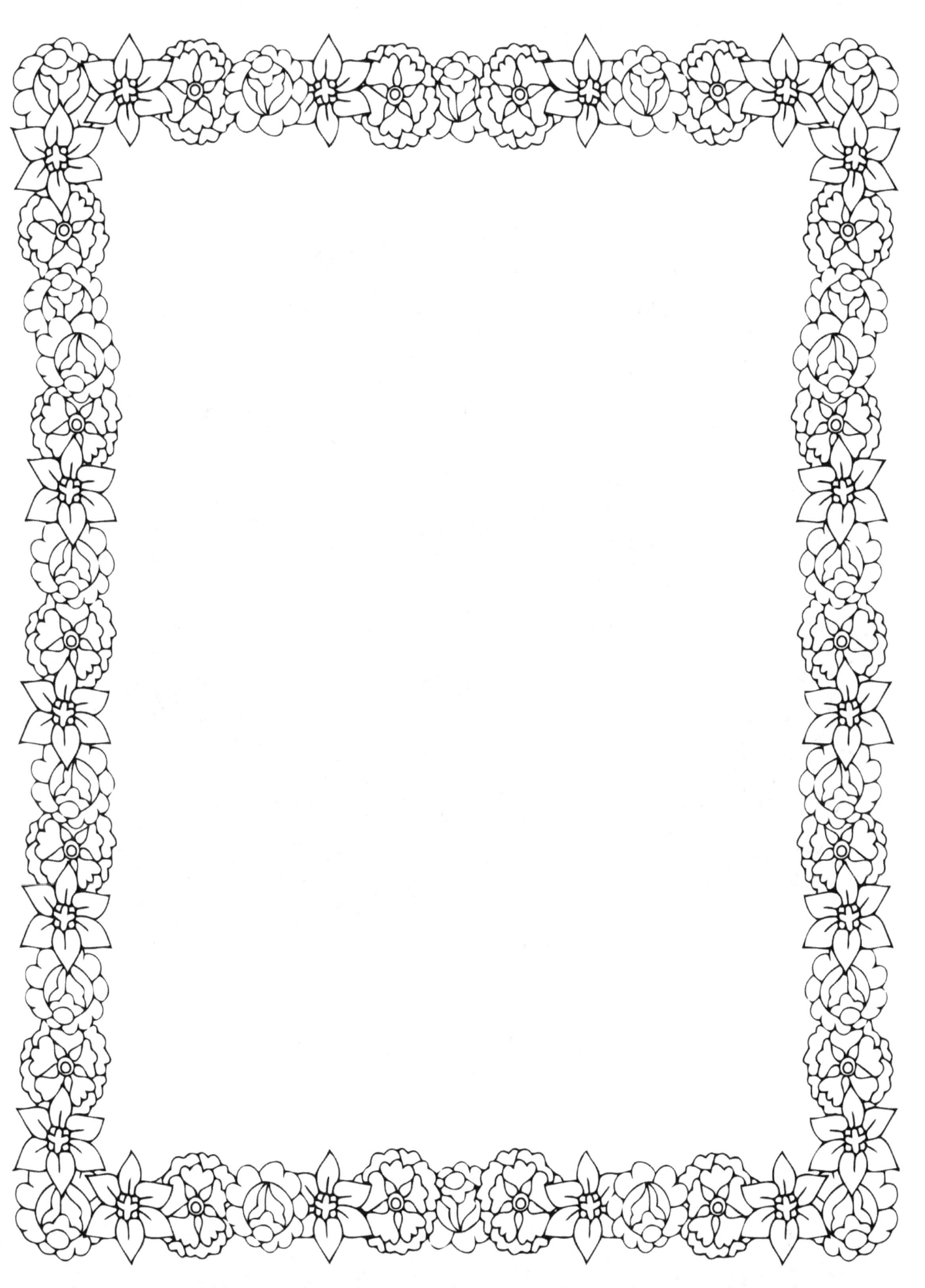

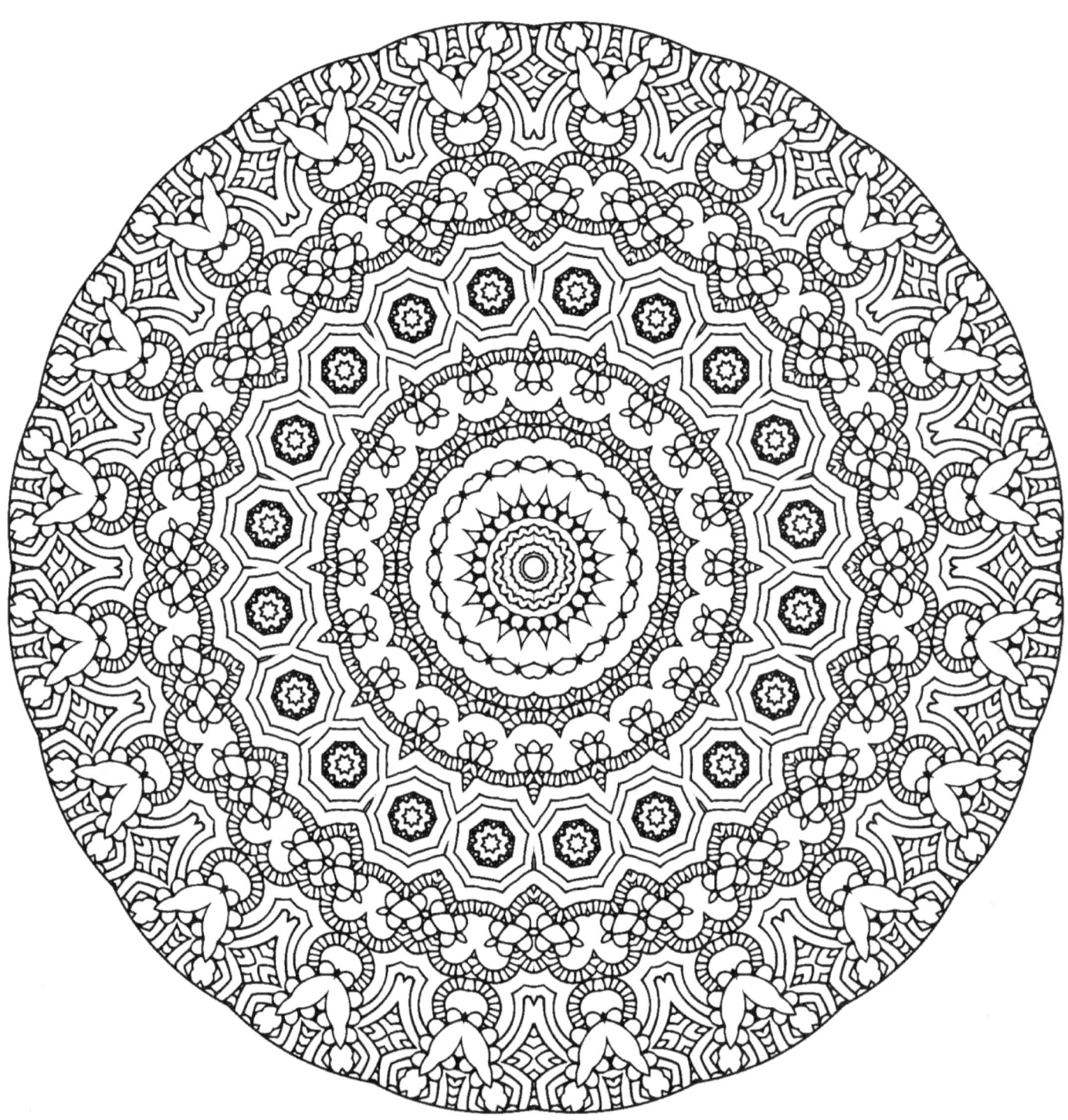

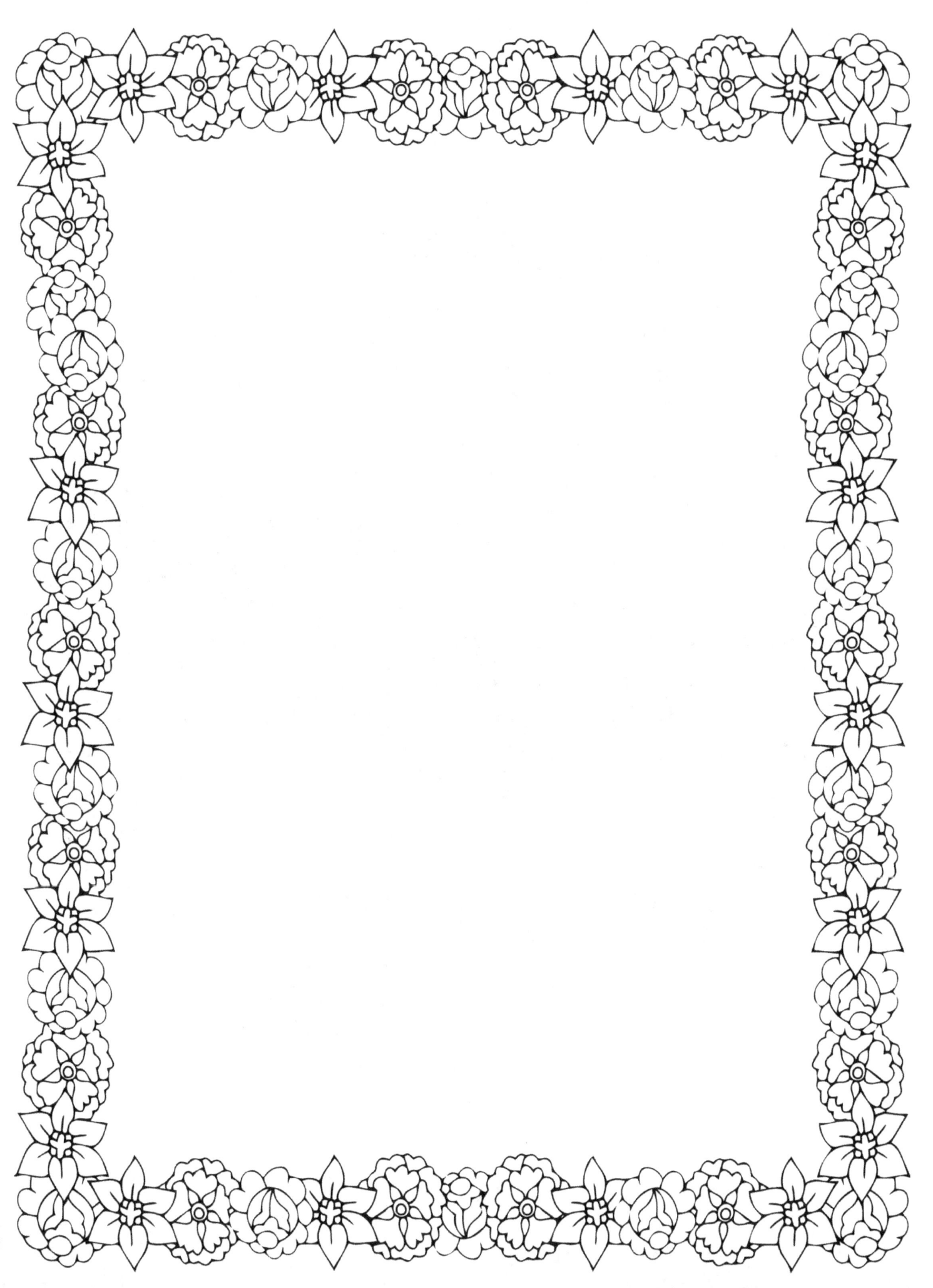

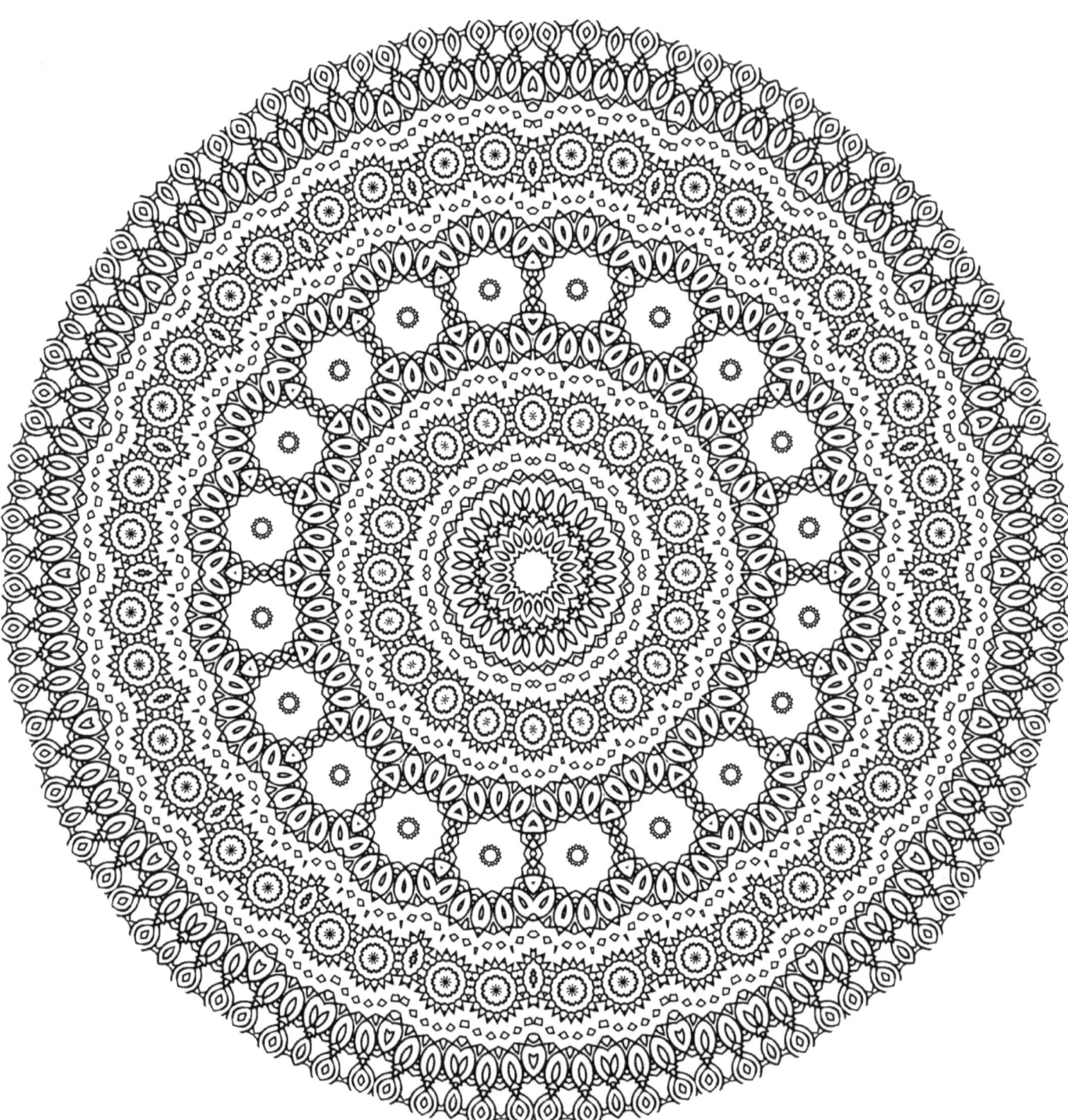

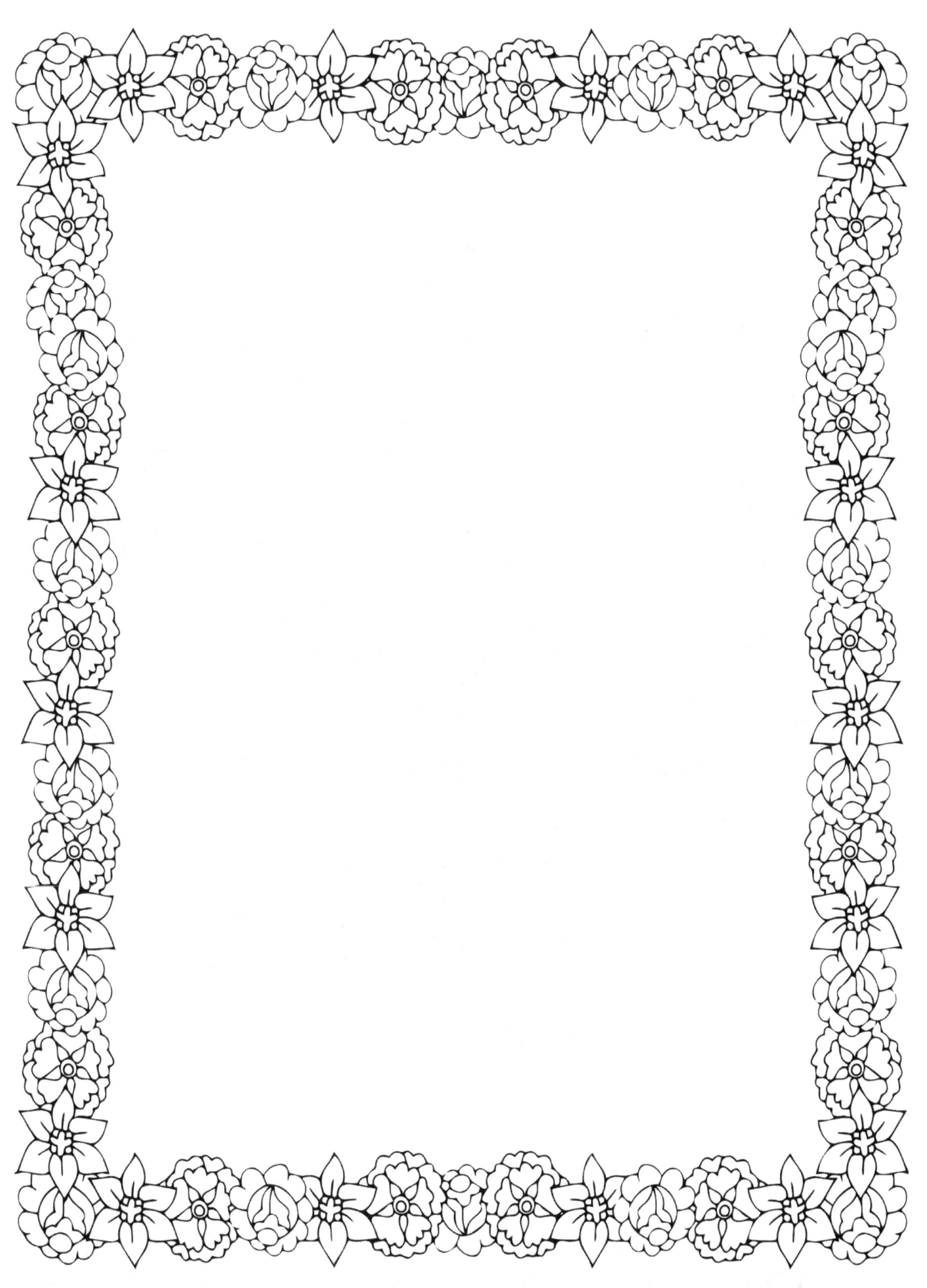

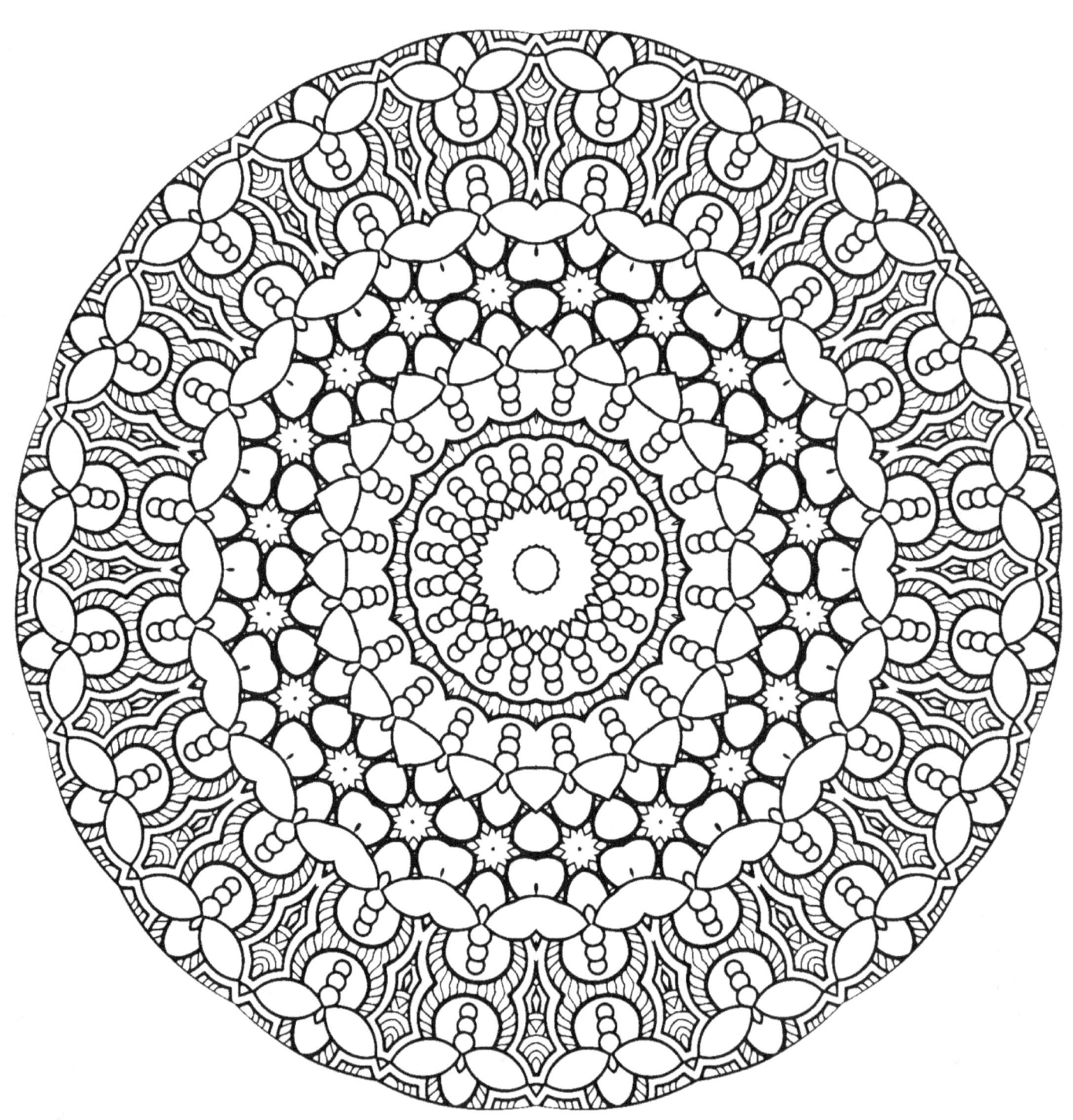

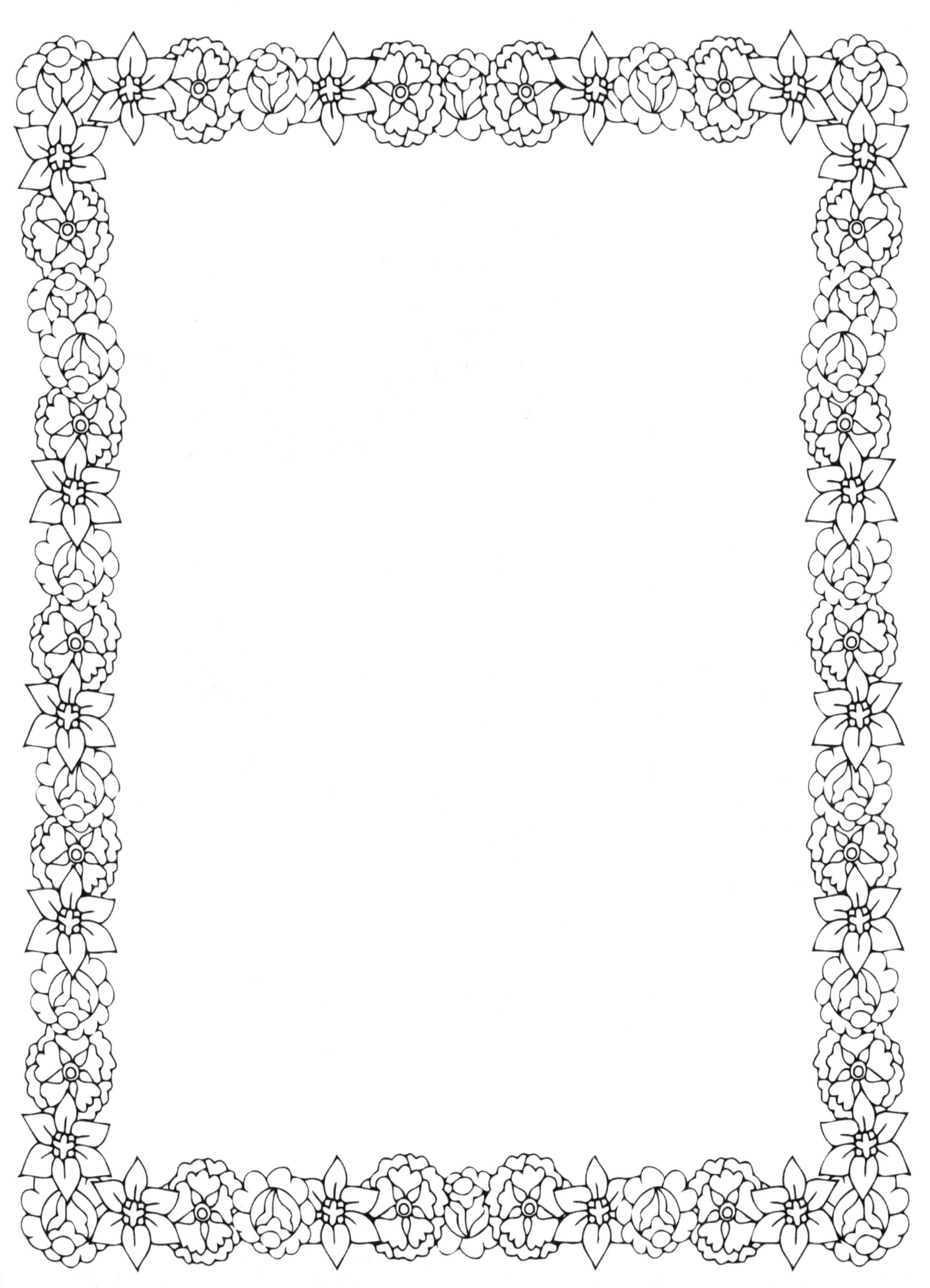

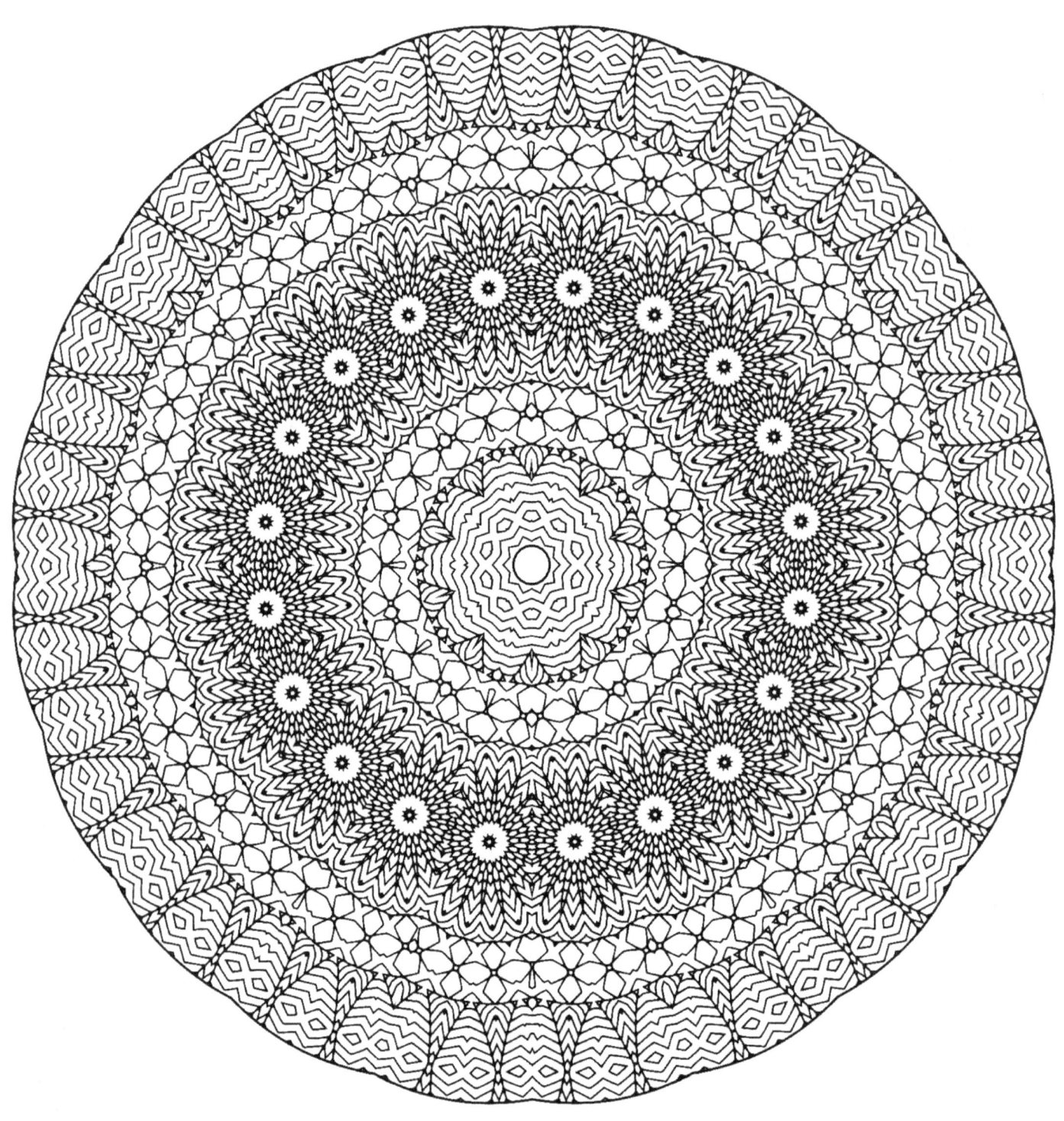

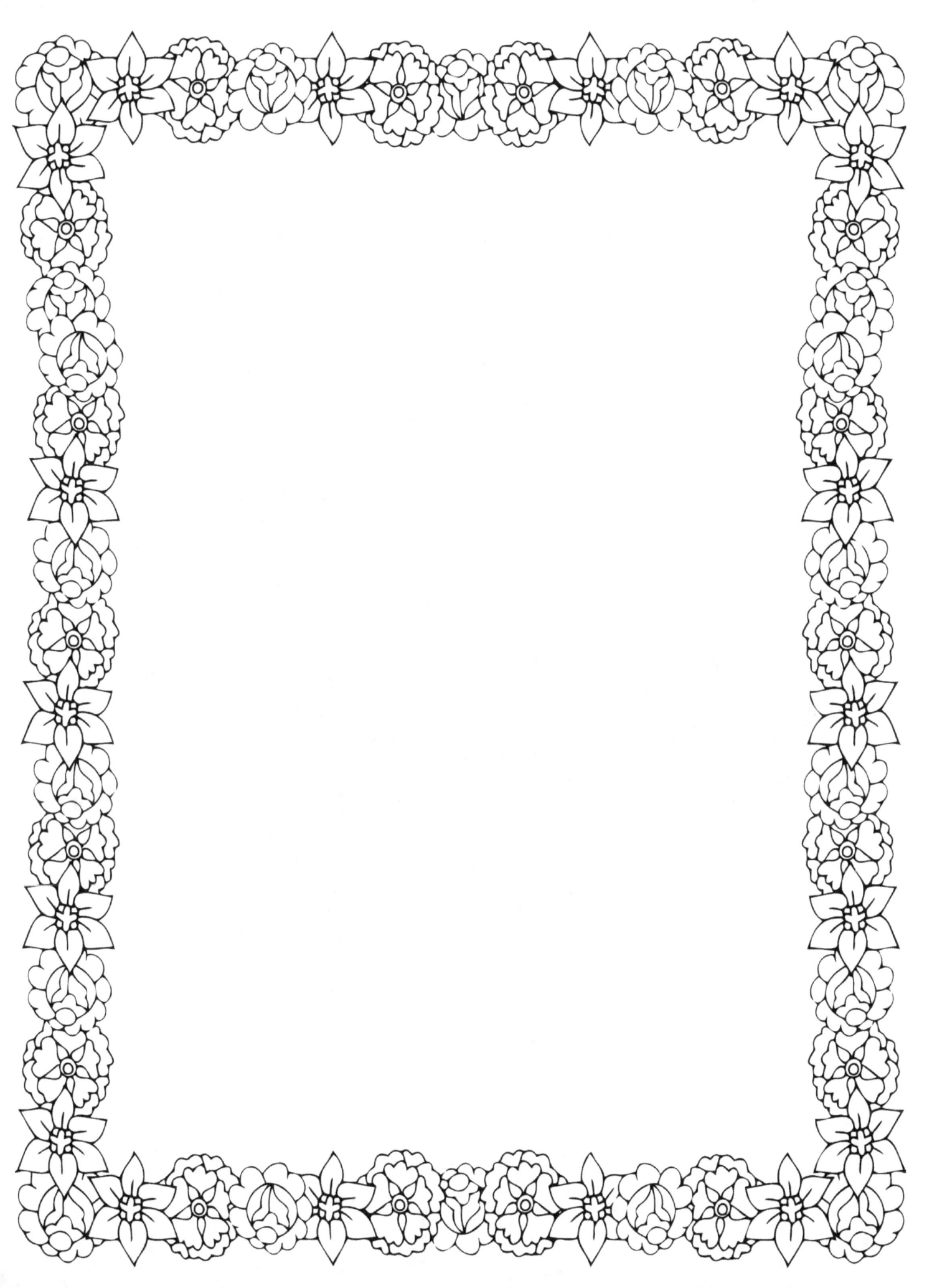

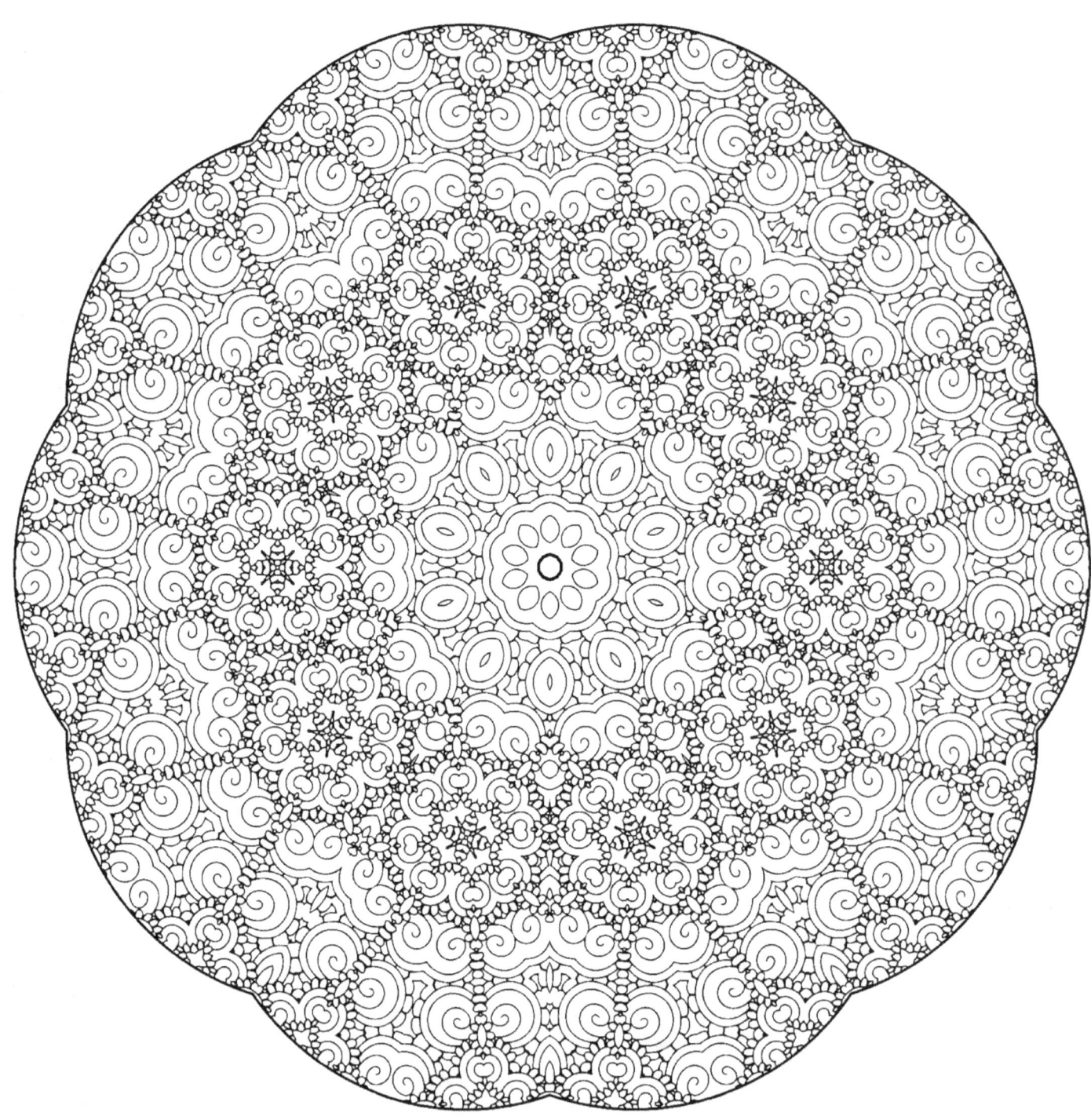

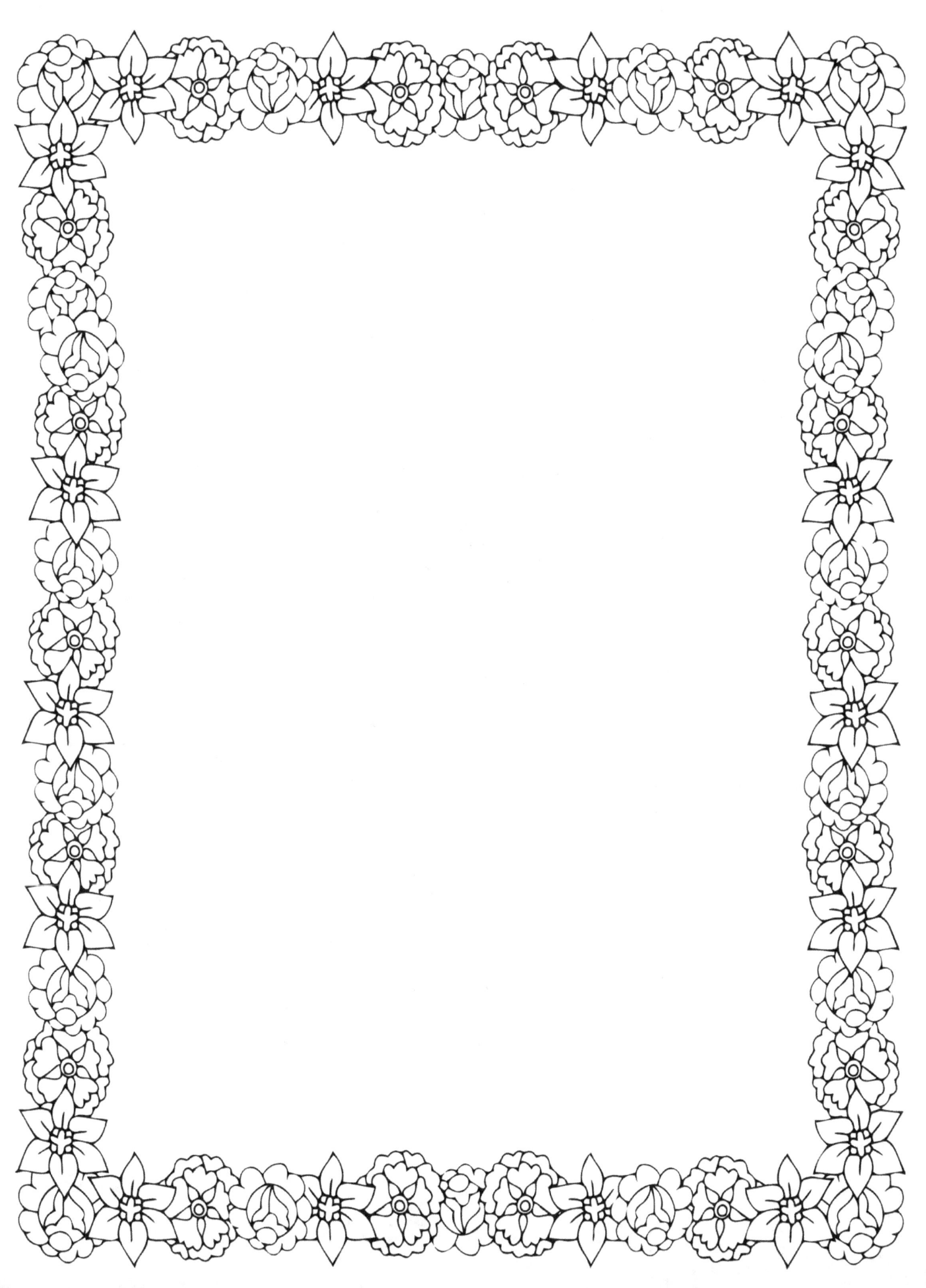

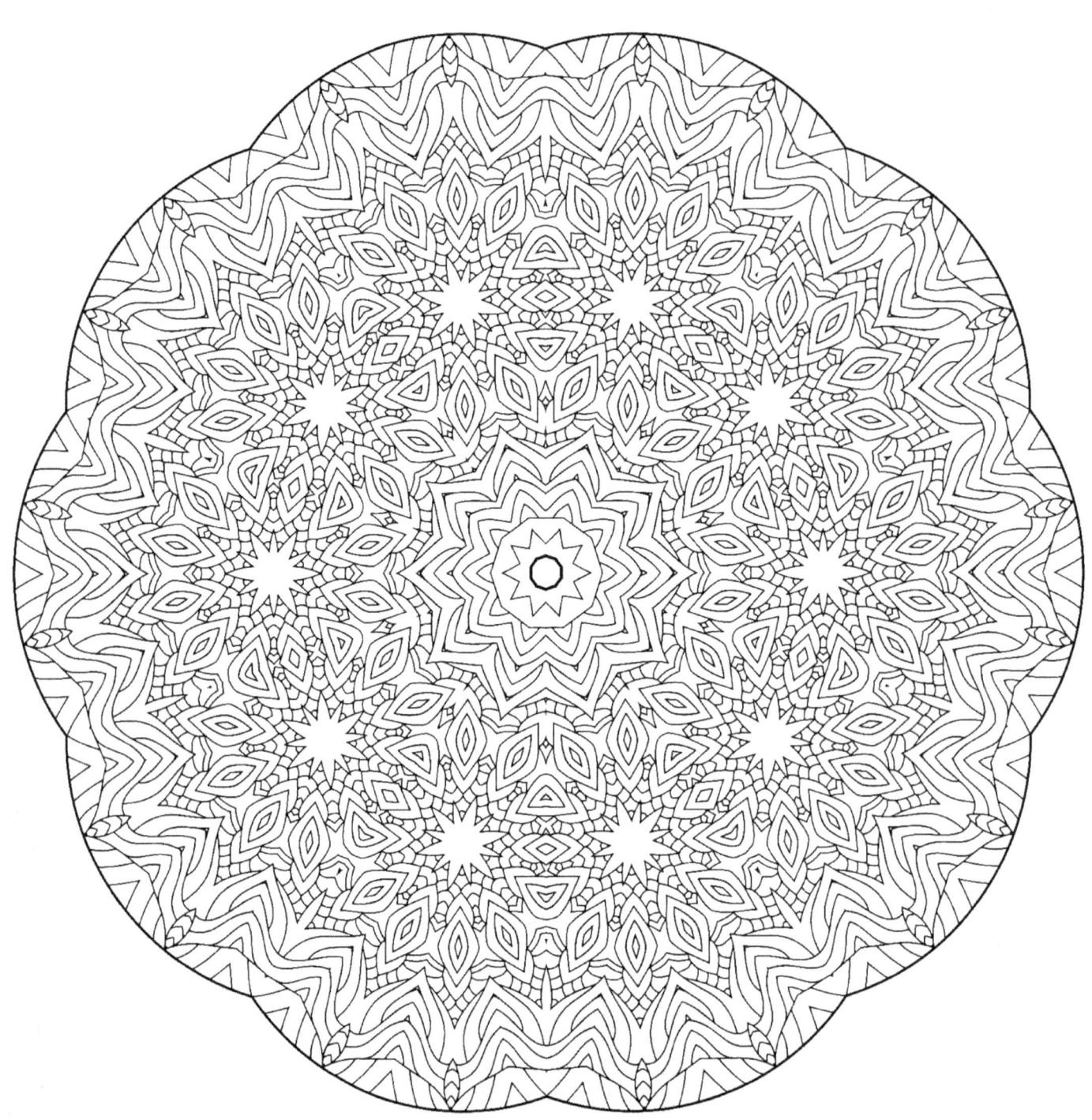

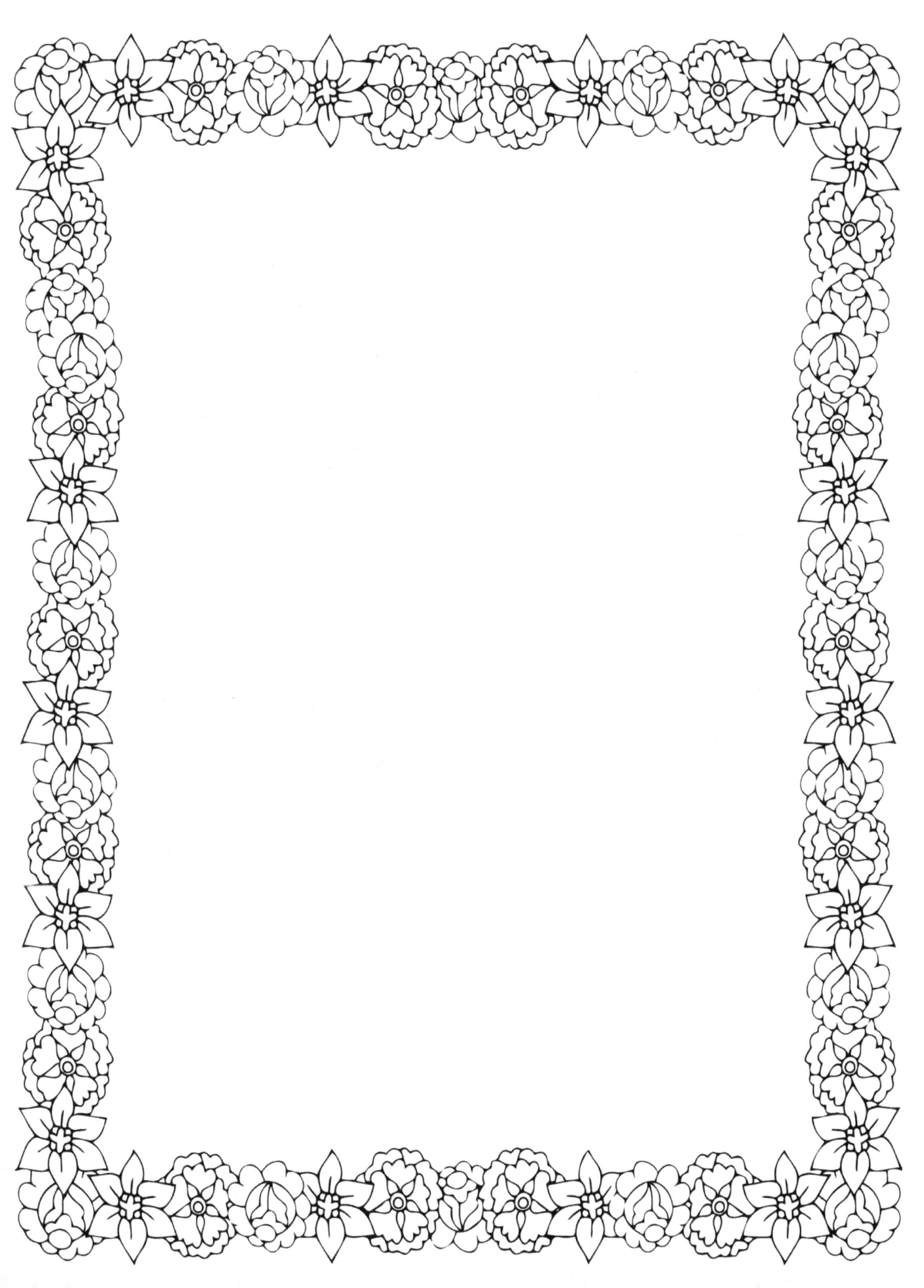

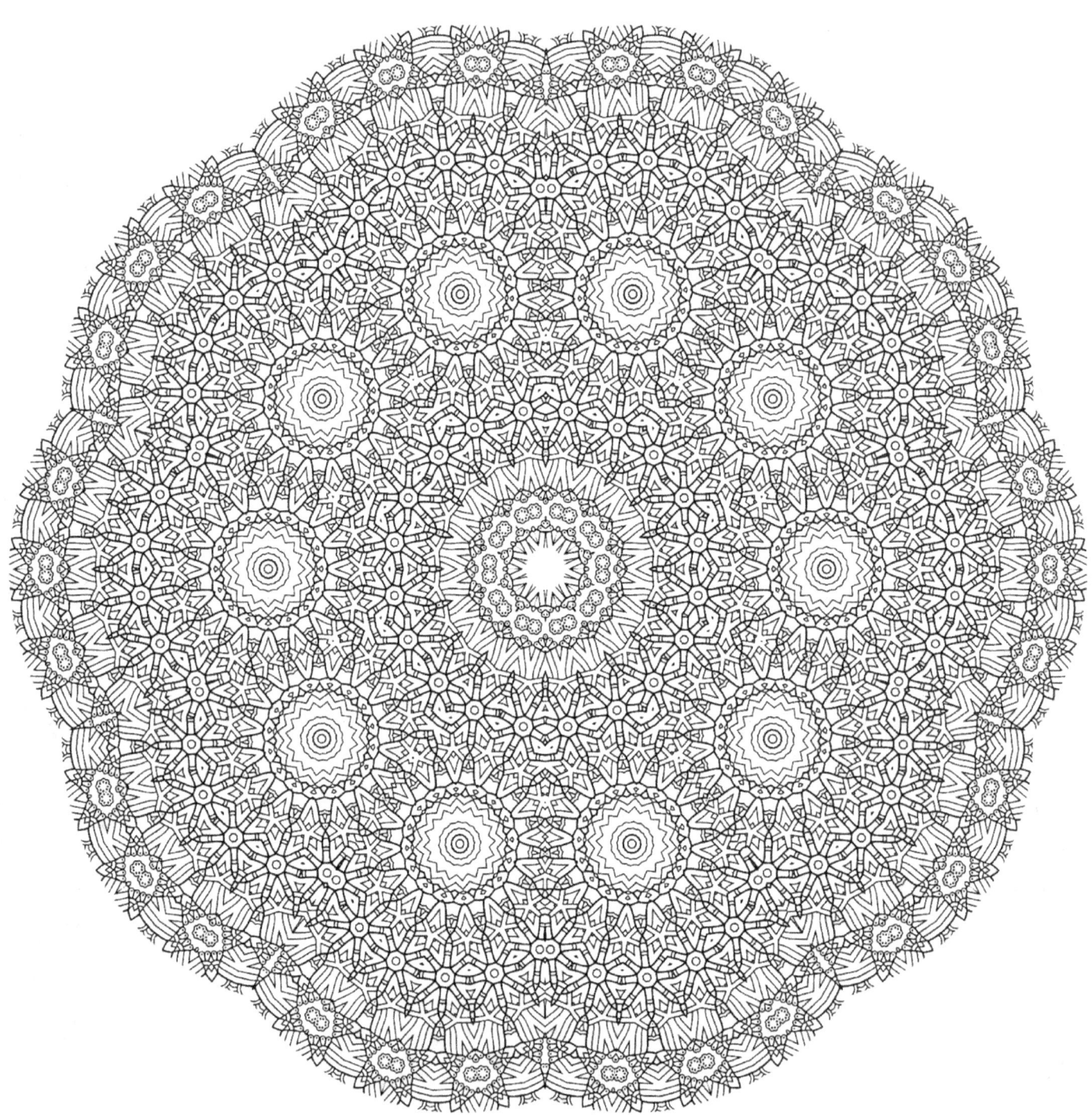

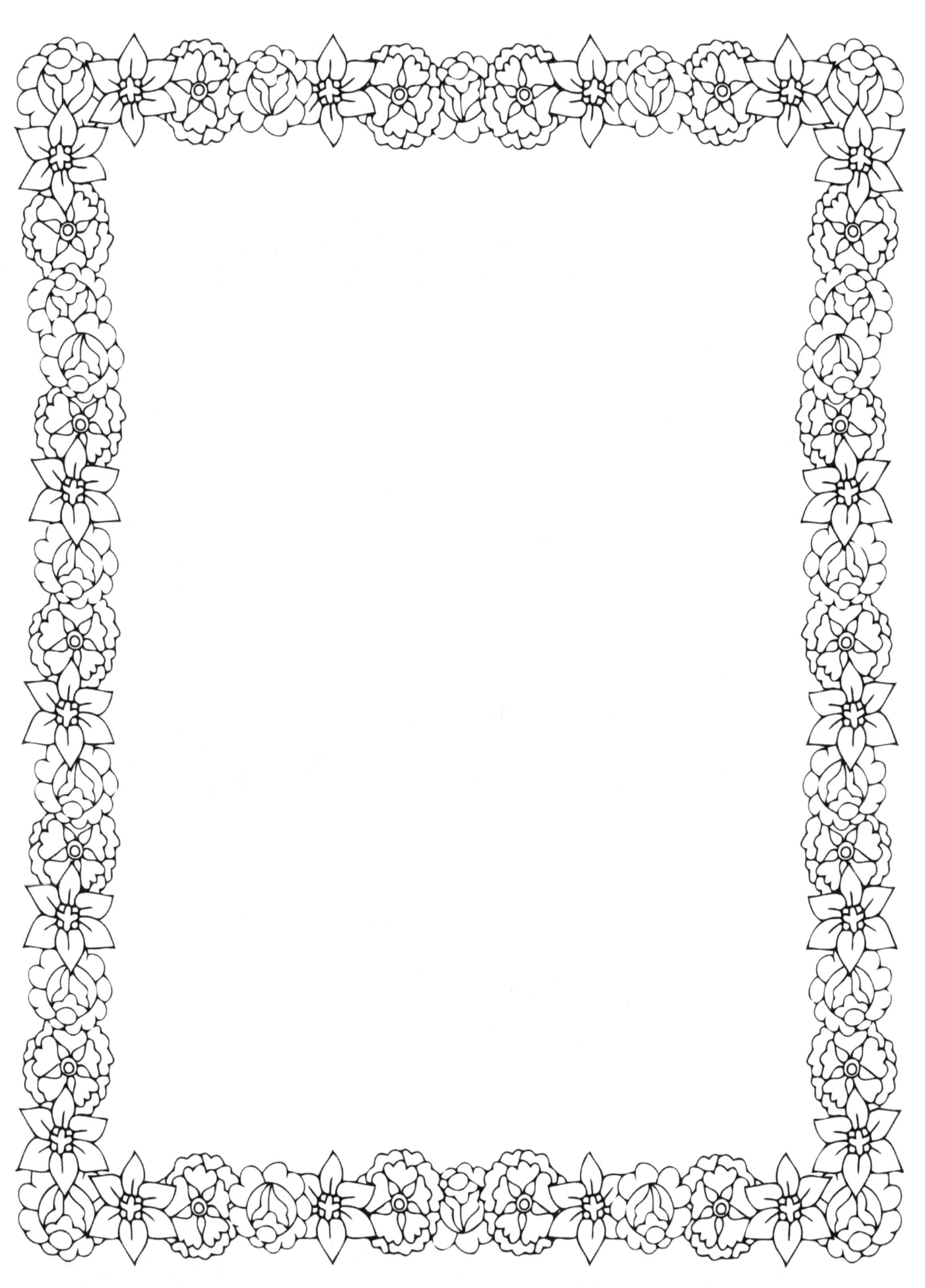

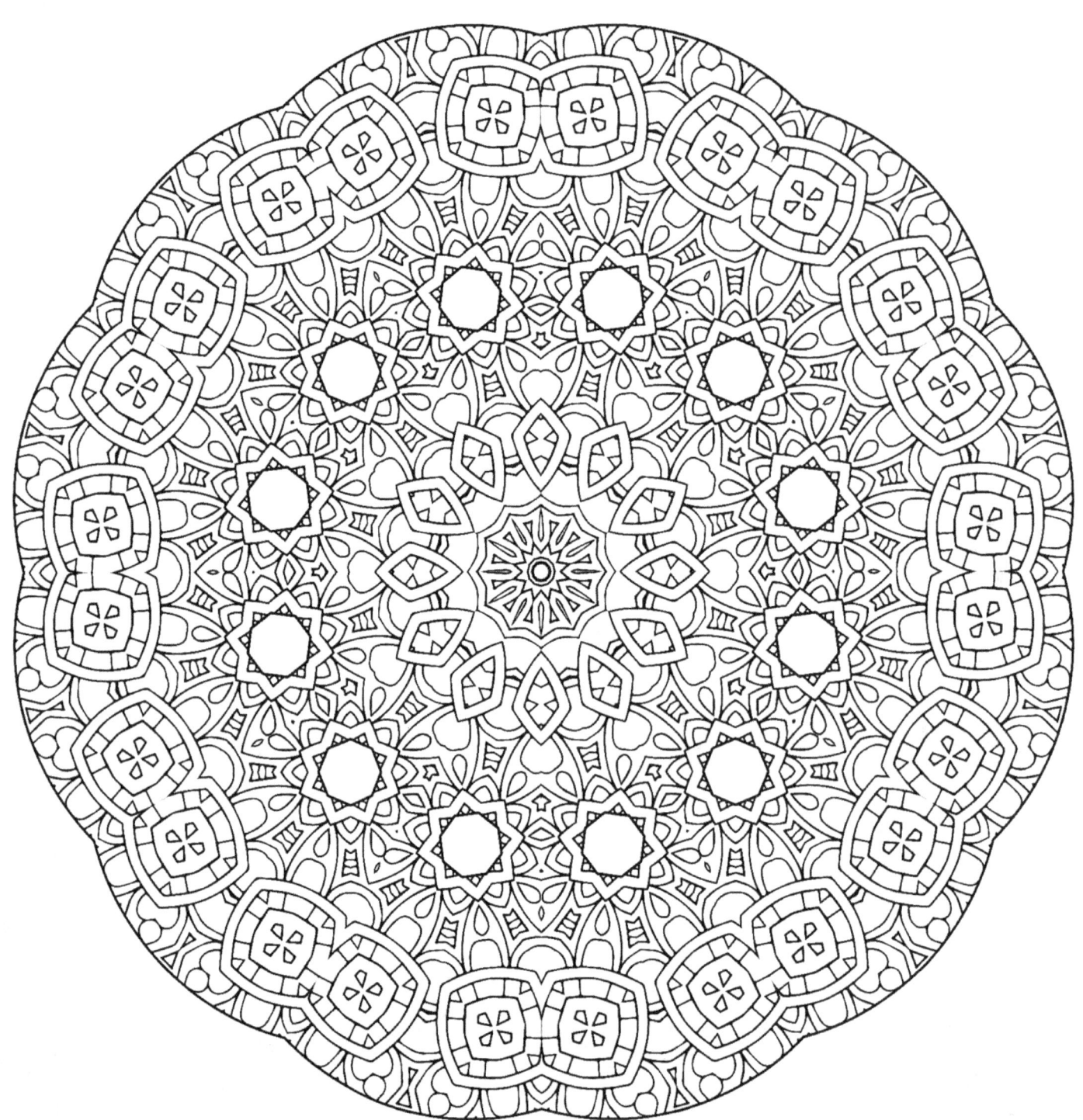

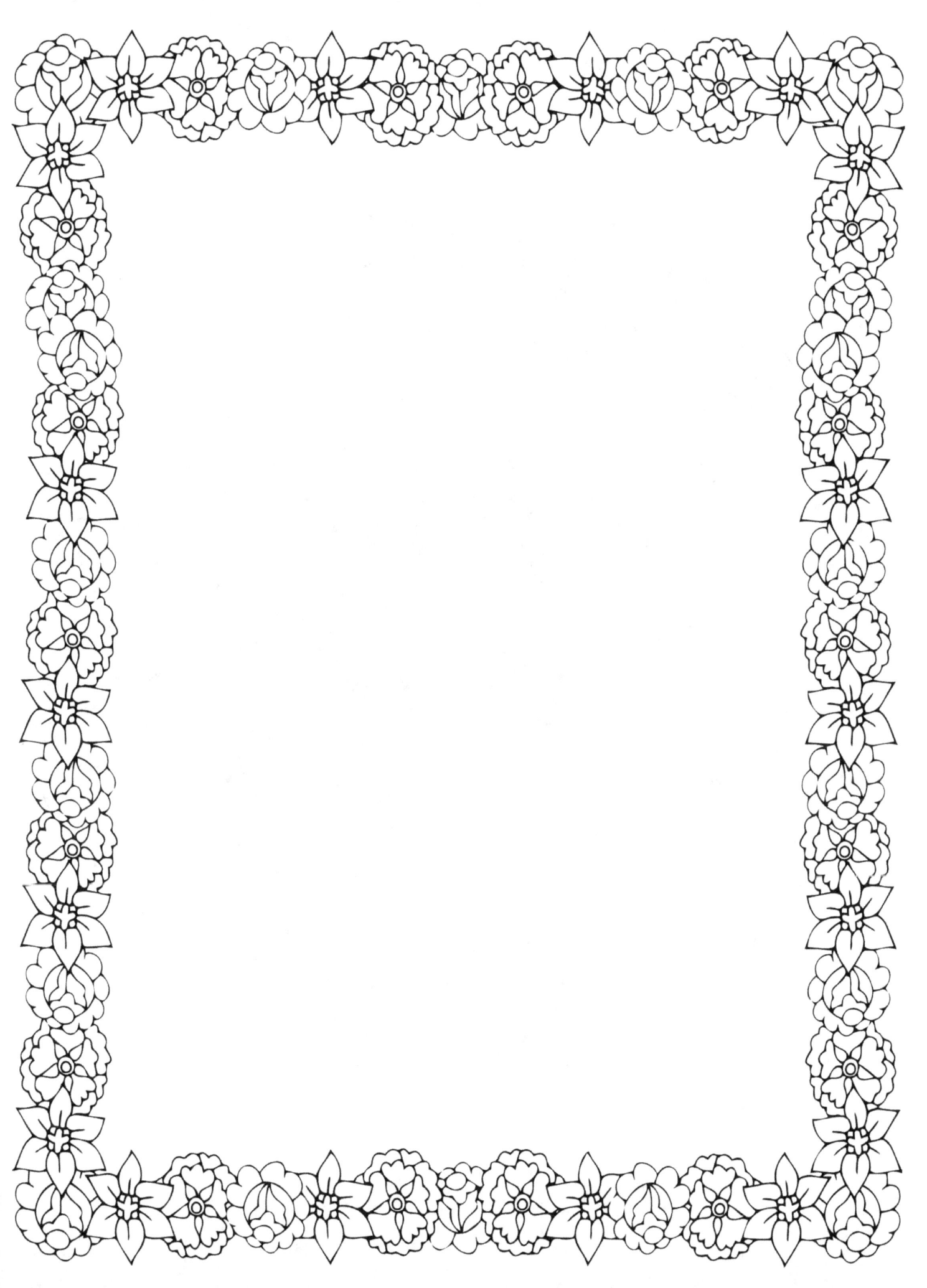

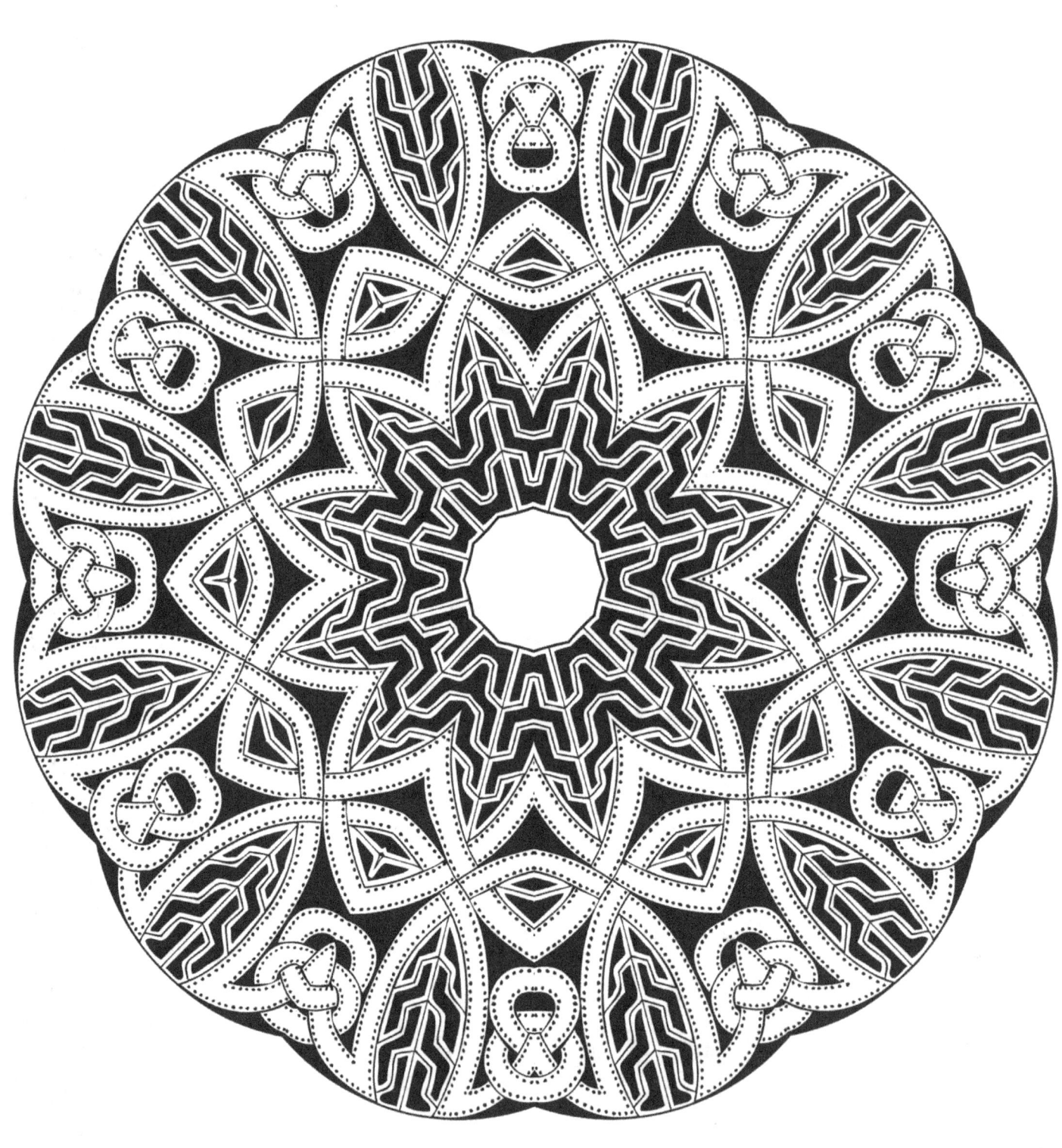

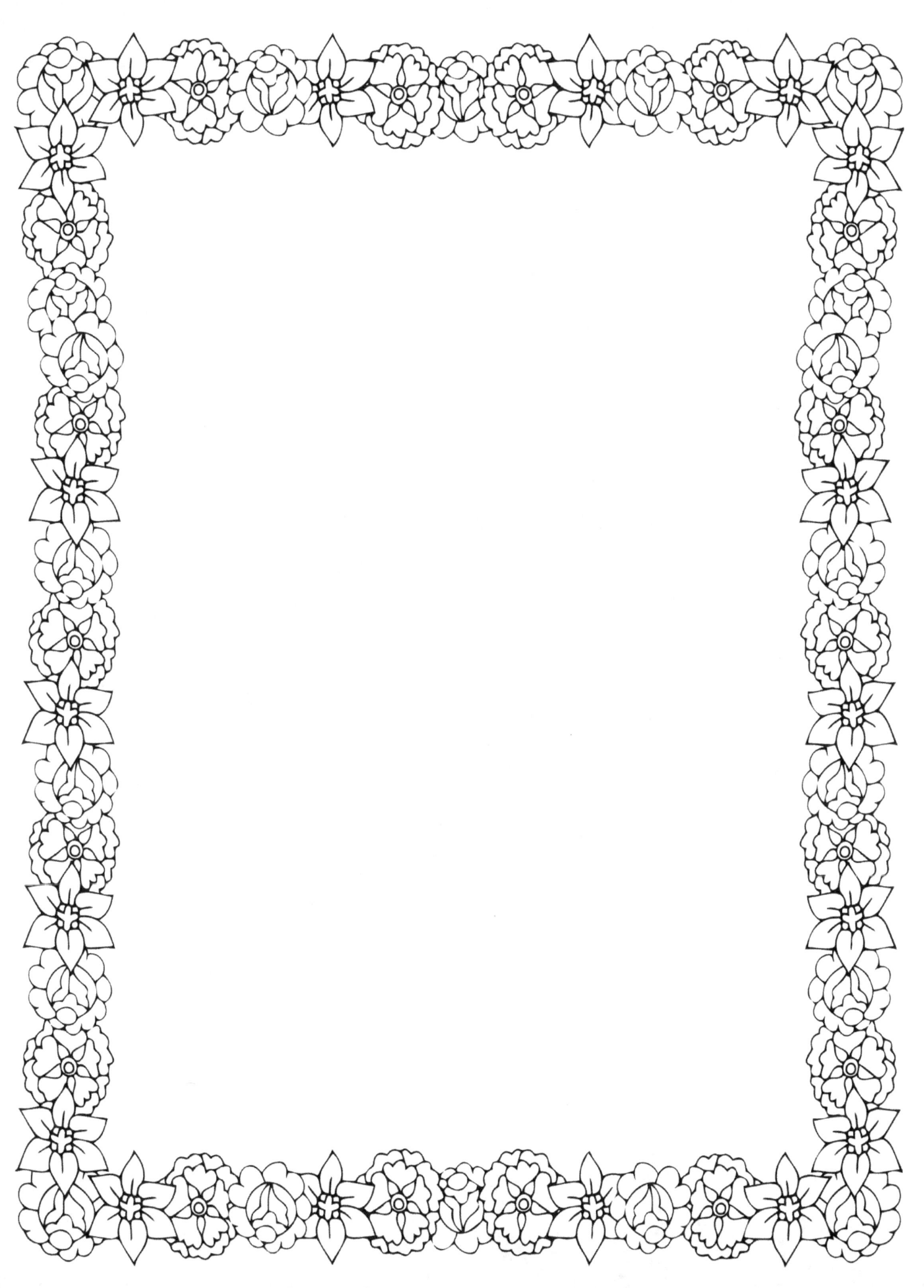

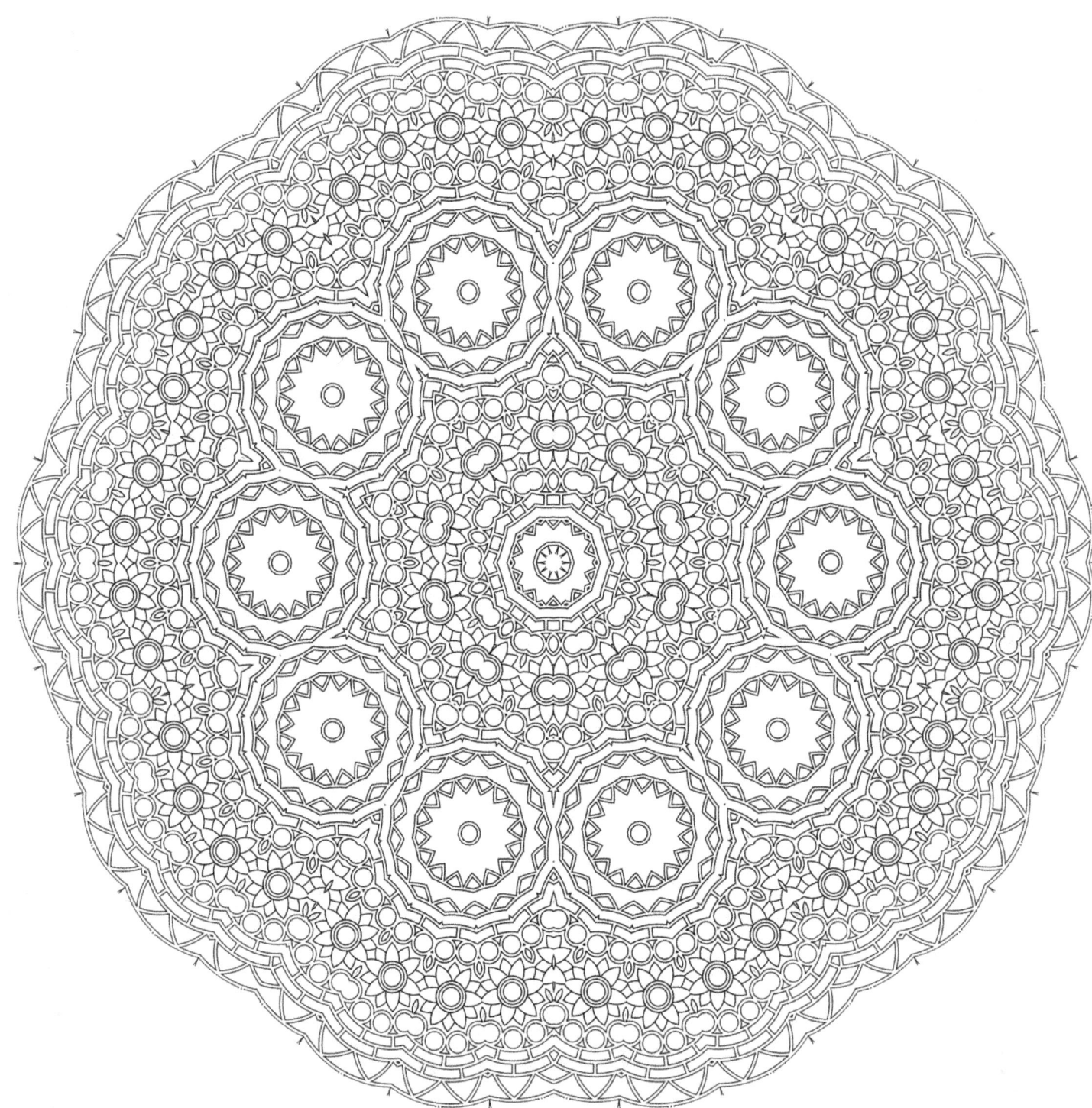

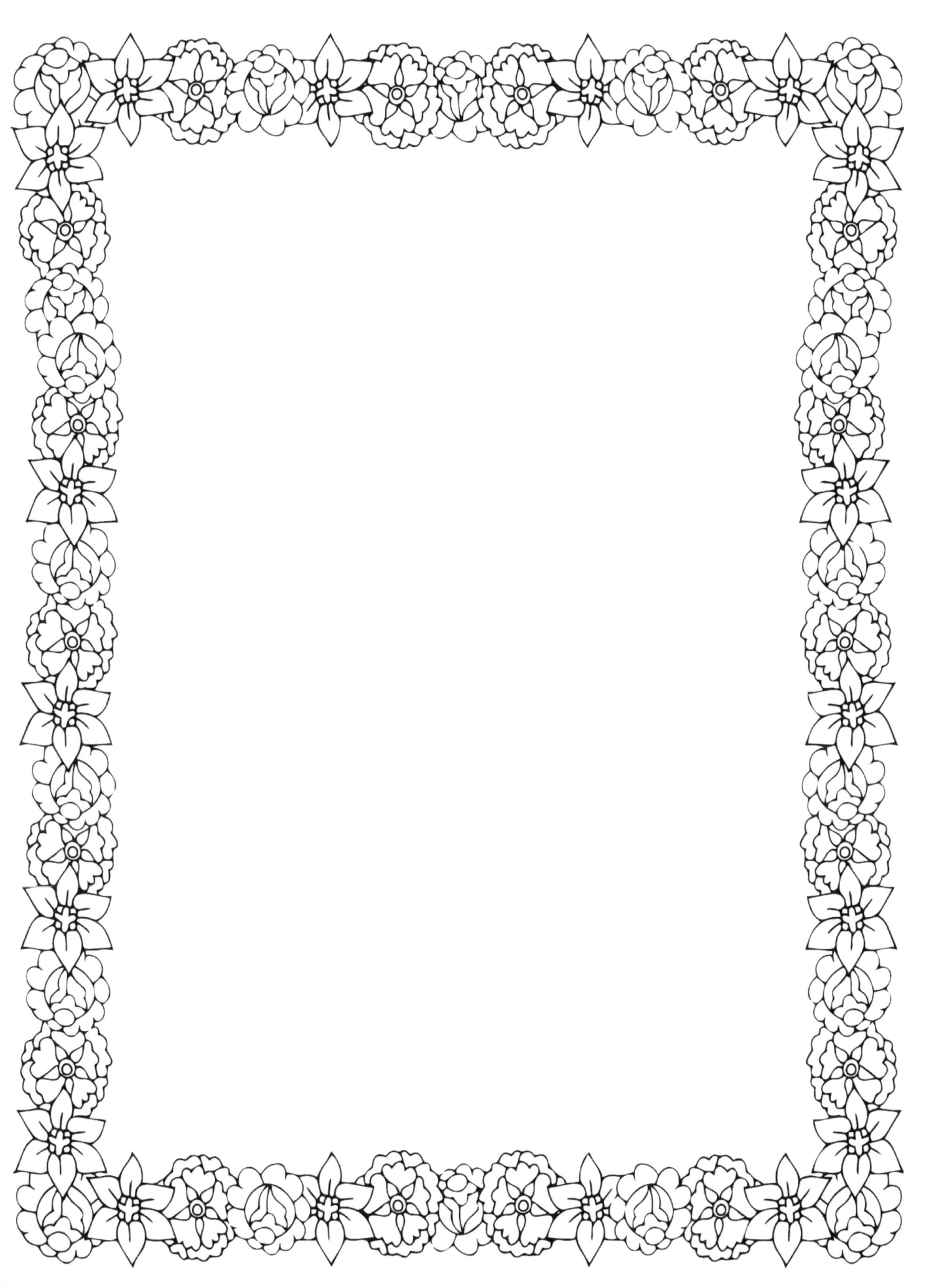

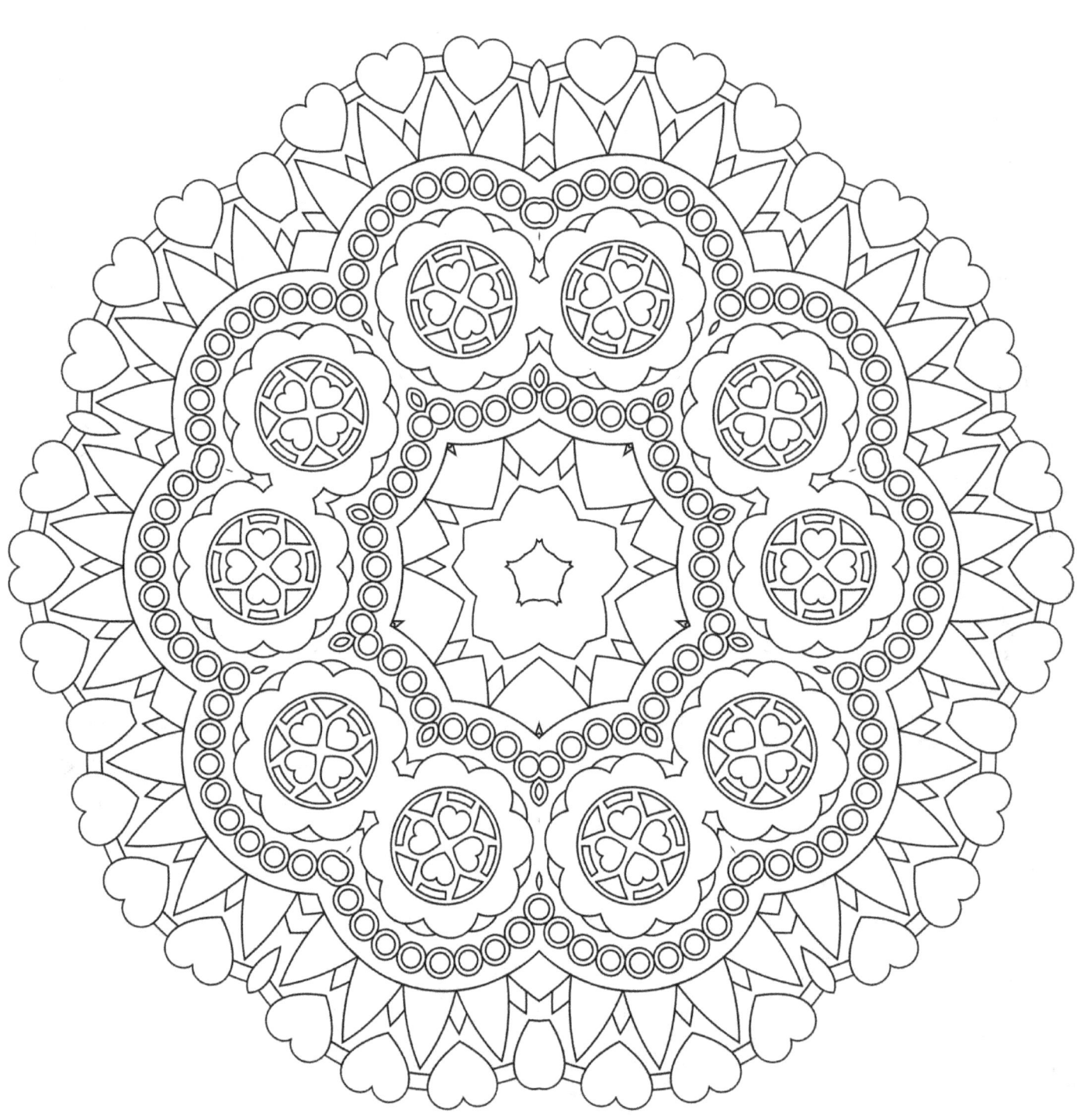

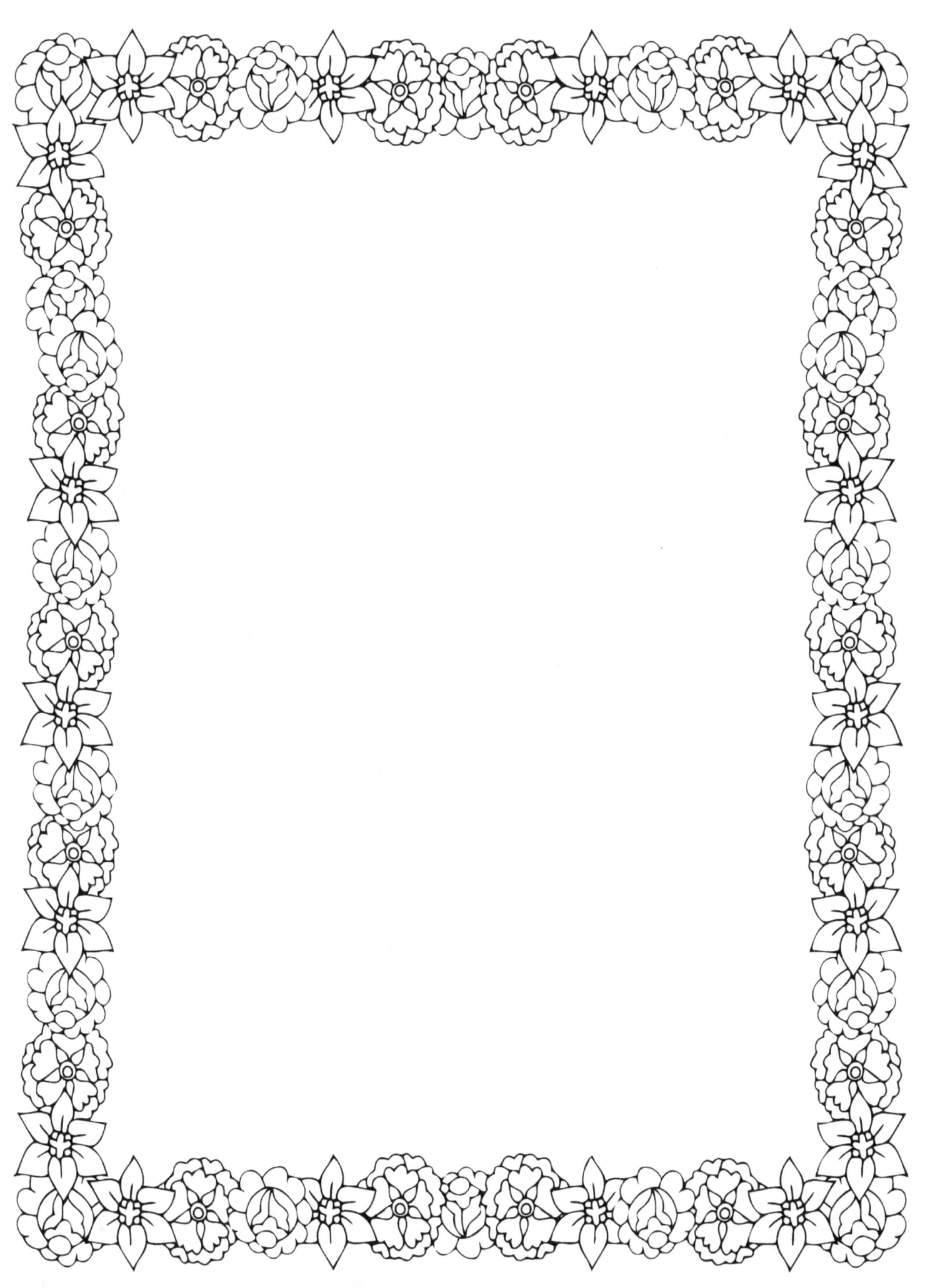

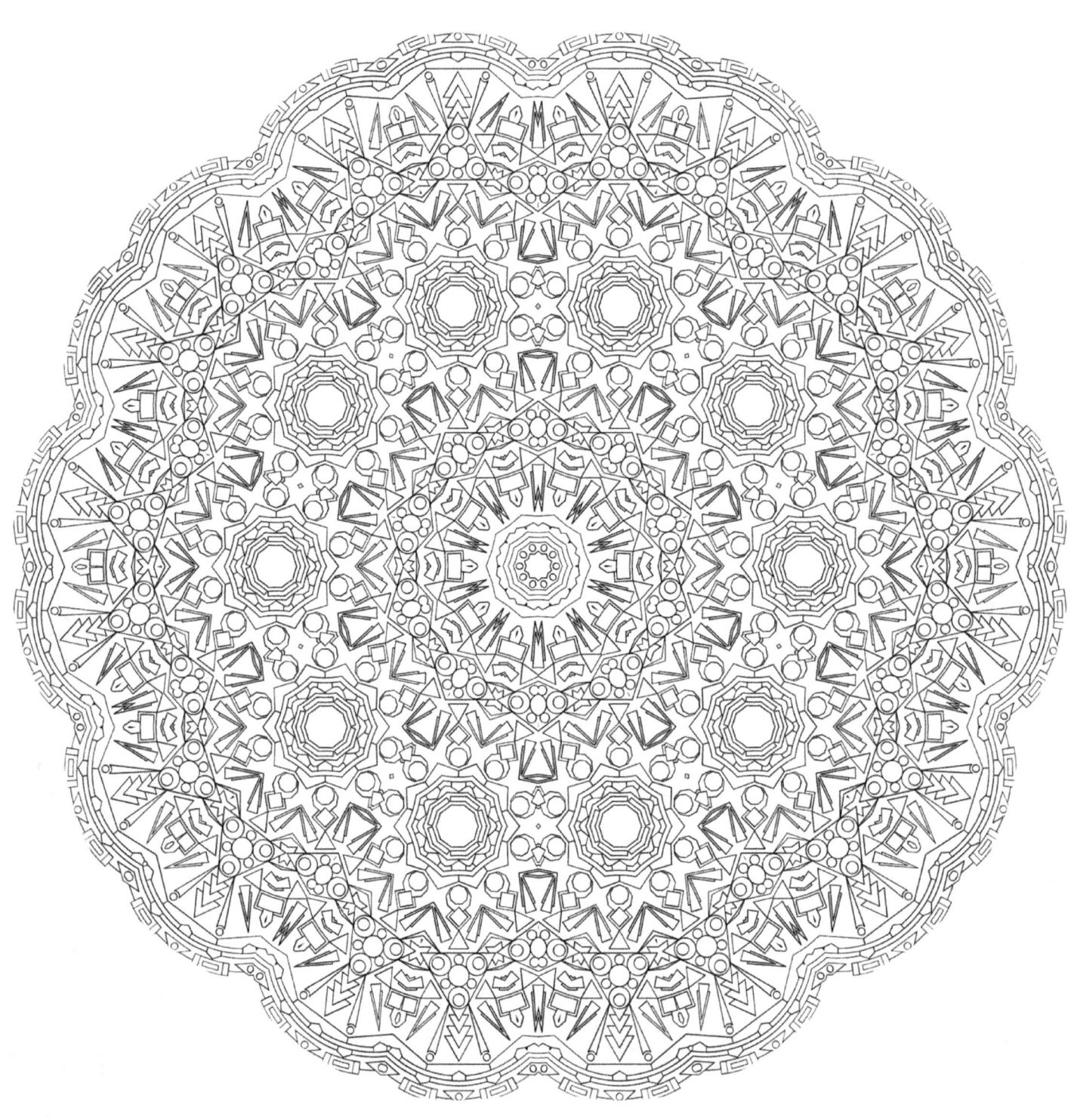

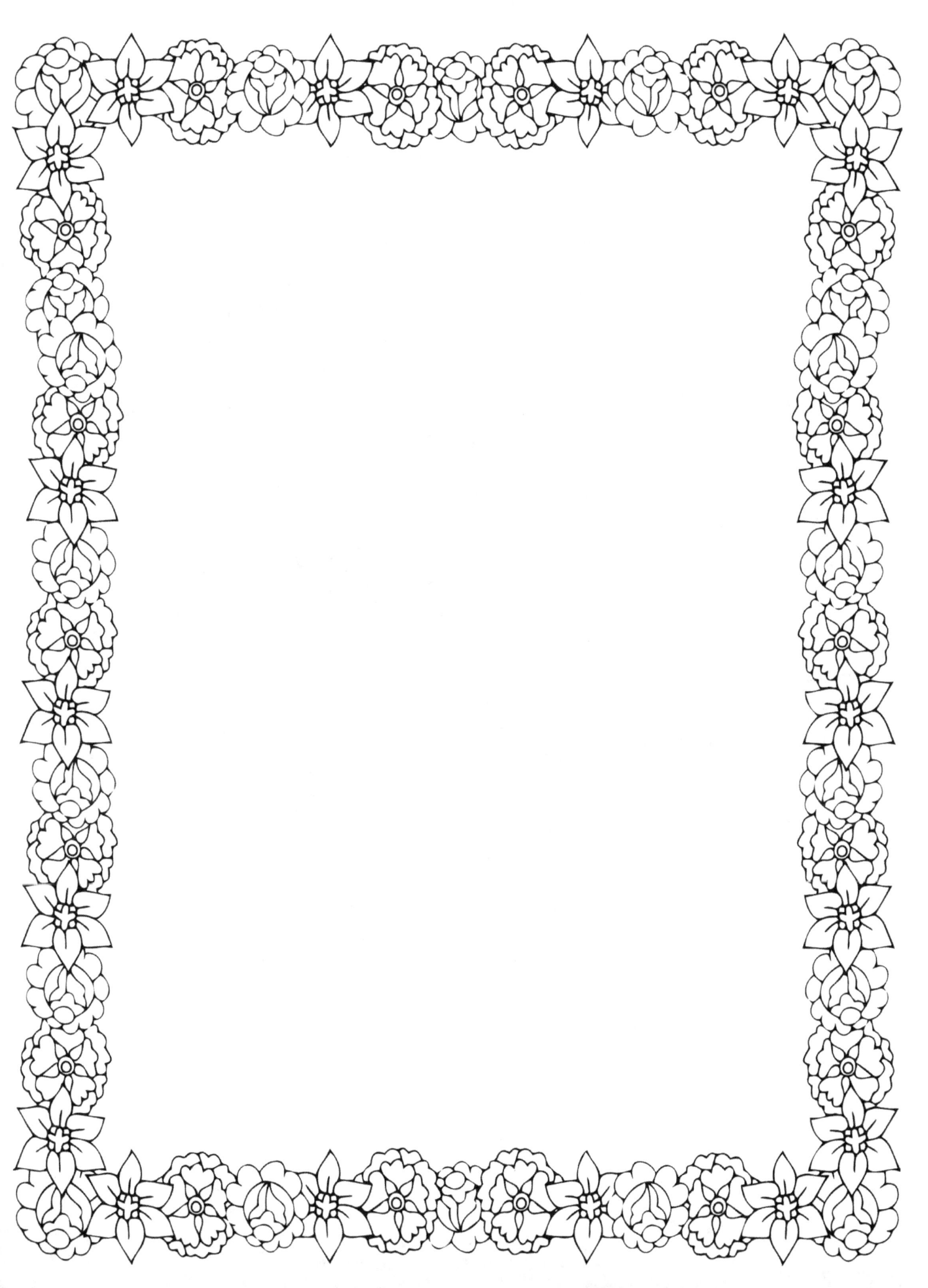

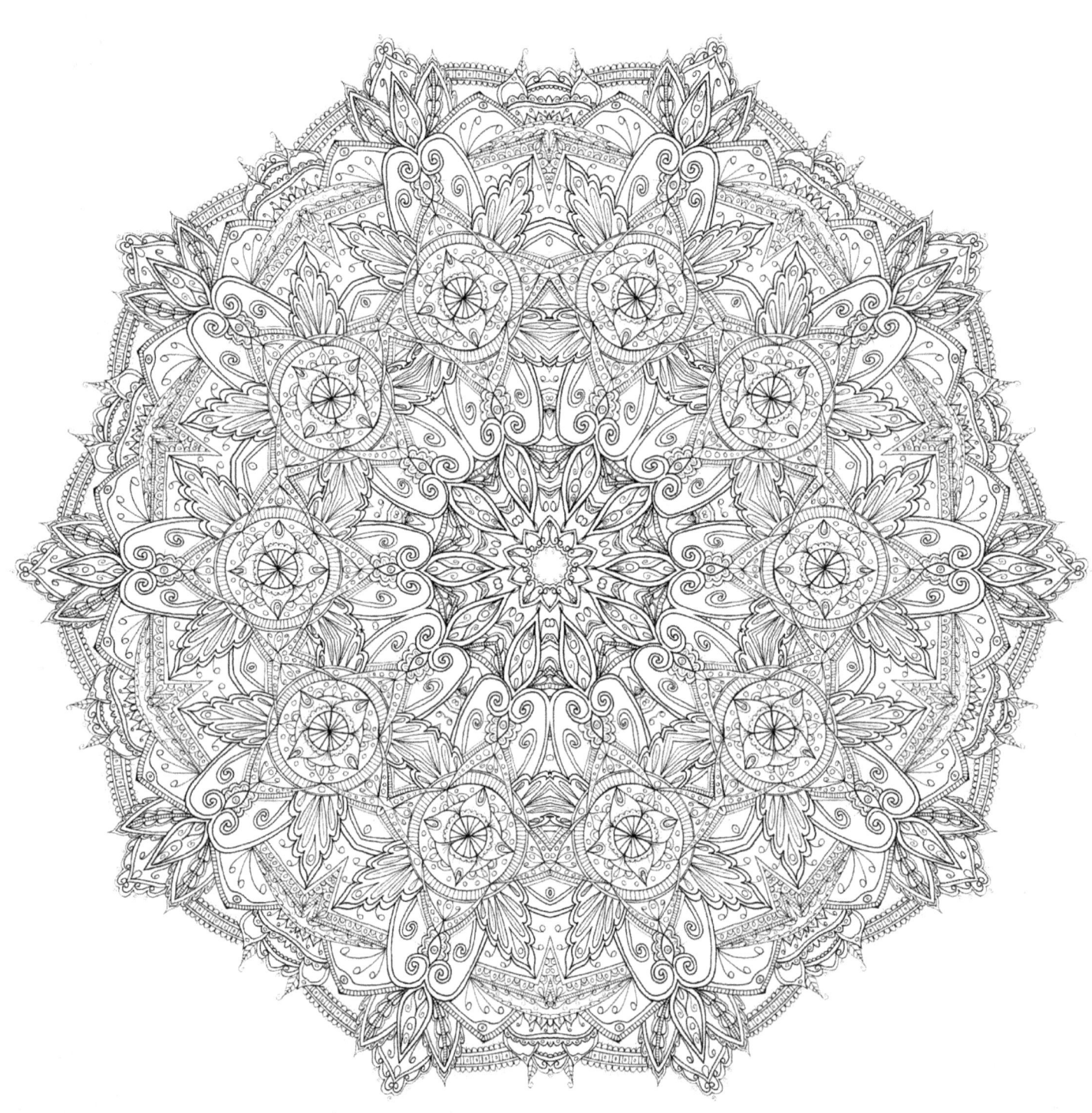

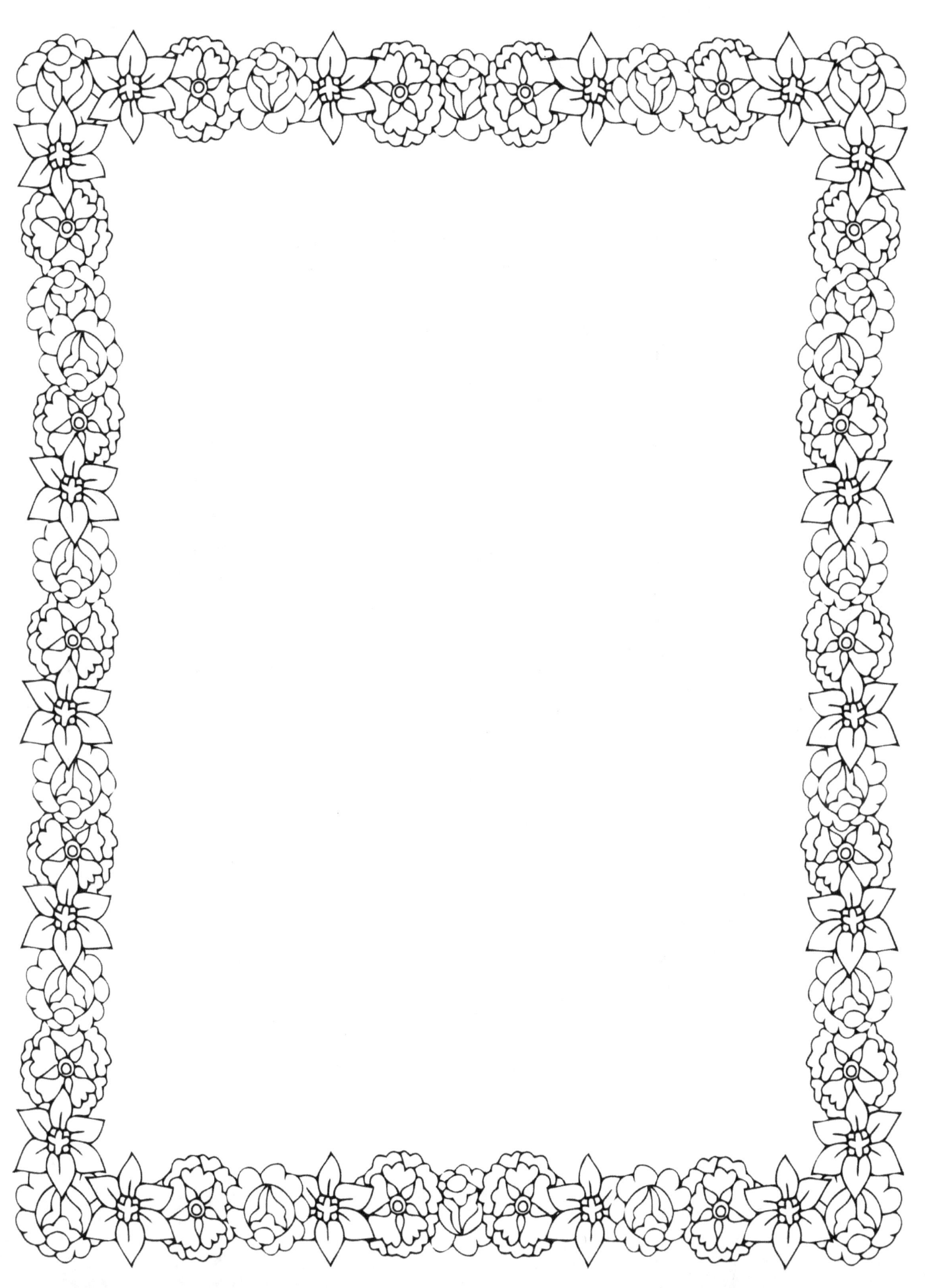

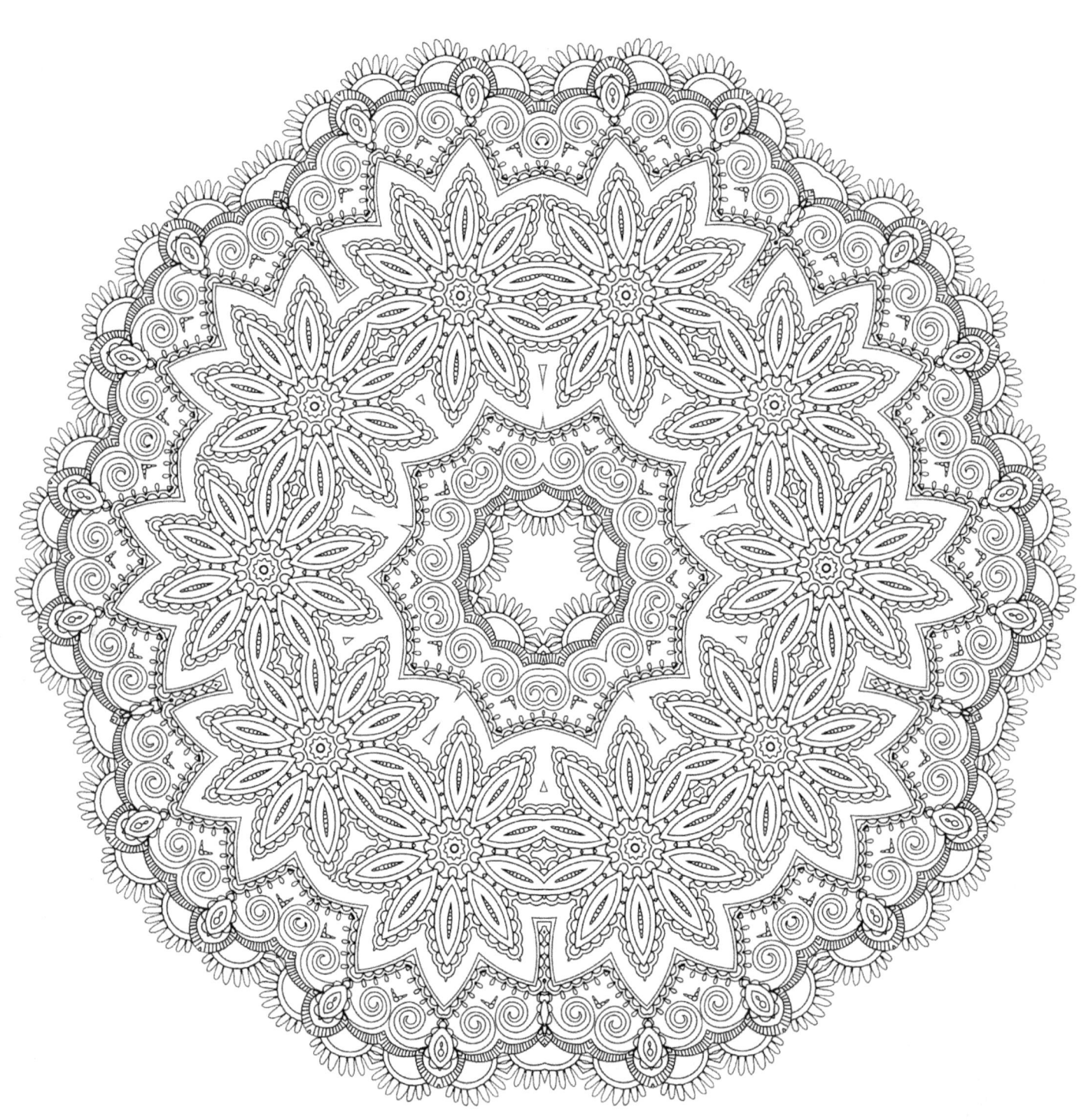

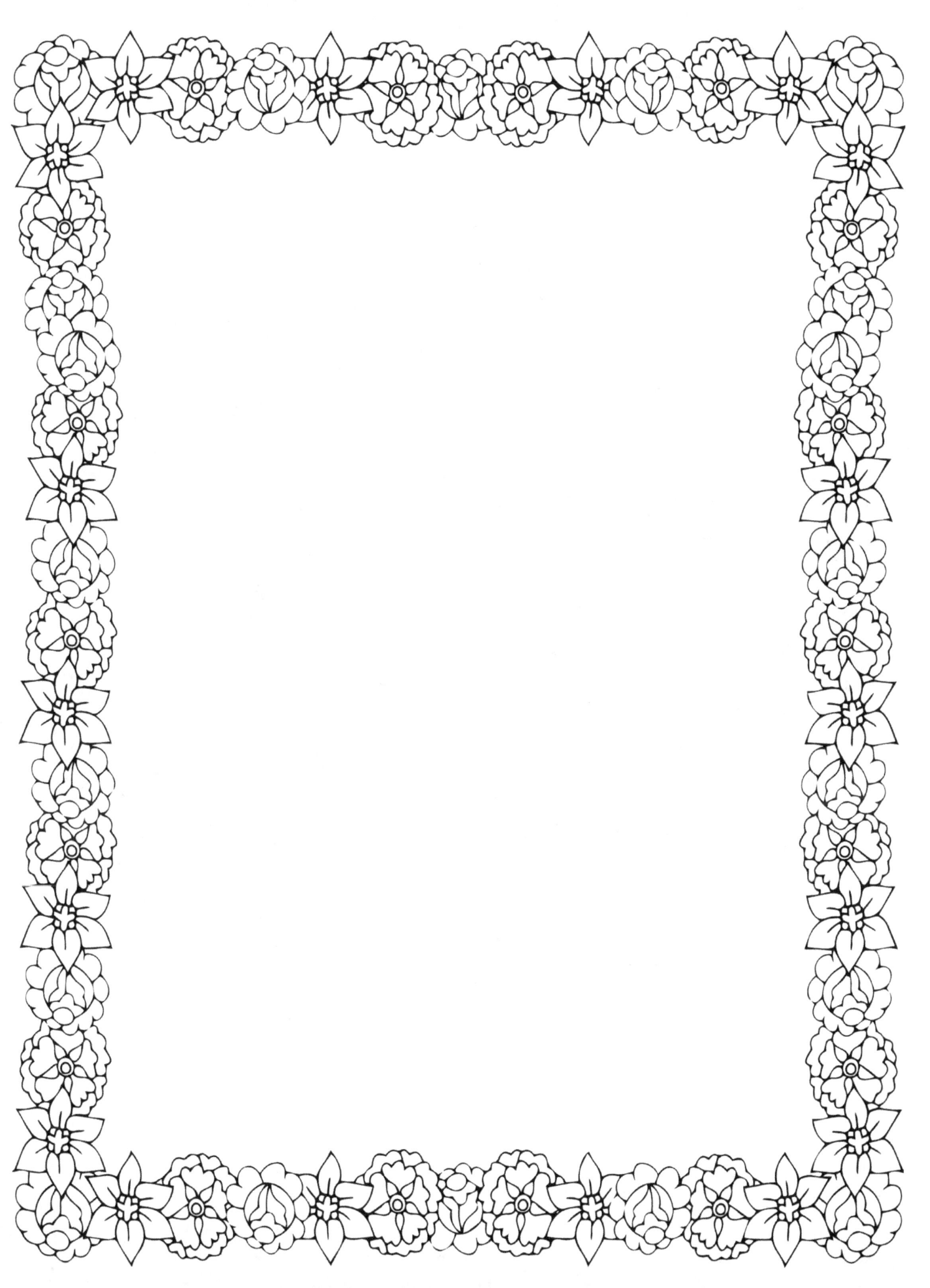

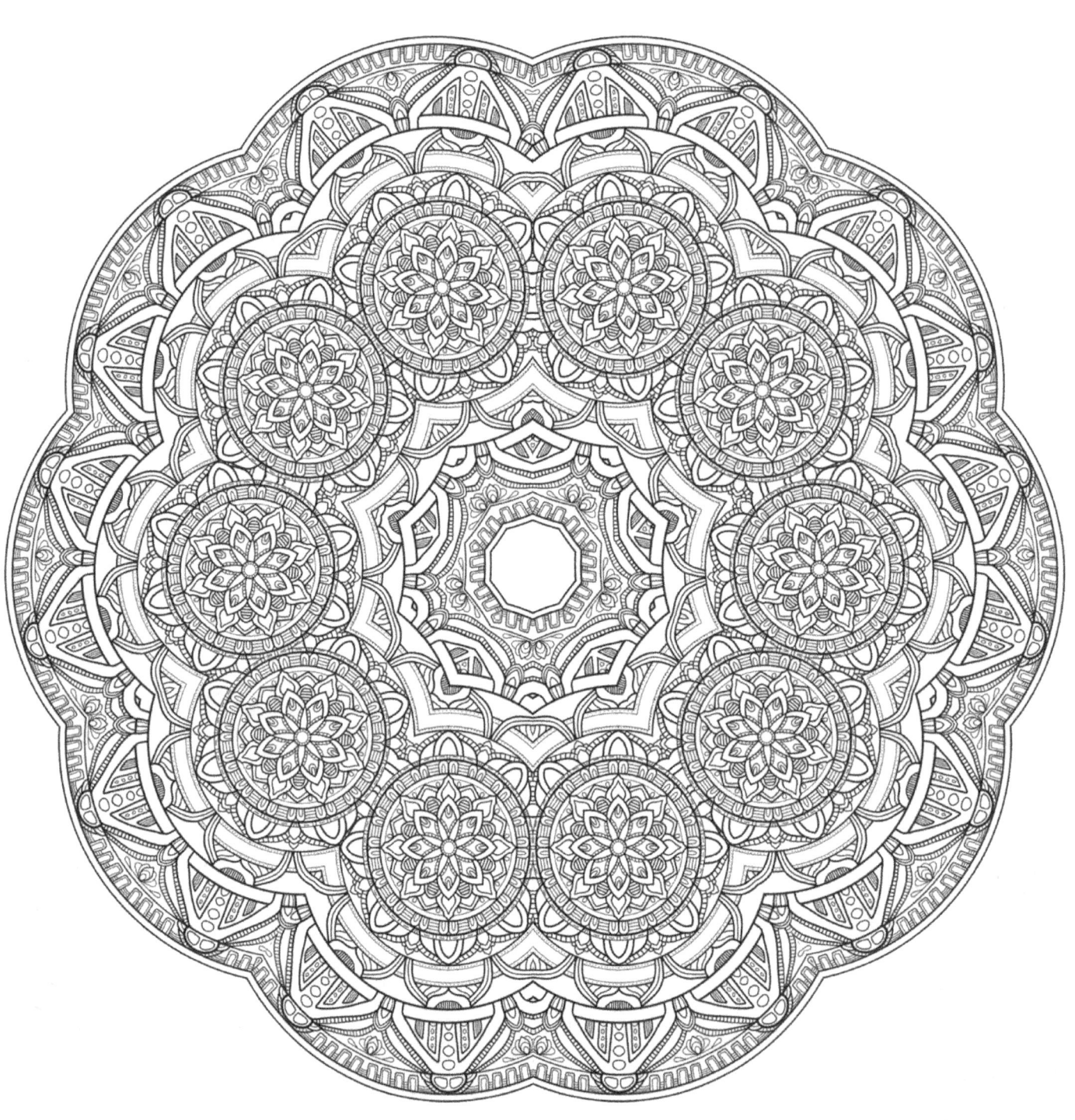

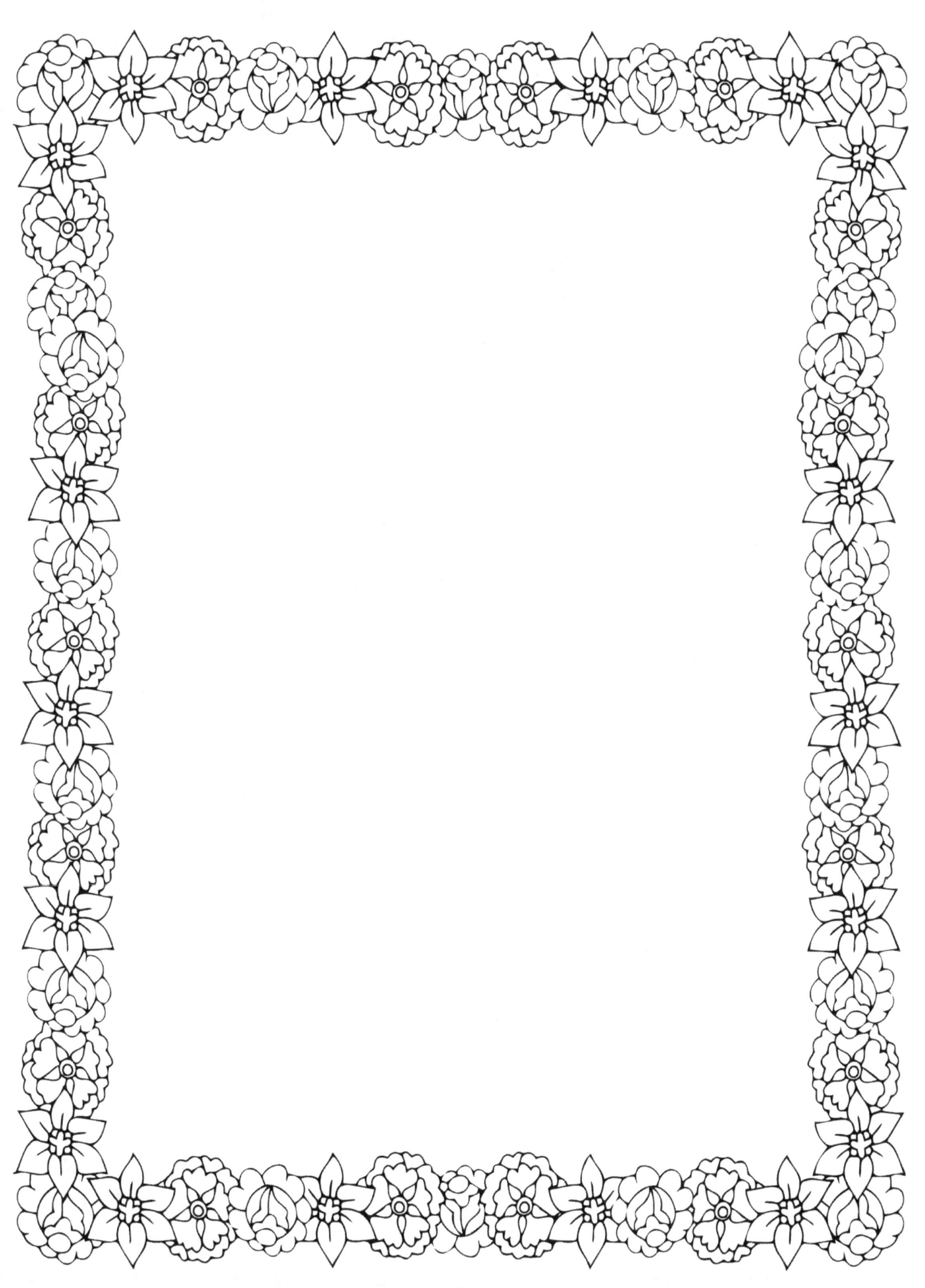

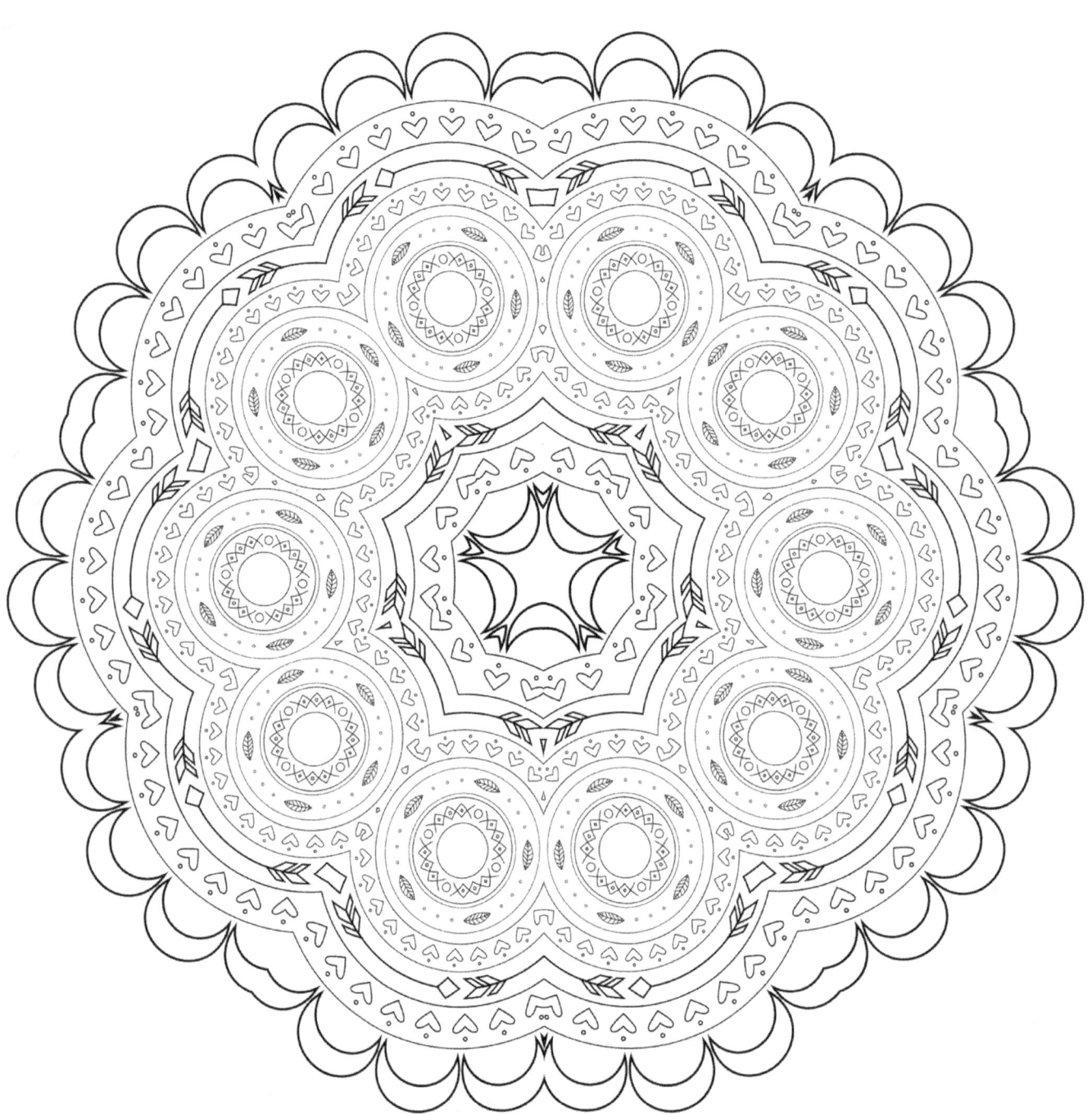

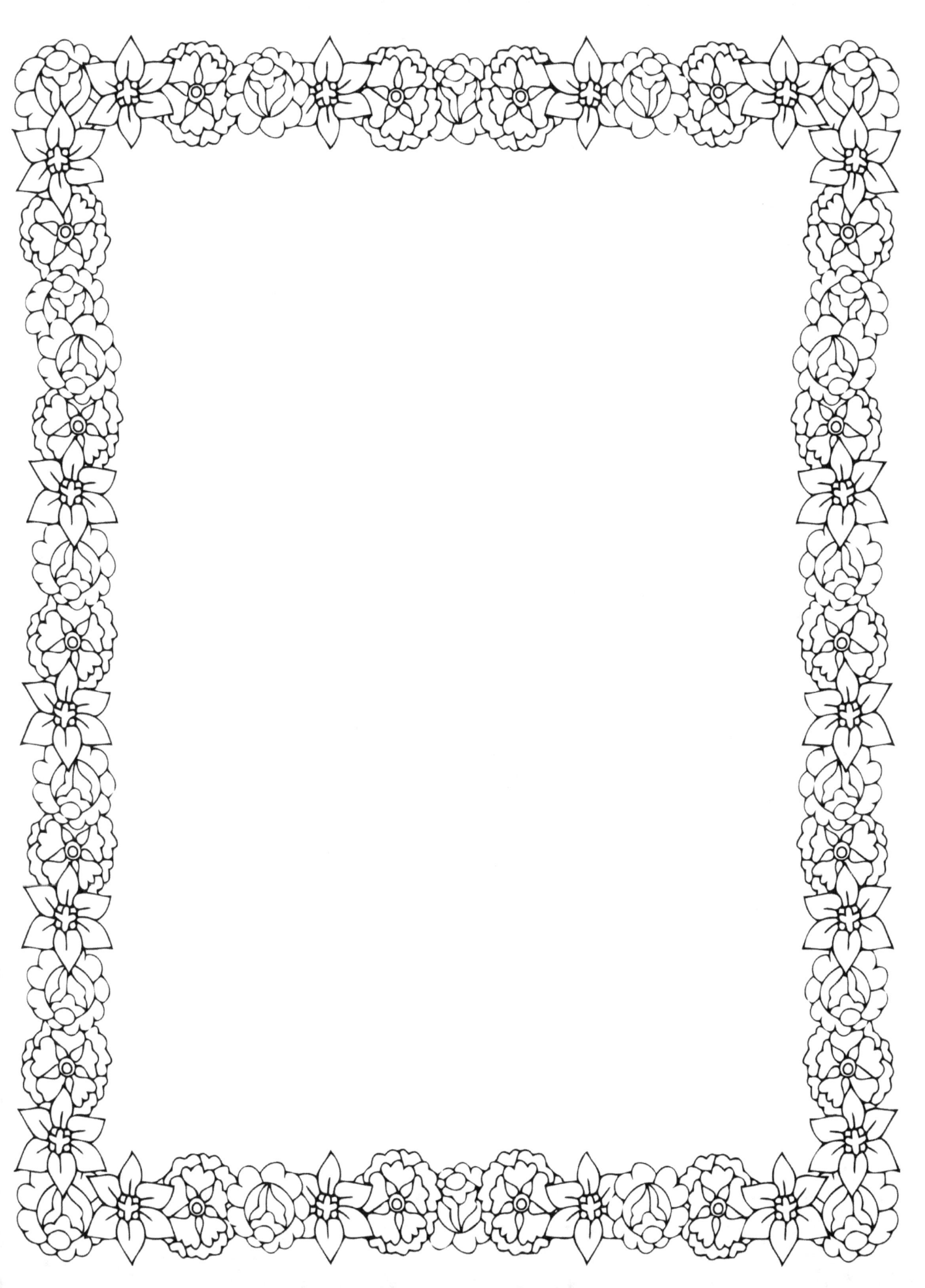

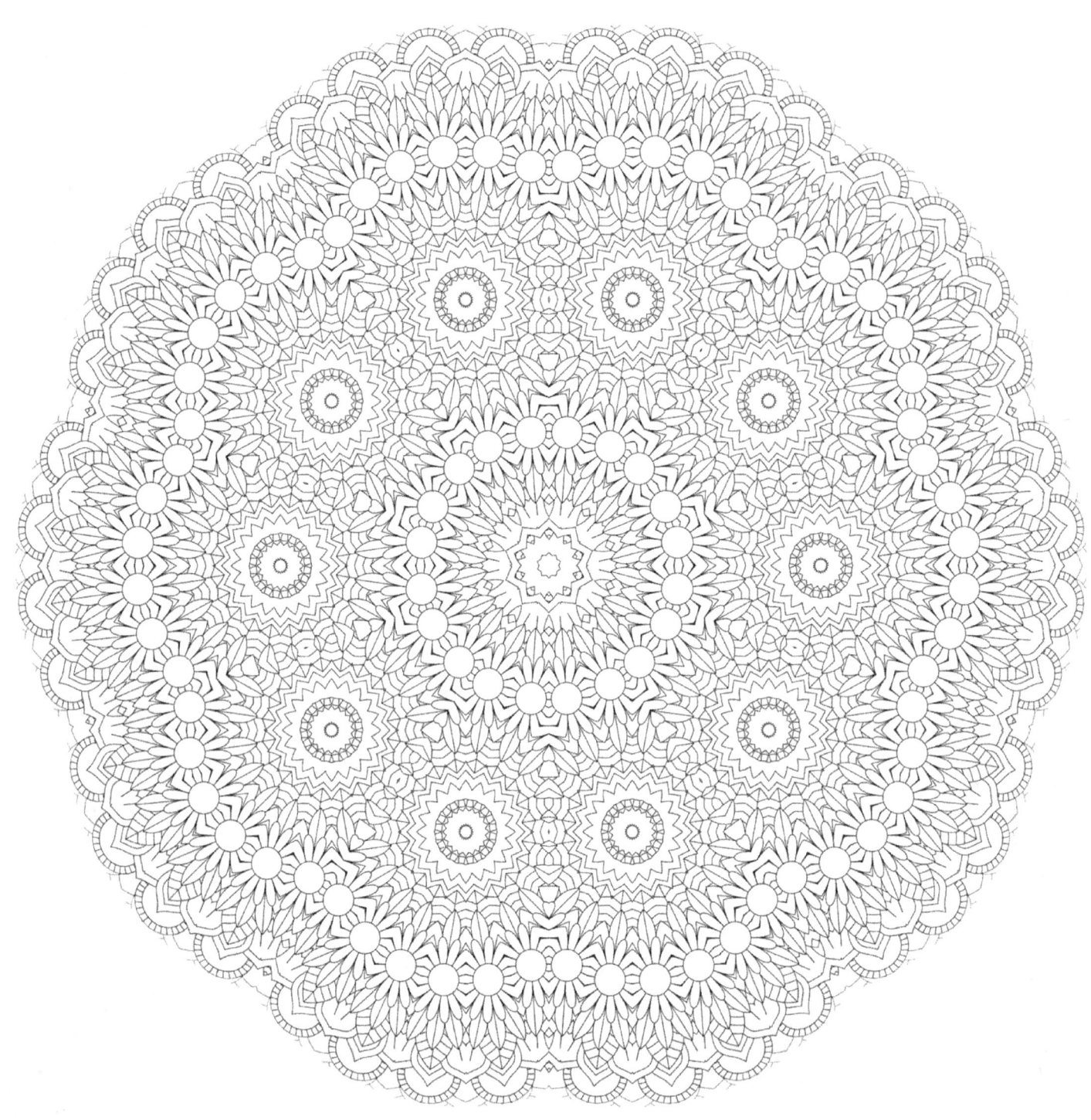

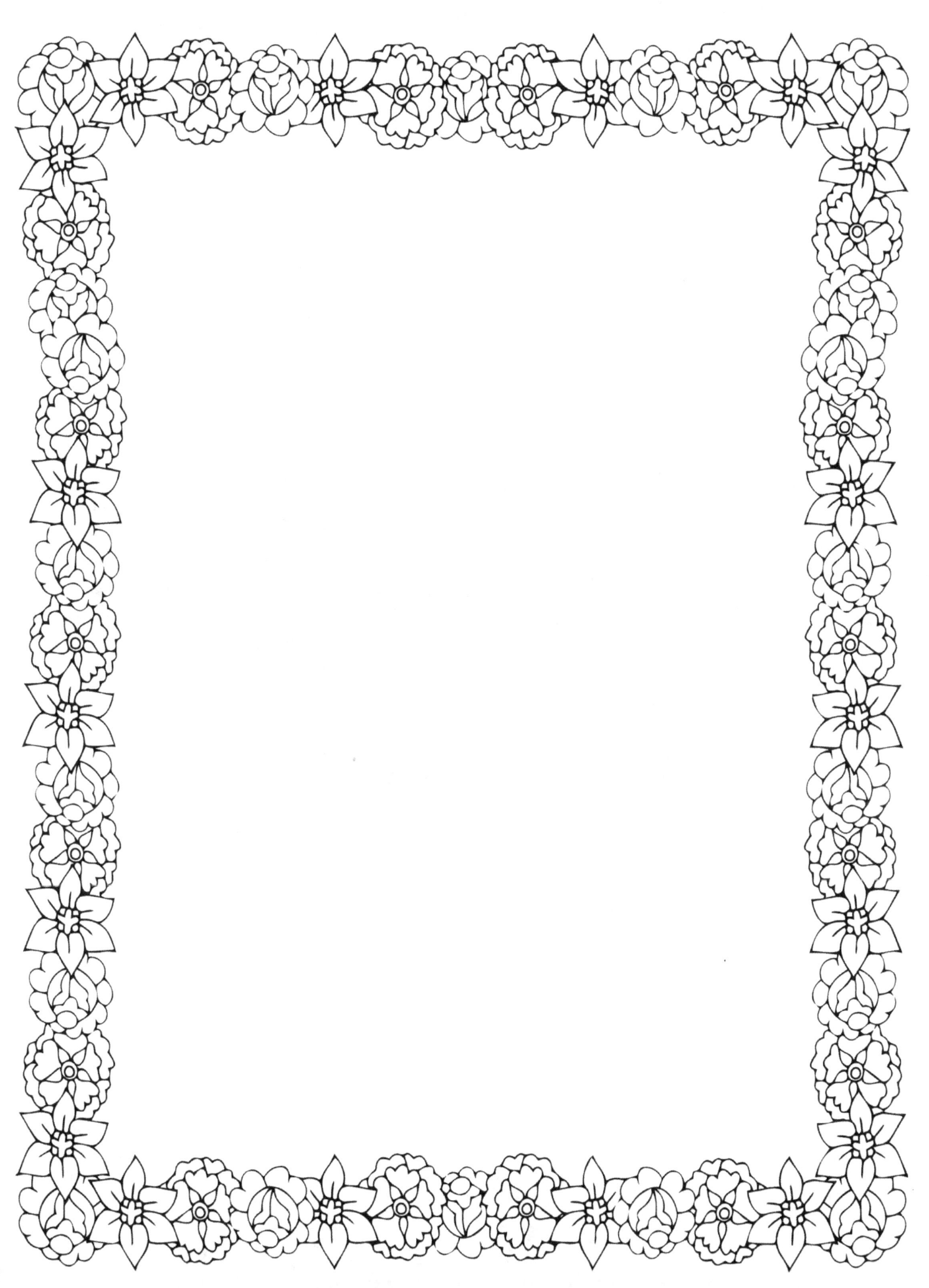

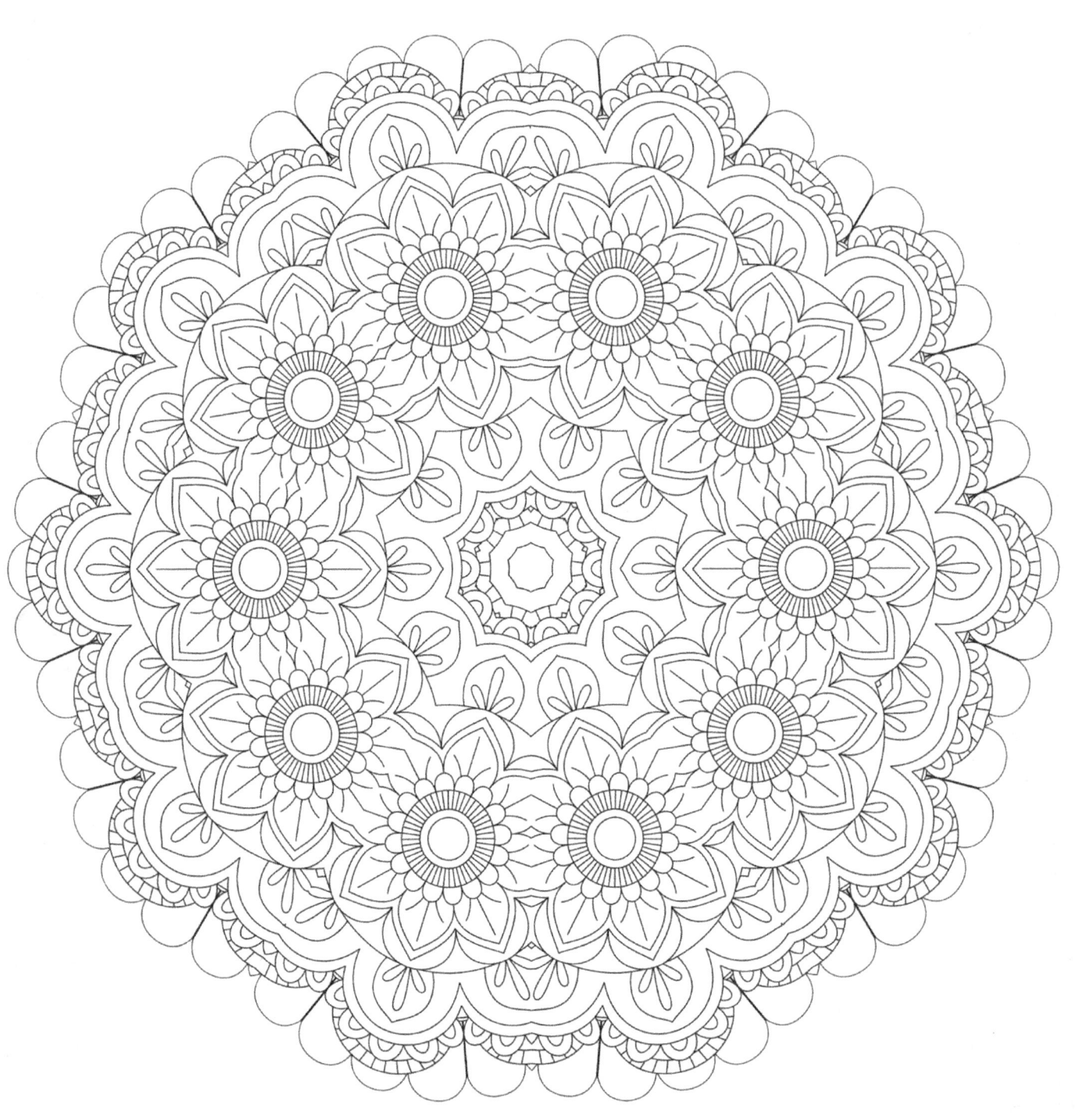

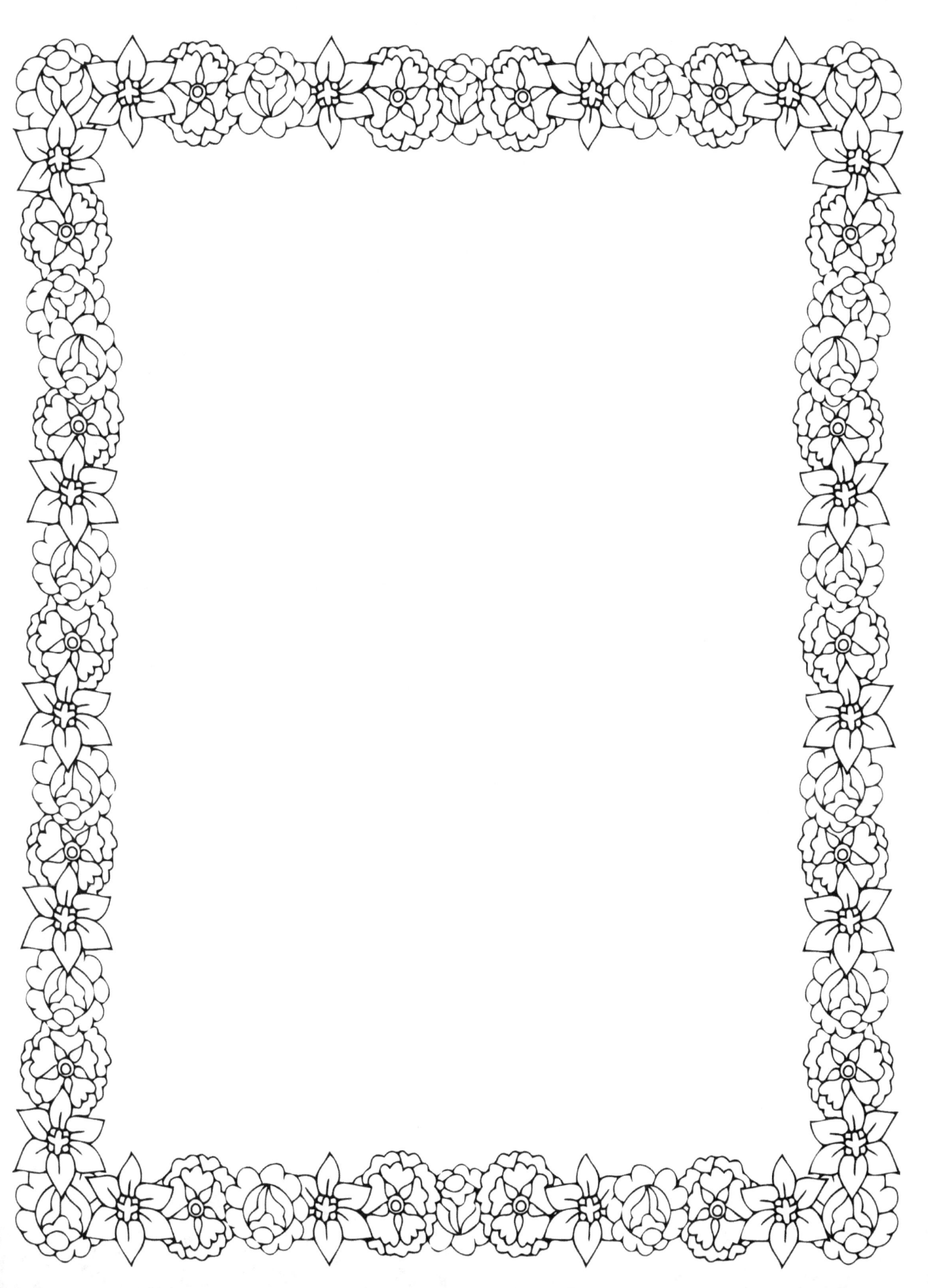

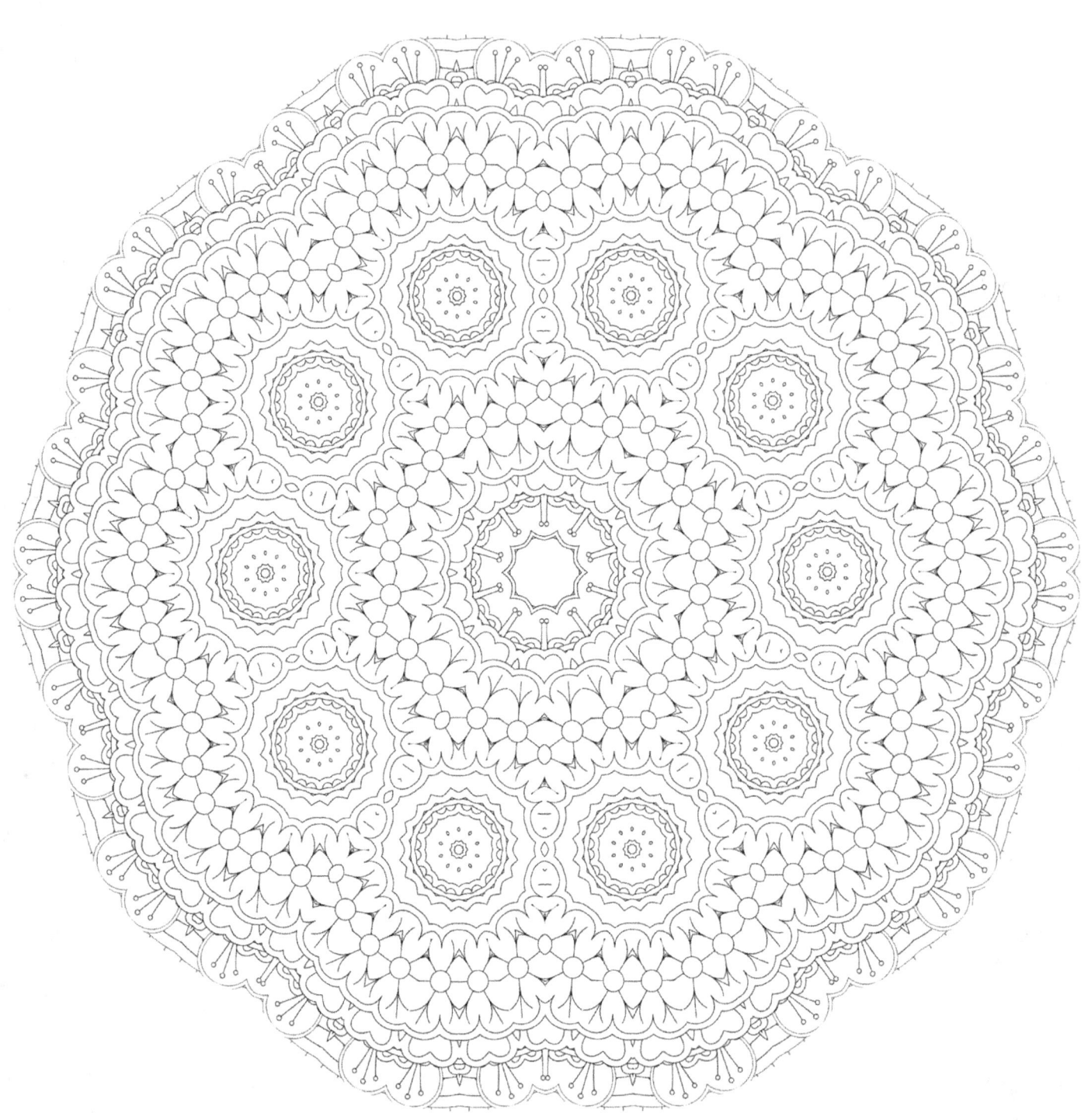

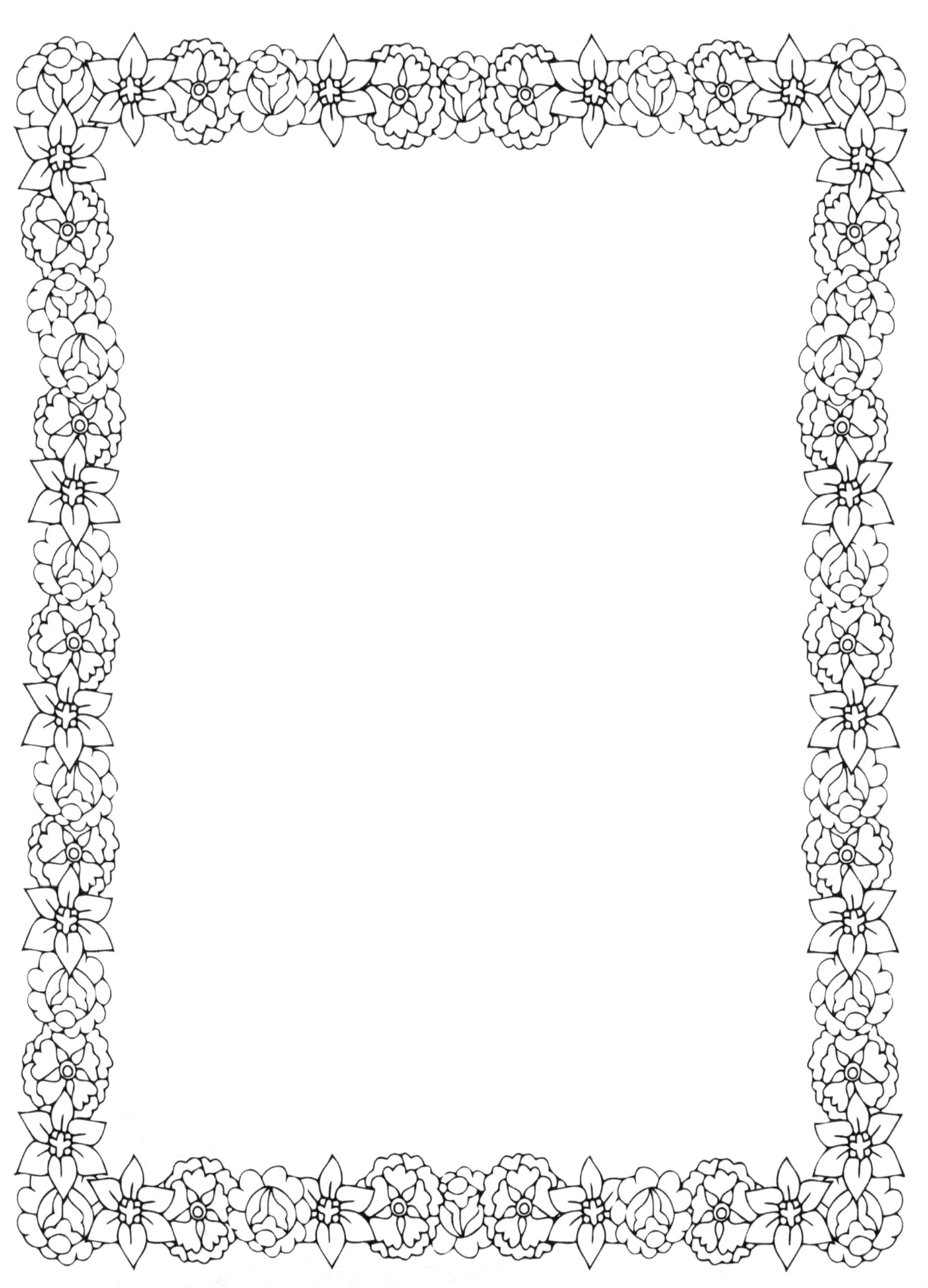

Notes

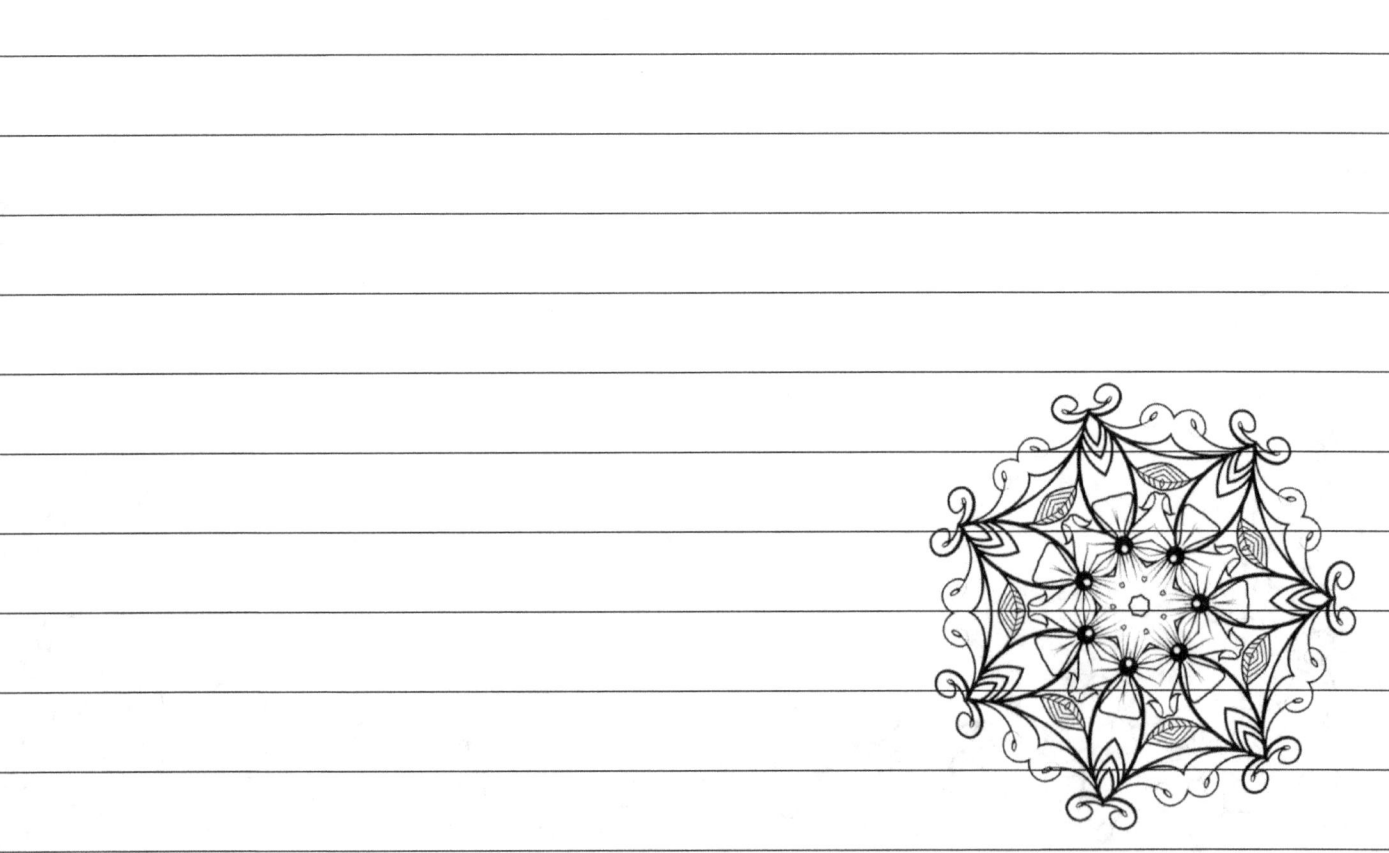

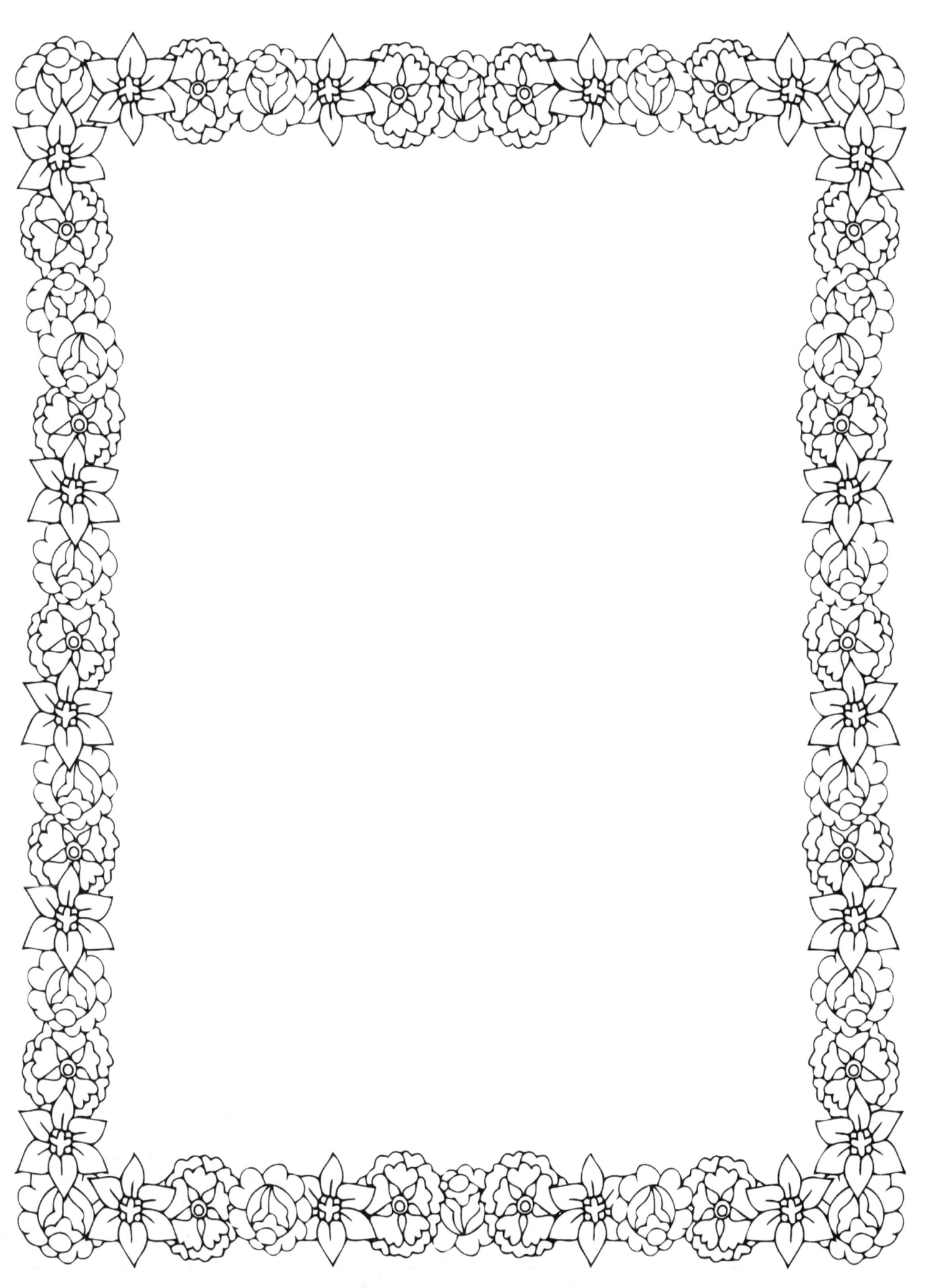

Notes

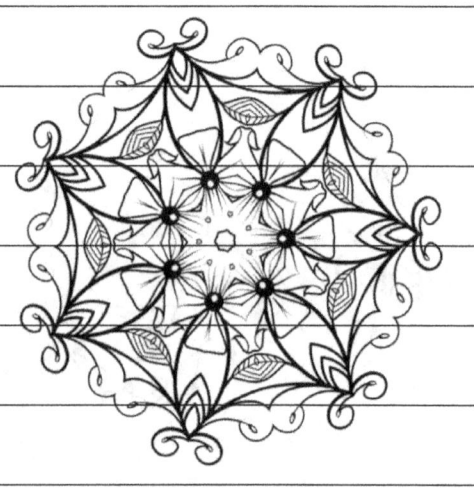

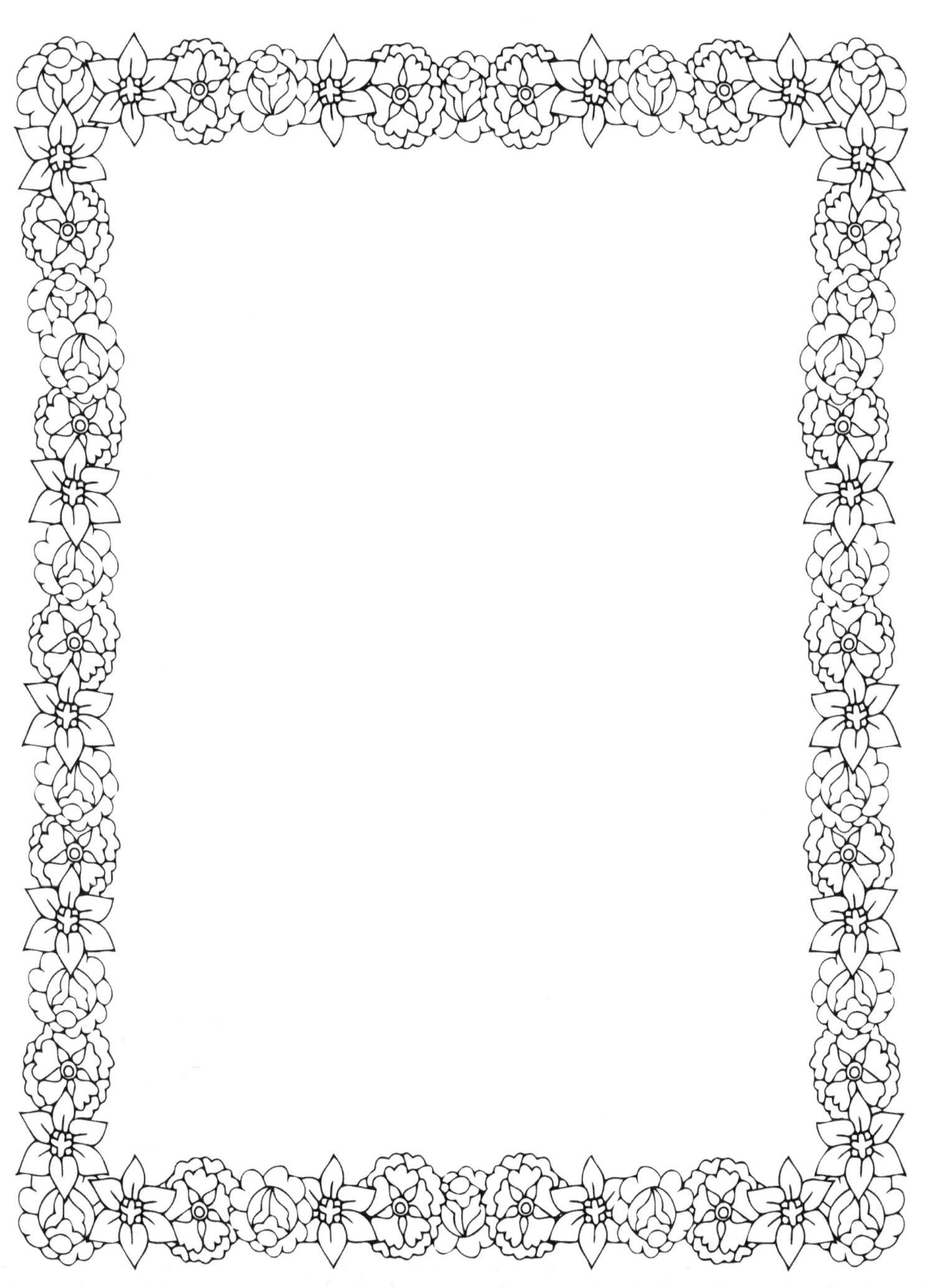

Notes